D0204037

Sports Governance, Development and Corporate Responsibility

Routledge Research in Sport, Culture and Society

Sports Governance, Development and Corporate Responsibility

Edited by Barbara Segaert, Marc Theeboom, Christiane Timmerman, Bart Vanreusel

Routledge
Taylor & Francis Group

NEW YORK   LONDON

First published 2012
by Routledge
711 Third Avenue, New York, NY 10017

Simultaneously published in the UK
by Routledge
2 Park Square, Milton Park, Abingdon, Oxon OX14 4RN

*Routledge is an imprint of the Taylor & Francis Group,
an informa business*

Library of Congress Cataloging-in-Publication Data

Sports governance, development and corporate responsibility / edited by
Barbara Segaert . . . [et al.].
 vp. cm. — (Routledge research in sport, culture and society ; 16)
 1. Sports administration. 2. Sports—Management. 3. Sports—
Social aspects. 4. Sports and state. I. Segaert, Barbara.
 GV713.S67785 2012
 796.06'9—dc23
 2012003712

ISBN13: 978-0-415-52249-6 (hbk)
ISBN13: 978-0-203-10602-0 (ebk)

Typeset in Sabon
by IBT Global.

Printed and bound in the United States of America on sustainably sourced
paper by IBT Global.

Contents

PART I

Building Communities and Social Responsibility—
Rising Stakes on Sport's Social Role

Figures

Tables

Preface

There is a widespread trust in the 'value of sport'. This trust goes beyond sport's recreational benefit and its often proclaimed contribution to the enhancement of physical health. For example, many believe that involvement in sport is beneficial to character building and moral education. It is also regarded as a means for social integration and is considered to play a political, economical and developmental role. Attributing a distinct social role to sport is, however, not a new phenomenon. During the Victorian era, it was generally accepted that sport enhanced character and morality, and there are numerous examples in history where sport has served a political purpose. For instance, 2011 marks the fortieth anniversary of the 'ping-pong diplomacy', a breakthrough in U.S.–China relations that started with an invitation from China to the U.S. table tennis team.

Although sport has long since been regarded as much more than a 'physical game', more recently an increased awareness of its social role has gained eminence among policy makers around the globe. Whereas many of today's politicians are known to 'ride the waves' of sport's increased popularity to boost their own public image, they also seem to have (re)discovered the potential of sport's contribution to society at large. Official statements are made and campaigns have been devised to emphasize the social value of sport and to stimulate various agencies and structures in society to use sport as a mediator or as an instrument in relation to a variety of pressing social issues. At present, many examples of this renewed interest in sport's social role are to be found both at local and global levels provided by various agencies and structures, such as governments, the non-profit and profit sectors. There is also a wide diversity in approaches to the use of sport, as an 'eye catcher', a mediating tool or a practice in its own right.

It is significant how sport's contribution has spread from the local or national context to the international arena (e.g., the United Nations' Sport for Development and Peace—UNOSDP). The diversity of agencies and institutions emphasizing the social role of sport have increased exponentially. For example, next to local, regional and national authorities setting up specific policy initiatives, inter-governmental agencies also take action (e.g., the European Commission's White Paper on Sport emphasizing the societal role of sport). There are also numerous examples illustrating the involvement of the private sector, both in the non-profit sector (e.g., various initiatives by non-governmental organisations), as well as in the profit sector (for instance in the realm of 'corporate social responsibility').

In examining these initiatives and programmes, different perspectives emerge concerning the implementation of sport.

From one perspective, sport is regarded as an eye catcher to draw attention to social problems, as illustrated by numerous cases in which sport is used to raise awareness or funding to fight diseases such as cancer and HIV/ AIDS or to tackle problems such as racism, discrimination and poverty.

From another perspective, sport is viewed as a mediator, whereby its universal character is used to facilitate other processes. The aforementioned diplomatic use of sport (illustrated by the ping-pong diplomacy case) can serve as an example here. Sport then becomes a kind of universal language to bridge social, religious, racial and gender divides.

A more critical and negative interpretation marks sport as an *instrument to distract the masses* (as *panem et circenses* in totalitarian regimes) or support extreme ideological or political actions (such as the terrorist attack during the 1972 Olympics).

Sport as a practice in its own right is also used to provide *added social value*. For example, the outcome of direct personal involvement in sport goes beyond the mere acquisition of sporting skills and improved physical fitness and is also viewed in terms of personal and social development.

These differences in perspectives result in a variety of aims, contexts and envisaged target groups for sport as a social instrument. In recent years, an increased number of initiatives, campaigns and programmes have been set up for specific deprived groups in developed, developing and/or divided societies (youth at risk, people in poverty, homeless people, refugees, ethnic minorities, juvenile delinquents, former child soldiers, etc.). Similarly, a variety of aims have been formulated for these initiatives (e.g., social integration/cohesion, crime reduction, community development, peace building, disease control, education).

Today, sport is considered to be far more than a mere leisure pastime. High stakes have been put on its social value. The first part of this book, 'Building Communities and Social Responsibility: Rising Stakes on Sport's Social Role', critically reflects on the social role of sport on a local as well as on a global level. It brings together research from a number of scholars from a variety of backgrounds. By looking into various contexts at different levels and in different countries around the world and zooming in on a number of deprived groups in society, this section attempts to provide more insight into the extent and the circumstances under which sport can take up a social role.

Drawing upon research undertaken in different regions, Richard Giulianotti explores the main analytical and practical issues surrounding the intersection of sport and peace of sports-based interventions in the promotion of peace building, reconciliation and reconstruction in divided and post-conflict societies throughout the world. Giulianotti places the 'sport and peace' movement within its historical context and looks at the main issues that are faced by sport and peace agencies in planning and conducting their work.

In her chapter 'In Africa for FIFA & Sons', Cora Burnett analyses the 2010 FIFA (men's) World Cup in South Africa and the roles played by stakeholders who contributed to key public debates. Burnett uses a critical discourse analysis perspective in which mediated social identities are (de-)constructed in terms of power relations and hegemonic practices.

Joel Rookwood describes a case study of an NGO-led play park / football project established in Mingachevir in Azerbaijan and examines the suitability and applicability of sport and play in contributing to the peaceful advancement of Azerbaijani society. Based on participant observation and interview data obtained from local and international personnel, Rookwood identifies lessons that can be learned for those wishing to run similar projects in other political settings.

By using the theory of social vulnerability as a framework, Rein Haudenhuyse and Marc Theeboom critically explore existing research on the conditions for coaching and organising 'sport plus' interventions aimed at attaining positive effects among socially vulnerable youth. They put forward the question whether socially vulnerable youngsters become less vulnerable by doing sports or not.

In her chapter, Bettina Rulofs focuses on the question of how social inclusion of diverse groups in German and other European sports clubs can be achieved. Based on the existing literature, as well as on data collection in Germany, Rulofs investigates the specific conditions and requirements that need to be taken into consideration when transferring the concept of diversity management to sport organisations. Lian Malai Madsen discusses the understandings of integration processes reflected in sports-political initiatives and public discourse in Denmark. She builds on a study of situated interaction and language-use among minority youth members of a martial arts club in a heterogeneous area of Copenhagen.

Finally, Fred Coalter draws on extensive fieldwork experience in Africa and India to explore the context for, and assumptions underpinning, sport-for-development programmes. Coalter raises critical questions about implicit deficit assumptions about participants and their 'development' needs and looks at the assumed relationship between a highly individualised definition of 'development' and more general processes of development.

The first part of this book approaches the social aspects of sport from a constructive, yet critical, perspective. Whereas policy makers and other stakeholders tend to idealise the contribution of sport—thereby referring to broad and general concepts to be pursued such as social integration—there is a common belief among the authors that sport's social value is not unconditional. Sport can only serve a social role if certain conditions are met.

Even though the stakes on sport's social capital are being raised, one may wonder how sport can be conceived to meet all these social issues at stake.

The second part of the book, 'Sport Corporations at Play. Doing Business in Sports: Who's Added Value?', offers new perspectives on the way today's sport is formally managed in an increasingly mixed arena of economic profit and social benefit. The focus is on the governance of mega sport events and on global sport organisations.

It was common to frame the management of sport policies and practices in a triangular model, between governments and their public policies, markets and their search for profit and civil society and its active citizens. However, this triangular model no longer adequately covers today's complex network and the power relations operating in sports, connecting local and global agencies and public and private interests. Indeed, several objections can be raised against the traditional triangular model of sport management.

First, governments, markets and civil society can no longer be identified as separate agents with an independent focus and a well-defined agenda. On the contrary, the governance of sport nowadays is characterised by multiple interconnections between these agents. Second, the triangular model completely underestimates the political and economic power at play in the actual production and consumption of sport events. Third, the triangular model does not take into account the network spanning local, national, international and transnational agents in sport. For example, in bidding for and hosting mega sports events, these three elements perform a crucial role.

Today, sport organisations not only interact with governments, but often as governments and sometimes with the power of governments in an ever-changing interplay. Governments share their power with local and transnational private corporations in order to achieve their aims as public authorities driven by politics. At the same time, corporations link up with sports organisations to support their objectives and to make a profit out of it. The role of active citizens in all this often tends to be reduced to being supportive and willing tax payers and consumers. Sport and the corporate world are traditionally presented as look-alikes and as act-alikes with a competitive and meritocratic model fitting and shaping both. However, the relationship between sport and the corporate world has dramatically intensified, from superficial similarity to profound interconnectedness. In an era of globalised sport, the corporate world is shaping sporting organisations, sport events and their public and private stakeholders. Corporations are now doing business in sport, with sport and as sport. These interconnections lead to a growing awareness of corporate social responsibility in sport. Is there a chance, for example, that corporate sports will serve social values, community building and a social economy? The second part of the book explores such new interconnections between sport, the corporate world, governments and active citizenship.

Physical contests such as football have been transformed into global arenas of power. Foucault's concept of bio-power might be helpful to understand this development of football as a global contest, not only as a physical game, but also from an economic, social and political perspective.

The concept of bio-power is often used in sport research to refer to health and body-related aspects of sports. However, the global competition for the production and consumption of mega sport events can be studied as another example of bio-power. The power position of global organisations with corporate features will be addressed from the perspective of governance, issues of law and fair business.

In his introductory chapter on sports governance, Hans Bruyninckx analyses three different approaches to the concept of governance: governance as steering, governance as rule and norm setting and good governance. He relates these concepts of governance to professional sport and at the same time he clarifies why governing sport is a tough challenge and how the world of sports had traditionally expressed its aversion to regulatory processes.

Jens Sejer Andersen, well known from his work as founder of Play the Game, follows up on this conceptual chapter with a piece of investigative journalism on the absence of transparency and accountability and on the lack of good governance in international sports organisations. The call for a global coalition in support of good governance in sports is an immediate response to his observations. At the same time, it puts into practice the conceptual approach of governance as developed in the first chapter by Bruyninckx.

Bert Meulders and co-authors pursue the focus on governance in sport. Their analysis of the complex governance arrangement in today's mega sport events is translated to the case of the 2010 FIFA World Cup in South Africa. The question is raised of how a governance approach deals with both the transnational agenda of (sport) corporations and the local agenda of development. Notwithstanding their focus on the 2010 World Cup in South Africa, the presented conceptual model of governance is designed to fit future mega sport events in general.

The next two chapters present an economic perspective on governance models of sport organisations. Sport economist Stefan Késenne discusses how economic impact studies of mega sport events, based on dubious and debatable economic assumptions, still have a decisive impact on public opinion and political decision making. He calls for more adequate economic analysis of mega sport events in order to make justified policy decisions as a crucial step in good governance.

Jeroen Schokkaert and co-authors present research on the economics of football player migration from developing countries. They use an economic rationale based on two recruitment strategies: establishing a football academy in developing countries or recruiting foreign players on the transfer market. Empirical evidence is provided by observations gathered in Senegal and South Africa. Again, the principles of governance allow us to analyse football player migration from developing countries.

Finally, Frank Hendrickx draws on his work in labour law to discuss how the business of sport needs to, and can, implement an ethical perspective. Sports law seeks to strike a balance between the quest for autonomy on the part of sport organisations and the need to intervene and regulate of public authorities. Hendrickx offers new perspectives on the quest for this balance of principles of soft law, self-regulation and responsive regulation. The open method of coordination promoted in this chapter as a regulatory strategy is a promising new approach in sports law, useful in an increasingly complex network of sports governance.

Although several chapters in part two present a discourse that is critical of the powerhouses of sport, they also provide new concepts and methods for positive future developments in sports governance. The loud call for good governance and transparency and accountability in sports is the common thread that runs throughout all the chapters. This call is expressed in a variety of ways throughout the book.

This book would not have materialised without the support of the University Centre Saint-Ignatius Antwerp (www.ucsia.org), not only in terms of financial and practical means, but foremost through the organization of the international and interdisciplinary conference 'Sports, a Matter of Peace?' at the University of Antwerp on 15 and 16 October 2010, which brought together all these experts whose presentations form the core of this book.

Part I

Building Communities and Social Responsibility

Rising Stakes on Sport's Social Role

1 Sport and Peace Making
Initial Promises, Social Scientific Issues and Practical Challenges

Richard Giulianotti

In recent years, the field of Sport for Development and Peace (SDP) has grown into a global sector of policy, practice and research. A critical component of this field has centred on the intersection of sport and peace, wherein diverse sports-based interventions are deployed in order to promote peace building, reconciliation and reconstruction in war-torn or post-conflict settings. A wide variety of institutions and agencies have supported and initiated these interventions, including national governments, inter-governmental organisations (such as the United Nations and the European Union), international and national non-governmental organisations, new social movements, corporate social responsibility units within private corporations and businesses and also individual philanthropists and benefactors.

In this chapter, I explore some of the main analytical and practical issues surrounding these sport and peace initiatives. The chapter is divided into four main parts. First, I briefly set out some of the main initial promises and possibilities of sport as a positive potential tool of social intervention in promoting peace making. Second, I examine in more critical terms the social history of sport's complex and greatly varied relationships to peace and violent conflict. Third, I explore the emergence of the 'sport for development and peace' sector, with particular reference to two main issues: the historical issues relating to sport in the making of global society and with regard to processes of globalisation, the making of 'global civil society'. The fourth part of the paper sets out four general issues and problems which sport and peace projects need to deal with in order to enhance their efficacy.

The chapter builds upon my prior research and practice within this field. This involvement has included personal consultancy and monitoring and evaluation work for sport and peace projects in conflict zones, advisory work with international and national sport and peace agencies, including the co-writing of the section 'Peace 1: Sport, Violence and Crisis Situations', in the Magglingen Declaration and Recommendations on sport and development (Giulianotti, Armstrong & Hognestad, 2003)[1] and various publications and conference papers on sport and peace work (e.g., Giulianotti, 2004; 2011a; 2011b; 2011c; Giulianotti, & Armstrong, 2011). This work has also been underpinned by fieldwork with 'sport and peace' projects and project officials, undertaken primarily in the Balkans, the Middle East, South Asia, and southern Africa.[2]

SPORT AND PEACE: THE INITIAL
POSSIBILITIES AND PRACTICES

There are a variety of ways in which sport-based interventions initially appear to have the capacity to assist peace-building exercises and initiatives in war-torn and post-conflict settings.

First, sports such as football are global cultural forms which are familiar to most social groups in very diverse social settings. Given that sport is centred on physical play, language barriers between participants are relatively unimportant when compared to other cultural forms such as theatre. Moreover, if appropriately implemented, sport facilitates potentially pleasurable forms of self-expression, creativity and corporeal self-development.

Second, many peace-building sport initiatives are targeted at young people as this broad user group is particularly vulnerable to future conflict (whether as combatants or victims) and also represents the future long-term body of citizens in a post-conflict zone. Their relative popularity with young people indicates that sports are a potentially valuable cultural medium for engaging these user groups in projects in order to build cross-society contact. Moreover, sport-based peace-building exercises may have the potential to demonstrate to other community members, who are not necessarily participating in these activities, the possibility of pursuing a 'normal' civilian life, particularly by the younger or 'future' generations, as regards engaging with previous enemies or opponents.

Third, the practice of sport may assist in psychological and social terms, in regard to the rehabilitation and re-socialisation of participants. At the individual level, sports may function as a form of personal therapy, which can help to rehabilitate psychologically those traumatised by war. At the social level, where appropriately and carefully implemented, sport may be able to demonstrate the benefits of redirecting deep-seated conflicts from actual violence into the mimetic sphere. The implementation of sports may also facilitate the making and enforcing of rules, while underlining the importance of these regulations for the facilitation of a meaningful, pleasurable, and peaceful interaction among participants or competitors.

The growth of the sport and peace field in recent years is such that these projects and initiatives now span most continents. War-torn regions are the most obvious targets for sport and peace initiatives:

- In sub-Saharan Africa, the region of West Africa (around Liberia, Ivory Coast and Sierra Leone) has been particularly prominent in receiving sport-related interventions (see Armstrong, 2004; 2007; Richards, 1997); South Africa has also attracted such initiatives, notably to pursue reconciliation in the post-Apartheid era (Höglund & Sundberg, 2008; Keim, 2003);

- In Europe, the Balkan region has been the focus of sport and peace projects following the break-up of Yugoslavia, notably in Bosnia and Kosovo (Gasser & Levinsen, 2004; Giulianotti, 2011a; 2011b);
- In the Middle East, sport and peace projects have been employed in Israel/Palestine, Jordan, Lebanon and other settings (see, e.g., Whitfield, 2006);
- In Asia, different kinds of sport and peace initiatives have been introduced in Afghanistan, Sri Lanka, Nepal, Korea, and Vietnam (Schulenkorf, 2010);
- In South America, projects have been deployed in locations where high levels of urban violence have been apparent, notably in Colombia and Brazil.

The projects vary greatly as regards their respective philosophies, scales, methods of intervention and the types of agencies and institutional partnerships which are involved. In Korea, for example, sport has been used at the diplomatic level, as part of the 'thawing' of political relationships between the North and South, with national governments and sports federations playing critical roles in planning and organising cross-border sporting initiatives, often through high-profile sport fixtures between elite teams from both nations. In contrast, in Sri Lanka, peace-building sport projects among Sinhalese, Moor and Tamil populations tend to be more grassroots, involving diverse organisations (ranging from local community organisations to international non-governmental organisation), and often featuring peace-building 'camps' in neutral territories, with a large range of social and cultural activities for participants, including sports.

Overall then, there has been a remarkable growth of sport and peace projects over the past decade or so. Much of this has been underpinned by an attempt to accentuate the positive possibilities that appear to be afforded by sport. However, if we are to advance a social scientific understanding of the peace-building possibilities of sport, then we need to explore more fully the complex historical and sociological relationships between sport, peace and conflict, and I shall now consider those issues.

SPORT, PEACE AND VIOLENT CONFLICT: A COMPLEX SOCIAL HISTORY

Any social scientific analysis of the interface between sport and peace needs to approach the subject with caution and realism and avoid making any over-generalised and essentialist claims. Like any other domain of socio-cultural practice, the everyday social 'realities' of sport are dependent upon how it is interpreted and implemented and in which manner it is subject to the complex power relations within and between different societies. Much social scientific research has highlighted the ways in which, in different historical and cultural contexts, sports possess distinctive social meanings, techniques, and organisational frameworks for diverse populations (cf. Giulianotti & Robertson, 2009; Guttmann, 1994). Thus, the relationship of sport to forms of social stability (or peace) and forms of social conflict varies very substantially according to historical and cultural contexts.

Accordingly, we have to note that many claims regarding sport's 'inherent' universal properties are too simplistic and quasi-functionalist in character. In this sense, we should certainly be wary of making any unwarranted claims, without examination of the evidence, that sport 'functions' in a purely positive way to promote social stability and consensus, and that it meets underlying societal needs, for example in regard to assisting social integration, fulfilling material prerequisites, and transmitting cultural values.

In contradistinction to these functionalist claims, we might begin by probing the extent to which, in line with Orwell's famous dictum that sport is 'war minus the shooting'. In considering the evidence, we find many illustrations of how sport has had a distinctive relationship to patterns of social domination and conflict. For example, historians have highlighted the links between many sports and frameworks of imperialism and colonialism: the spread of British sports such as cricket and rugby through the colonies, in contexts in which indigenous peoples were subjugated or annihilated provides a particularly potent illustration (cf. Booth, 1998; Mangan, 1986; 1987; Perkin, 1989). Across the British Isles, we might also point to examples of ethno-nationalist and ethno-religious conflict, most obviously relating to the 'Irish Question'. In 1920, when Ireland was occupied by British forces, the Royal Irish Constabulary opened fire on crowds of spectators and players at a Gaelic football match, fatally wounding fourteen people (Cronin, 1999). Moreover in many ways, throughout the late nineteenth and twentieth centuries, the Gaelic Athletic Association (GAA) sought to promote Irish cultural independence and nationalism through sport, in direct opposition to the 'colonial' sports which the British had introduced and inculcated (Sugden & Bairner, 1993).

Looking beyond Britain, we see many further instances in which nationalist conflicts have underscored the meaning and manifestation of sport at particular historical junctures. Turning to Orwell's time, in the run-up to the Second World War, sport often served as a socio-cultural proxy for the expression of virulent and violent nationalisms. We might think automatically here of the 1936 Berlin Olympics, intended as a showcase for Aryanism and Nazi ideology. Yet consider too the strongly nationalistic and often violent football fixtures played by England against Italy and Germany during the 1930s (Beck, 1999). Nationalistic barbarism made a violent return to Europe in the 1990s, amidst the break-up of Yugoslavia, particularly in the disputed territory of what is now Bosnia-Herzegovina. One significant flashpoint in the run-up to the Yugoslav civil war was the football fixture between Dinamo Zagreb and Red Star Belgrade in Zagreb in May 1990, when supporters, players and police fought running battles on and off the pitch. At the outbreak of war, many of the militant football supporter formations in Serbia and Croatia were transformed into militias to fight in the conflict and many of these groups were strongly implicated in the mass killings, rapes, ethnic cleansing and other crimes against humanity which subsequently followed (Vrcan & Lalic, 1998; Sack & Suster, 2000). Less dramatically but rather more routinely, we might point to the many, everyday cases of violence in and around sports events, most notably in incidents at football fixtures, involving hooligan movements and often police and security forces. These further highlight the socio-historical connections between sport, conflict and violence (cf. Giulianotti, Bonney & Hepworth, 1994).

It would be wrong to argue, of course, that sport is inherently violent and predisposed to igniting conflict. But what these historical insights provide is confirmation that the relationship between sport, peace and conflict is socially constructed out of the power relations between different social groups. Keeping in mind this 'other' history of sport, peace and conflict also enables us to avoid falling into the traps of sport 'evangelism' and essentialism (Giulianotti, 2004).

THE SPORT FOR DEVELOPMENT AND PEACE SECTOR: THE CONTEXTS OF GLOBAL SPORT AND GLOBALISATION

As I noted at the outset, we also need to position the work of sport and peace agencies and institutions within what is now known as the 'sport for development and peace' (SDP) sector. The SDP sector has grown markedly in recent years, particularly since the United Nations appointed the former President of Switzerland, Adolf Ogi, as the Special Advisor on Sport for Development and Peace to the UN Secretary-General in the year 2001 (cf. UN General Assembly, 2006; SDP IWG, 2008). Subsequently, the UN established the year 2005 as its International Year of Sport and Physical Education, with a major focus of that initiative centred on development and peace. The UN in turn has created its own office for SDP and has been a crucial catalyst in promoting partnerships, programmes and initiatives on this theme across the world.

I would argue that the SDP-sector emerges out of two broader contexts: first, with respect to global sport, and second, with reference to processes of globalisation.

Global Sport and Peace/Conflict: Three Key Phases

Let us first consider how the SDP-sector has emerged out of the making of global sport. I would argue here that there have been three broad historical phases in the making of global sport.

Phase one lasted from the eighteenth century up to the mid-twentieth century, and was marked by violent colonisation and imposition of Western 'civilisation', as new territories were conquered by European powers (particularly the British), thereby enabling the wider diffusion and institutionalisation of sports and other forms of physical culture. This phase lasted until subjugated peoples, particularly in Africa, began to achieve more politically independent forms of nationalism. Thus, this period was marked by the interface of sport, colonisation and 'civilisation', as British imperial sports were established in the Asian sub-continent, southern Africa, Australasia and the Caribbean (Holt, 1989; Mangan, 1986). The violent conquest and re-population of North and South America—marked by the extermination of many indigenous peoples—also provided the conditions for the modern establishment of nation-building sport traditions (such as football in South America, ice-hockey in Canada, and American football and baseball in the United States) (Guttmann, 1994).

Phase two was marked by colonial struggle and post-colonial independence and ran roughly from the 1940s through to the 1990s. Sport thus came to be positioned significantly within these ethno-national and ethno-religious struggles. In colonial Africa, for example, majority black populations often struggled to exercise forms of political autonomy and cultural identity through sport, perhaps most notably during the apartheid era in South Africa (Armstrong & Giulianotti, 2004; Baker & Mangan, 1987; Booth, 1998). The sport of cricket was also a locus of strong national pride for many former British colonies, notably in the Asian sub-continent and West Indies, with victories over England having a very potent symbolic significance (Appadurai, 1995; Beckles & Stoddart, 1995). Once independent, many former colonies established their national sovereignty on the world stage through membership of international sports governing bodies. Sport in these nations, like other social spheres, was subject to the pressures of modernisation and development; thus the focus was on the development of sport, for example through athlete training, team professionalisation and infrastructure projects such as stadium building.

Phase three has been marked by the emergence of the sport for development movement, and may be seen as running from the mid-1990s onwards. Arguably, this phase has itself featured two main periods thus far.

The first period ran up to and included the UN 2005 dedication and featured the introduction of many SDP-projects that tended to be short-term, weakly monitored, and relatively uncoordinated (cf. Armstrong, 2004; 2007; Lea-Howarth, 2006).

The second period, since 2005, has featured a far more coordinated SDP-sector, with stronger long-term planning for projects, closer monitoring of the impacts and results of projects, along with better networking across different agencies undertaking SDP work.

It should be added here that these three phases point to significant or dominant trends in the making of global sport. This does not mean that these phases are mutually exclusive. In other words, at any one historical moment, it is possible to find significant elements of each of the three phases. Thus, in phase three, whereas sport for development projects have taken off, we also find that significant (and often dominant) strains of post-colonial nationalism, modernisation and the development of sport (phase two) are still evident, as well as aspects of colonialism and tradition building (phase one).

Locating the work of sport and peace agencies and institutions within the SDP sector enables us to trace the relationships of sport to peace and conflict through different historical phases. This also enables an understanding of how different settings, in which sport and peace projects may be implemented, have experienced specific sports in particular historical ways. Thus, in many sub-Saharan contexts, sports like cricket and rugby may have been strongly associated with colonisation (phase one), whereas other sports like football may have been favoured by the majority population, thus being more strongly associated with the nationalist struggle and the post-colonial context (phase two). On this basis, it makes sense for sport and peace projects (phase three) to draw on sports like football in order to include majority populations, rather than other pastimes which have an inherently colonial heritage.

Sport, Peace and Conflict: The Role of Processes of Globalisation

The second context in which we need to locate the SDP-sector relates to processes of globalisation. I have argued elsewhere that the SDP-sector may be understood as part of one aspect of globalisation, namely the 'global civil society' (Giulianotti, 2011a, 2011b, 2011c). Global civil society tends to be associated with social programmes and initiatives that are intended to provide social goods, particularly for dispossessed or disadvantaged social groups in the global South. I understand 'global civil society' largely in line with Kaldor (2003a; 2003b), who argues that this is a highly contested political field, in which diverse social groups enter into struggles and conflicts over 'the arrangements that shape global developments' (Kaldor, 2003b: 591). In my analysis, the relevant institutional and political forces which shape global civil society include nation-states, intergovernmental organisations (IGOs), non-governmental organisations (NGOs), new social movements, and transnational corporations (notably through 'corporate social responsibility' programmes).[3]

Each of these institutional and political forces will harbour their own distinctive interests and ideologies, which will underpin how they seek to shape and to define the field of global civil society and globalisation more generally. For example, transnational corporations are most likely to favour a relatively neo-liberal version of the global civil society. In this model, humanitarian projects are to be funded privately by individuals and agencies through voluntary donations and are implemented by NGOs according to the directions of the donors; these initiatives and projects are also not intended to undermine commercial interests.

Conversely, a more politically active form of global civil society is pursued by new social movements and radical NGOs. This model favours the pursuit of social justice, such as human rights, gender equality and fair industrial relations in developing nations and is more likely to challenge the interests and policies of global North institutions and agencies.

In the SDP sector, the different aspirations and functions of agencies and institutions are often clearly manifested. Some transnational corporations in the sport sector (e.g., Nike) have their own 'corporate social responsibility' programmes which are understood in part as promoting the long-term commercial success of the enterprise. The more neo-liberal types of SDP agency and institution tend to have a strong 'business-like' approach towards SDP work; they are also very effective in building partnerships with corporations as well as leading sports federations, governments and intergovernmental organisations. Moreover, these neo-liberal agencies tend to favour a particular type of sport-based intervention which is 'top-down', in terms of drawing heavily on established manuals and universal methods and in making the most of publicity opportunities, particularly through using world celebrities to endorse programmes.[4]

Conversely, smaller NGOs in the SDP sector tend to draw their support from different sources which are less likely to pursue particular commercial agendas; for example, private donors with liberal and humanitarian values tend to be strong partners. The work of these NGOs is usually relatively small scale, in being focused on specific locations and a particular number of SDP projects. The projects themselves are essentially focused on meeting the needs of local actors, with relatively little emphasis given to external publicity. Moreover, local actors tend to be engaged in strong dialogue with NGO officials when planning and implementing projects; indeed, the NGO officials are often drawn from the local population and given prior training before project implementation. The work of new social movements in regard to sport and the global civil society is more likely to focus on pursuing social justice, for example in advancing the labour rights of workers in sport merchandise factories in developing nations (see, e.g., Yimprasert, 2006).

Overall, then, SDP-work is one significant component of the wider sphere of global civil society. The different organisations and strategies within the SDP sector provide an insight into the institutional and political diversity of global civil society. It is also worth noting that many SDP agencies and officials have close and complex ties to institutions associated with wider global civil society. For example, many charitable NGOs have become more actively involved in sport-related work in recent years, whereas employees on SDP projects are often drawn from the wider NGO sector.

SPORT AND PEACE: KEY ISSUES FOR
INTERVENTIONIST PROJECTS

My research in a variety of sport and peace interventionist projects points to four broad issues and problems that need to be confronted and which could most effectively be resolved with reference to the contextual issues discussed above, in regard to global civil society, processes of globalisation, and the wider historical making of global sport.

Aims and Objectives

To begin, the project's aims and objectives need to be clearly defined. Within the sport-focused agency, it is highly beneficial if a clear set of core values and principles are established in order to underpin these aims and objectives. Officials need to establish what they are seeking to achieve and how these goals may be best realised through specific practice. For example, is the work to be focused on peace making or health promotion or improving gender equality, or perhaps a particular mixture of all three? More specifically, what particular results and impacts does the project seek to have among user groups?

In clarifying these aims and objectives, projects should take full account of how, within the site of intervention, sport has interconnected historically with processes of peace building and war. It is also beneficial for project workers to have an understanding of the different phases of sport history within their site of intervention, for example with reference to colonialism, nation building and the development of sport, and also how 'sport for development' initiatives have been introduced in the past in these locations. This historical reflexivity also leads more sophisticated project officials to recognize that the results of their work can only be assessed over the long term.

Resources

Sufficient resources—in terms of finance and labour—are essential for these projects to be implemented. Project officials need diverse forms of social capital in order to access finances from different funding sources, such as sports federations, private donors, corporations, larger NGOs, and governmental organizations (at national and international levels). Project officials need to exercise significant care in their relations with powerful partners and donors, as these latter groups may be 'hands-on' and seek to shape the project according to their particular interests. This can prove problematic if there are underlying conflicts over the philosophy, strategy and operational techniques within the project.

In regard to labour, the training of project workers serves to maximise their understanding of the project's objectives, principles and the wider socio-cultural context. The 'training the trainers' method enables local people to organise and to implement sport and peace projects in their home settings. Monitoring and evaluation initiatives are also widely reported by project officials to be helpful in terms of assisting the long-term effectiveness and critical improvement of initiatives. An effective utilisation of financial and human capital can also help projects to enhance their sustainability, thus tackling a problem that was particularly evident in the SDP sector in the 1990s and early 2000s, as we noted earlier.

Overall, understanding of, and responsiveness to, resource issues may be significantly enhanced if project officials have a good grasp of the range of 'global civil society' institutions and agencies which are operating within their sphere of operation.

Socio-Cultural Issues Surrounding Participation

A range of more practical socio-cultural issues needs to be addressed by project officials. The project needs to clearly identify its user groups and how they may be reached and engaged on an equitable and consistent basis. Key questions here are: is it the case that all participants are equally involved, or is one side privileged over the other? Do the coaches and helpers on these programmes derive from one particular side of the conflict rather than the other? Are there initiatives in place to train these situated actors in the values and ethics of the programme, in order to override previous sectional interests?

Questions also arise regarding the location of events. Context and the scope for reciprocity between user groups may be crucial in this regard. In some circumstances, a 'neutral' setting is essential to guarantee security and to demonstrate the equal status of participants. Alternatively, the project's work may be undertaken in different communities, to foster forms of reciprocated hospitality between participants from the different sides of a conflict. Securing local political support and establishing strong social capital can also be crucial. Many projects will depend upon backing and contacts from well-connected organisers and stakeholders. Local NGOs are often critical in terms of adapting international initiatives to the local context, something that is necessary to make these projects work.

Project officials need to think carefully about the sports which are to be used and how these are to be implemented. Do project officials favour traditional sports (e.g., cricket in South Asia, or football in Latin America), which are familiar to most participants, but which may also serve to continue to exclude key social groups (e.g., girls, those with less interest in these sports)? Or do project officials favour new sports which are unfamiliar to all participants and which are less attractive to some potential service users, but which may maximise the scope for equal participation? Additionally, the nature of social contact within the sport needs to be considered. For example, are 'invasive' sports like football to be favoured or more clearly demarcated sports, such as volleyball, where the two teams are divided by a net? Moreover, it might be possible to transform some traditional sports in order to safeguard the full participation of hitherto marginal groups, for example, by adjusting the rules of football to ensure that the involvement of girls in play is rewarded.

Finally, a key issue is how participants are engaged in designing, implementing and evaluating projects. Is it the case that the project users are fully consulted in relation to the projects? Do they generate strong senses of ownership? This form of dialogical engagement is not only an ethical imperative for projects but also serves to promote their success among prospective user groups.

Responses to these questions are facilitated if project officials have a good understanding of the historical interplay between sport, conflict and peace within the targeted setting. For example, an awareness of histories of colonialism, or the connections between particular sports and violent conflict, can serve to guide projects in their choice of sports and their method of implementation.

The Project's Wider Location: Global Civil Society and Political Environment

Too often, among agencies associated with global civil society, there is a lack of cross-institutional coordination and communication when work is being undertaken in a single geographical location. Therefore, most immediately, sport and peace project officials need to locate themselves fully with respect to other relevant agencies, particularly those working with broad development and peace-building agendas. Consideration also needs to be given to hitherto under-utilised institutional resources. For example, where relevant, military peace-keepers may play a useful role in some settings, in terms of organizing sports events, providing equipment and assisting in the teaching of practical skills (see Giulianotti & Armstrong, 2011). Networking with all of these relevant agencies is critical if the project is to make a full contribution to the wider peace-building context.

Additionally, consideration needs to be given to the deeper socio-political environment in which the project seeks to operate. Project officials may find themselves in contexts in which apparently extreme asymmetries exist between different social groups in terms of power, resources and the human costs of conflict. Issues of social justice and human rights may come into conflict with the need to establish peaceful and stable social relations between different peoples. On this matter, project leaders and officials need to reflect on the particular historical context in which they are working, consider how they resolve these issues of social justice and conflict with reference to the project's aims and objectives and consider how these issues impact upon the kinds of partnership that are pursued with specific institutions in global civil society, ranging from corporations through IGOs and NGOs to radical new social movements.

CONCLUDING COMMENTS

There has been a rapid growth in the number of sport and peace projects and initiatives since the early 1990s. There are a variety of ways in which sport would appear to have positive potential impact on peace-building exercises. Social scientists are able to apply historical and sociological approaches in order to obtain a fuller understanding of the interrelationships between sport, peace building and conflict. Clearly, there are significant historical periods when sport has been associated with violent conflicts. Moreover, we might explore the historical roots of global sport with regard to three broad phases which are marked, respectively, by colonisation and conquest, nation building and the development of sport and the rise of 'sport for development' from the early 1990s onwards.

The implementation of sport and peace projects features a variety of challenges that need to be confronted by project leaders and officials. Here, I have highlighted four broad sets of issues that need to be addressed: the project's aims and objectives, resources, socio-cultural issues surrounding participation and the wider location of the project with regard to global civil society and the political environment. Awareness of these historical and sociological issues can help to clarify the issues and challenges faced by project leaders and officials and help to enhance the implementation of these initiatives. Future work in this field would be enhanced through fuller consideration of how projects may promote forms of human emancipation and social justice within highly complex and diverse locations.

NOTES

1. See http://www.sportanddev.org/newsnviews/search.cfm?uNewsID=25.
2. This research was generously supported by a grant from the Nuffield Foundation.
3. On global civil society, see also Bartelson (2006) and Chandler (2005).
4. For potent critiques of neo-liberal ideologies and practices within the SDP sector, see Darnell (2008; 2010a; 2010b).

REFERENCES

Appadurai, A. (1995), 'Playing with Modernity: The Decolonization of Indian Cricket', in C. A. Breckenbridge (ed.) *Consuming Modernity: Public Culture in a South Asian World*, Minneapolis: University of Minnesota Press.

Armstrong, G. (2004), 'The Lords of Misrule: Football and the Rights of the Child in Liberia, West Africa', *Sport in Society*, 7(3): 473–502.

Armstrong, G. (2007), 'The Global Footballer and the Local War-Zone: George Weah and Transnational Networks in Liberia, West Africa', *Global Networks*, 7(2): 230–247.

Armstrong, G. & Giulianotti, R. (eds) (2004), *Football in Africa*, Basingstoke: Palgrave.

Baker, W. J. & Mangan, J. A. (eds) (1987), *Sport in Africa*, London: Africana Publishing.

Bartelson, J. (2006), 'Making Sense of Global Civil Society', *European Journal of International Relations*, 12(3): 371 395.

Beck, P. (1999), *Scoring for Britain: International Football and International Politics 1900 1939*, London: Routledge.

Beckles, H. McD. & Stoddart, B. (eds) (1995), *Liberation Cricket*, Manchester: Manchester University Press.

Booth, D. (1998), *The Race Game: Sport and Politics in South Africa*, London: Frank Cass.

Chandler, D. (2005), *Constructing Global Civil Society*, Basingstoke: Palgrave.

Cronin, M. (1999), *Sport and Nationalism in Ireland*, Dublin: Four Courts.

Darnell, S. (2008), *Changing the World Through Sport and Play: A Post-Colonial Analysis of Canadian Volunteers Within the 'Sport for Development and Peace' Movement*, unpublished PhD thesis, University of Toronto.

Darnell, S. (2010a), 'Power, Politics and "Sport for Development and Peace": Investigating the Utility of Sport for International Development', *Sociology of Sport Journal*, 27(1): 54–75.

Darnell, S. (2010b), 'Sport, Race and Bio-Politics: Encounters with Difference in "Sport for Development and Peace" Internships', *Journal of Sport and Social Issues*, 34(4): 396–417.

Gasser, P. K. & Levinsen, A. (2004), 'Breaking Post-War Ice: Open Fun Football Schools in Bosnia and Herzegovina', *Sport in Society*, 7(3): 457–472.

Giulianotti, R. (2004), 'Human Rights, Globalization and Sentimental Education: The Case of Sport', *Sport in Society*, 7(3).

Giulianotti, R. (2011a), 'Sport, Peacemaking and Conflict Resolution: A Contextual Analysis and Modeling of the Sport, Development and Peace Sector', *Ethnic and Racial Studies*, 34(2): 207–228.

Giulianotti, R. (2011b), 'Sport, Transnational Peace-Making and the Global Civil Society: Exploring the Reflective Discourses of "Sport, Development and Peace" Project Officials', *Journal of Sport and Social Issues*, 35(1): 50–71.

Giulianotti, R. (2011c), 'The Sport, Development and Peace Sector: A Model of Four Social Policy Domains', *Journal of Social Policy*, 40(4): forthcoming.

Giulianotti, R. & Armstrong, G. (2011), 'Sport, The Military and Peacemaking', *Third World Quarterly*, 32(2): 379–394.

Giulianotti, R., Armstrong, G. & Hognestad, H. (2003), *Sport and Peace: Playing the Game*, paper to Sport and Development: An International Conference, Swiss Academy for Development, Magglingen, Switzerland, 16–18 February 2003.

Giulianotti, R., Bonney, N. & Hepworth, M. (eds) (1994), *Football, Violence and Social Identity*, London: Routledge.

Giulianotti, R. & Robertson, R. (2009), *Globalization and Football*, London: TCS/Sage.

Guttmann, A. (1994), *Games and Empires: Modern Sports and Cultural Imperialism*, New York: Columbia University Press.

Höglund, K. & Sundberg, R. (2008), 'Reconciliation Through Sports? The Case of South Africa', *Third World Quarterly*, 29(4): 805–818.

Holt, R. (1989), *Sport and the British*, Oxford: Oxford University Press.

Kaldor, M. (2003a), *Global Civil Society*, Cambridge: Polity.

Kaldor, M. (2003b), 'The Idea of Global Civil Society', *International Affairs*, 79(3): 583–593.

Keim, M. (2003), *Nation Building at Play: Sport as a Tool for Integration in Post-Apartheid South Africa*, Aachen: Meyer and Meyer.

Lea-Howarth, J. (2006), *Sport and Conflict: Is Football An Appropriate Tool to Utilise in Conflict Resolution, Reconciliation and Reconstruction?*, MA

Dissertation, University of Sussex, accessed at: http://archive.sportanddev.org/data/document/document/238.pdf.

Mangan, J. A. (1986), *The Games Ethic and Imperialism*, London: Viking.

Mangan, J. A. (1987), 'Ethics and Ethnocentricity', in W. J. Baker & J. A. Mangan (eds) *Sport in Africa*, London: Holmes & Meier.

Perkin, H. (1989), 'Teaching the Nations How to Play', *International Journal of the History of Sport*, 6(2).

Richards, P. (1997), 'Soccer and Violence in War-Torn Africa: Soccer and Social Rehabilitation in Sierra Leone', in G. Armstrong & R. Giulianotti (eds), *Entering the Field: New Perspectives in World Football*, Oxford: Berg.

Sack, A. L. & Suster, Z. (2000), 'Soccer and Croatian Nationalism: A Prelude to War', *Journal of Sport and Social Issues*, 24(3): 305–320.

Schulenkorf, N. (2010), 'Sport Events and Ethnic Reconciliation: Attempting to Create Social Change in War-Torn Sri Lanka', *International Review for the Sociology of Sport*, 45(September): 273–294.

SDP IWG (2008), *Harnessing the Power of Sport for Development and Peace: Recommendations to Governments*, Toronto: Right to Play.

Sugden, J. & Bairner, A. (1993), *Sport, Sectarianism and Society in a Divided Ireland*, London: Leicester University Press.

UN General Assembly (2006), *Sport for Development and Peace: The Way Forward*, Report of the Secretary-General, A/61/73, New York: United Nations.

Vrcan, S. & Lalic, D. (1998), 'From Ends to Trenches and Back: Football in the Former Yugoslavia', in G. Armstrong & R. Giulianotti (eds), *Football Cultures and Identities*, Basingstoke: Macmillan.

Whitfield, G. (2006), *Amity in the Middle East: How the World Sport Peace Project and the Passion for Football Brought Together Arab and Jewish Youngsters*, London: Alpha Press.

Yimprasert, J. L. (2006), *The Life of Football Factory Workers in Thailand*, Thai Labour Campaign, accessed 8 March 2012 at: http://www.cleanclothes.org/documents/Life_football_workers_of_thailand.pdf.

2 In Africa for FIFA & Sons

Cora Burnett

The slogan for the 2010 FIFA (International Federation of Football Association) (men's) World Cup, 'In Africa for Africa', is an echo of the pan-Africanist credo, 'It's Africa's turn', which is laden with anti-colonial rhetoric as much as it is an expression of *neo-tribus* according to Maffesoli's post-modernist concept of social configuration (Maffesoli, 1996). The FIFA World Cup, on the one hand, represents a 'whole alternative world unto itself . . . an unreality zone of media and marketing mayhem' (Davies, 1991: 4), and on the other hand it is imbedded in society where the socio-political context is reflected in, and interwoven with, the very processes and products of the socially constructed and mediated world of sport. In a critical review about journalistic accounts of the FIFA World Cup, Sugden and Tomlinson (2007) refer to 'stories from Planet Football' in which the media is responsible for the construction of advertising this mega-event in such lucrative terms that the persuasive rhetoric is packaged as a powerful political narrative. Contradictory accounts and contextual realities (Kidd, 2008) are marginalised and silenced; almost any critical voice is publicly scrutinised and dismissed as a mere manifestation of Afro-pessimism (Black, 2007) or proof of disloyalty and ignorance, coming from outsiders or the non-informed (Burnett, 2009).

Often public debates are transfigured into this discourse, with all the mystery and myth packaged in a development discourse that addresses the perceived needs of the poor as an abstract collective (Kersting, 2007). The absence of the voices of the politically marginalised is evidenced in the induced ideology of how they are to benefit from the 'paradoxical blending of inclusive, transcendent or cosmopolitan narratives', and the construction of a national (sport) identity encapsulated by a notion of nationhood and world class citizenship (Black, 2007: 261).

In this chapter the case under discussion entails the 2010 FIFA (men's) World Cup and the roles played by stakeholders who contributed to key public debates. A critical interpretative mode of sociological inquiry is utilised which is anchored in an objective and realist epistemology. The narratives that are constructed around this mega-event in terms of political symbolism and the discourse of 'development' are interrogated as an alternative to existing epistemologies and to 'self-serving rhetoric' (Sugden & Tomlinson, 1999: 393). The localised production of knowledge should thus not be reduced to the social or linguistic imperatives of the stakeholder who produces them, but find a theoretical middle ground ('associational epistemology') (Ward, 1997: 83–85).

The question of the social construction of reality is, in first instance, investigative (prototyped by the penetrating activism of Andrew Jennings which focuses on the 'dark side' of the Fédération Internationale de Football Association), yet also pragmatically seeks to influence hegemonic policies, structures and practices (McDonald, 2002). This critical pragmatism (Mann, 1986; Kadlec, 2007) embodies the dissenting voices of the marginalised as much as it seeks to uncover the enshrined codes of entitlement and conduct that are rooted in the particular time and place of the 2010 FIFA World Cup (Sugden, 2010).

The graph in Figure 2.1 provides a structural overview of the rationale for this discussion of the mediated and real manifestations, according to what is widely propagated as a national sport legacy in which the sport component is the catalyst and link to the 2010 FIFA World Cup. The manifestations are recognised as an effect, rather than an impact, as they found expression in infrastructure development and quality of life components that influenced the lived realities of local communities and civic society through and for sport (see Figure 1).

Figure 2.1   Impact of 2010 FIFA World Cup.

RATIONALE FOR 2010 FIFA WORLD CUP-
RELATED MANIFESTATIONS

The residue of mega-event related interventions, propagated as 'legacy', speaks of limited community uptake and exclusion, despite the inclusive and pan-African rhetoric of regional and global unity spoken in a 'universal' language of sport (Mandela, 2000). What narratives are blended to portray and deconstruct a divided nation's reality where powerful political ideologies colour its own rainbow? South Africa pulled off the first event of such magnitude presented on African soil. Recognition of success found symbolic meaning in the proverbial 'pat on the back' by Sepp Blatter, who publicly acknowledged that South Africa would always be 'Plan B' for future FIFA World Cup events. As host, it was the rising star in the constellation of first world nations which was no small feat for a developing country, even if it is one with the largest economy and a "Big Brother" to other African nations.

PROFILING AFRICA AND SOUTH AFRICA

Wrapped up in the global configurations of power, inequality, and identity, South Africa has emerged as a survivor of apartheid, a victim turned victor and as a main player on the global stage where capitalist imperialism is contested, embraced and ever-changing. As a semi-peripheral continent, one of the largest 'first order' mega events launched would help Africa in its quest to overcome 'a historic sense of marginality and peripheral-ness' (Black, 2007: 265). The continent is home to thirty-two of the thirty-eight most heavily indebted countries in the world and Egypt and South Africa emerged as the only economically viable options to host the 2010 FIFA World Cup. It was no easy feat for South Africa, which received fourteen of the twenty-four votes, whilst both countries depicted themselves as the gateway to Africa, with bids wrapped up in post-colonial rhetoric and causing intra-continental polarisation of African nations (Cornelissen, 2004).

For South Africa, being awarded the 2010 FIFA World Cup provided the country with the opportunity to shed the residual legacy of apartheid ostracism within and beyond Africa and the racial politics that underpinned it. To counter this image, mega-events have persuasively helped brand the coming of age of a new democracy, as South Africa hosted (and won) the 1995 Rugby World Cup, the 2003 Cricket World Cup and Pan-African events such as the African Cup of Nations and the All Africa Games (Grundlingh, 1998).

The scene was set for moving from nation building and reconciliation (era of Mandela), to the promotion of an African identity through cultural renewal or African Renaissance (era of Mbeki) to 'inclusive and tribal emancipation' (era of Zuma). Hosting the 2010 FIFA World Cup was a coming of age for the South African black majority government (the

African National Congress, ANC) that signified, by proxy, the arrival of the African continent. This was vividly expressed by the South African Minister of Sport when he said that this event placed South Africa in the spotlight and that 'we dare not disappoint ourselves as South Africans and Africans' (Stofile, 2007).

The event became an instrument signifying continental unity, solidarity and collaboration, the arrival of a dignified and confident continent that would change 'Afro-pessimism'. The letter of Thabo Mbeki expressed the motivation of a continent's yearning for global inclusion and stated that being a host would write the history of 'a moment when Africa stood tall and resolutely turned the tide on centuries of poverty and conflict' (Black, 2007: 268 citing the South Africa 2010 official Web site).

The highly profiled *Ke Nako Africa* ('the time has come') platform during the World Cup, hosted by Sport and Recreation South Africa (SRSA, 2010a) in collaboration with various international and national partners, leveraged cooperation between influential and diverse stakeholders from the sport, corporate, public, cultural and development sectors. Associative clustering emerged, such as the Southern African Development Community (SADC) which promoted the region's investment opportunities as expressed by Dr. Augusto Tomáz Salomão, Executive Secretary of SADC by saying:

> The natural endowments in minerals, oil, abundant raw materials for manufacturing and value addition, coupled with a combined population of about 257 million with an estimated GDP of US\$ 465 billion, makes the region an invaluable investment partner. (SRSA, 2010a: 6)

Conflict and dissenting feelings were put aside as comrades rallied against Western capitalist powers in constructing and mediating a continent-wide legacy. Forgotten were feelings of animosity and the criticisms of South African arrogance that had compelled CAF-representatives (Confederation of African Football) from Cameroon, Botswana, Mali and Tunisia to vote for Morocco as the host country. The African political and economic elite stood united in the romanticised portrayals of potential pan-African benefits in all spheres of society. The region's identity and cohesion found expression in slogans such as *Simuny* ('We are one'), national identity and pride (Kersting, 2007).

Pan-Africanism constituted an Afro-barometer of identity formation and national pride—of being South African and African. The multiple, yet intersecting identities were socially constructed as feelings of pride found symbolic expression in a shared geographical setting and an event of historical significance (Norris, 1999). A hegemonic value system was constructed around values of reconciliation, collaboration (*ubuntu*) and assertion (Makoba, 1999). The rhetorical effect ignited a unique brand of sport patriotism as the 'beautiful game' belonged to the indigenous populations of Africa—the working man's sport—with little recognition of the imperialistic past. The divisions between African and non-African populations became an invisible subtext as African heads of state celebrated Africa's humanity.

The six African states that were represented in the tournament brought out the strengths and weaknesses of their preparations, yet contributed to the 'deepening of the bonds of solidarity and internationalism' (Campbell, 2010b: 1). The symbolic relevance of these teams transcended the victories and losses (Campbell, 2010a). Thick symbolism and pride underscored the much acclaimed opening and closing ceremonies, the beating of drums, blowing of vuvuzelas and a tribal identity with world-class players achieving totemic status. Hope was placed on the youth to liberate a continent full of strife, suffering and corruption, and FIFA became the strategic partner for all the contradictory narratives of a celebrated tribalism mandated by neo-liberal capitalism. It was a celebration of the 'people's game' acted out against the development agenda of political heavyweights with little regard for national priorities, marginalised communities and grassroots realities (McKinley, 2010).

In an address, the Minister of Sport and Recreation of South Africa acknowledged, during the Plenary of the International Olympic Committee 7th World Forum on Educational and Social Legacy of the FIFA World Cup (SRSA, 2010b), that the economic projections were overestimated and the benefits and costs were underestimated, yet he ignored the fact that the majority of impoverished communities had little to show from this legacy translated in an improved quality of life. The socio-political and developmental discourses constructed by decision-makers form a stark contrast with that of the majority of South African citizens who were left wanting and suppressed.

THE SOCIO-POLITICAL DISCOURSE AND 'DEVELOPMENT'

Sport-Related Development

Sport cannot address many of the development issues laid at its door and similarly, mega-events have limited reach and development potential. The sport-related legacy was driven by Sport and Recreation South Africa's legacy programme, alongside other national sport mass participation programmes, located in impoverished communities (*Siyadlala* hubs) and schools (School Sport Mass Participation Programme). As part of the legacy programme, FIFA launched Football for Hope programmes and centres in local communities where civic or non-government organisations already mainly ran health and educational projects and sport-for-development programmes (Campbell, 2010b: 2). Such projects include the LOC, South Africa's Legacy Project of erecting fifty-two Football Turfs in all the different SAFA-regions (SRSA, 2010a; 2010b), to which the National Lottery

Distribution Trust Fund committed 170.1 million rand sponsoring 27 of them (LOC, 2010). Civic society was brought on board for a more long-term legacy. Key non-governmental organisations (NGOs) were identified in order to manage the centres for community-driven projects. However, the NGO-sector is inherently competitive as most are totally dependent on donor funding and giving them the custodianship of such centres increased local competition. Having several NGOs utilising the same spaces would almost certainly provoke some conflict in the long run.

The inclusive management and optimal community involvement poses challenges, as was the case with some artificial turfs which were erected but locked by local governments to avoid damage to the surfaces. The lack of financial and human resources left local communities completely excluded and provided no solution for the lack of local sporting infrastructure. One turf in the Limpopo Province, near Jane Furse, is one such white elephant. Next to the national road to the northern province of Limpopo, there is this very neatly fenced surface of bright green among a deserted landscape with some traditional houses in the distance. No ball has been kicked there since the picture shoot during the World Cup period. Upgraded fields are therefore there for show only or for more elite teams and no longer available to local stakeholders. One such field provided a local primary school in the inner city of Johannesburg regular access to physical activities, but they were banned from using it as the local government does not have the funding for its maintenance.

As evidenced by policy-driven initiatives and international stakeholder agencies, sport-for-development interventions are often entrenched in 'evangelistic' claims and symbolic legitimisation of professed achievements that lack the rigour of scientific scrutiny (Coalter, 2010). The international aid paradigm often ignores the socio-political and economic realities of local contexts, creating a universal language for assessment of impact, circular reasoning and producing NGO operators who dance to the tune of their donors with their eyes fixed only on contributing to the achievement of the Millennium Development Goals or serving their own ends (Burnett, 2010).

Sport as a medium for development, despite promising findings within the South African and 'other' African contexts (Coalter, 2010; Keim, 2003), still has not reached maturity as a movement, or been translated into a meaningful agency (Kidd, 2008; Sugden, 2010). World Cup-related initiatives, such as the Youth Development through Football programme implemented as a joint initiative of the German Development Corporation (Gesellschaft für Technische Zusammenarbeit, GTZ), the European Union (EU) and SRSA and implemented in ten African countries with the Nike Network for Social Change as another key partner, hold special promise for a 'ripple effect' (Sugden, 2010) of sustainable impact (Burnett, 2010).

Women and girls became part of the sport-for-development initiatives launched by multiple agencies (including the government, international developing agencies and the corporate sector). In a national programme known as 'A Chance to Play', the international agent, Terre des hommes, offered various programmes in the Limpopo, Eastern Cape and Gauteng Provinces (Burnett & Hollander, 2011). Girls' football received priority in the Eastern Cape and afforded the local female players in the impoverished rural area of Peddie the chance to take part in the local ABSA) league. Yet this was but a drop in the ocean, for the gender politics within football as bastion of male domination is still firmly in place (Clark & Paechter, 2007). The African Women's Championships that was held in South Africa from 31 October to 14 November was not able to obtain the rights to be hosted in any of the newly-developed FIFA (men's) World Cup stadiums. Clark (2010) explains:

> It was only on 21 September, a mere 40 days before the tournament kicked off that the venue and confirmed dates were revealed. Much to the dismay of football fans hoping to cheer on the National Women's team, Banyana Banyana, in one of the newly built stadiums, this does not appear to be so. Instead, the Sinaba Stadium in Daveyton (Benoni) and Makhulong Stadium in Tembisa were announced as the hosts of this prestigious tournament where Nigeria, Ghana, Cameroon, Algeria, Tanzania, Mali and Equatorial Guinea will compete for the Continental Title.
>
> In my two visits to the (Makhulong) stadium for a warm-up match before the World Cup between Nigeria and North Korea and to watch Banyana Banyana trample Tanzania after the World Cup, the R38 million (spent on upgrading) does not seem to have gone into making the game more comfortable for the fans. After almost getting caught in a stampede at the entrance for the first match, lights were missing in the women's toilets, and upon leaving you unwillingly took part of the stadium with you as a concrete residue from the seats remained on our trousers . . . While this may be positive use of the practice stadium, why are the women getting the second class once again?

It is clear that the powerhouse of football in South Africa promotes a male agenda despite a public announcement by SAFA (South African Football Association) through a statement of those host cities' (*Ekurhuleni*) Councillor Ndosi Shongwe, that the 'hosting of this tournament on the heels of the successful 2010 World Cup is testimony that the infrastructure built for the World Cup will not lie dormant'. The marginalisation of women's football is firmly entrenched in patriarchal values, a cultural determinism evidenced in a lack of media exposure and the socio-political will to make a difference.

Non-sporting Development

The measuring of other tangible and intangible benefits left by the World Cup suggests that the expenditure and infrastructure that boosted the economy and had a temporary impact on job creation were skewed in favour of the economic and political elite. According to Grant Thornton South Africa (2010), an influential consultancy firm, the final cost of the 2010 FIFA World Cup was in the region of R55 billion, or 6 percent of South Africa's GDP, with the national government as the main spender (around R33 billion). The R846 billion that was allocated for public infrastructure investment programmes between 2010 and 2013 does not only leave a large debt, but channelled funding away from pressing developmental needs such as water provision, electricity and housing in underdeveloped areas. Dimant (2010) acknowledged that, according to an assessment of the 2010 FIFA World Cup by the Bureau for Economic Research, only R19.5 billion of the R33.7 billion spent, could be regarded as potentially productive investment.

The majority of expenditure went towards infrastructure development such as the development of world-class stadiums, the upgrading of airports and the Gautrain and other transport links that have been part of the annual budgets since 2006 (Sylvester & Harju, 2010). There are few guarantees for host cities that the stadiums will be financially sustainable, with the real possibility of the ones in Johannesburg, Durban, Cape Town and Port Elizabeth ending up as liabilities rather than assets, especially the R4.5 billion Green Point Stadium for which an estimated average loss of R7.1 million yearly for the first three years is projected (Ndaba, 2010; Donnelly, Grossmann & Harbour, 2010).

Despite the stimulation to the economy and the creation of 130,000 contractual construction jobs, the expenditure of about R11.7 billion on skill development and salaries for stadium constructors and employees, South Africa still recorded a job loss of 232,000 in the first half of 2010 (Statistics South Africa, 2010) and 870,000 in 2009 (Isa, 2010). The most recent unemployment figure is still relatively high at being an 'official' estimate of 25.2 percent and a 'wide' measure (including discouraged work-seekers) of 32.4 percent (South African Institute of Race Relations, 2010: 22).

Despite the unequal benefit sharing and FIFA's banning of unlicensed 'informal traders' within one kilometre of match venues, the informal sector did enjoy an increase in business and projected an increase of 115,000 jobs (Sylvester & Harju, 2010). Yet, the progress is slim and not likely to change the trajectory towards socio-economic inclusion of the marginalised majority. Given the large proportion of unemployed youth (age 15 to 34 years) comprising 52.7% of the total unemployment figure, exploitative opportunities were afforded them to be 'once-off' volunteers or to earn a wage for the short-term implementation of sports-related programmes for various NGOs. Several sets of data confirmed that these youth volunteers mostly have access to trainings and experiences that do not provide any kind of career pathway or access to steady income-generating opportunities (Burnett & Hollander, 2011).

The mega-event is a unique happening wrapped up in a mystique of political symbolism and many empty promises that leave the majority relatively untouched, except to provide them with a mystified memory and illusions of having been part of an event that was never theirs in the first place. It is an event for and by FIFA whose male and political cavalry ambush a global and local public into being a receptive and captive audience.

FIFA & SONS

It is no secret that FIFA pressurised (to the point of anticipated global ridicule) the LOC and South African government to deliver world-class infrastructure development, deemed essential for the delivery of a 'successful' World Cup. The tourist and sports-focused infrastructure was inevitably going to benefit the socio-political elite who could afford to travel or buy tickets for major events, whilst existing class divisions were exacerbated. How can a government that has pledged to redress the past developmental inequalities of its 49 million citizens justify spending R24 billion on the Gautrain that mainly transfers passengers to and from the Oliver Tambo Airport in Johannesburg for R100 per one way trip? The burden of debt is of no consequence to FIFA which left South Africa with more than R26 billion in tax-free revenue earnings (Delonno, 2010; Wright, 2010).

The irony of the proclaimed success of the 2010 World Cup lies in FIFA's rhetoric echoed by the brotherhood of political (and governmental) stakeholders of host cities who exercised their bragging rights by legitimising their spending on self-identified branding. How can this branding exercise of R55 billion be justified in view of post–World Cup 'scandals' such as the proposed media act intended to silence public criticism of governmental actions, corruption charges and regional conflict (Sylvester & Harju, 2010)?

Identity formation as global role player, the 'feel good factor', sport and national pride might be some of the most meaningful intangible benefits. It is however questionable if it is shared by citizens of all or even participating African countries. Civil rights abuses and the marginalisation of thousands of informal traders, exploitative pricing by MATCH (the official agency arranging packages for visitors and teams) and the protection of its own commercial interests and underhand dealings are but the ears of the hippopotamus.

Possibly the most devastating fact is the impact of evictions on the lives of the 10,000 local people who were evicted from local townships in 2007 to be 'dumped' in concentration-style living areas, in Tin Town, for example, which was supposed to be a temporary dwelling (Abahlali, 2010). The beautification of the surroundings next to the national main road, the international airport and upgrading Green Point Stadium (contrary to overwhelming support for the Athlone Stadium in the heartland of low-cost council housing) bears evidence to a FIFA Legacy, for and by the institution, regardless of the social devastation it produces.

The scale is largely tipped in favour of the exclusionary practices of an undemocratic entity, whilst legacy projects are published to demonstrate the development agenda of FIFA and its partners (SRSA, 2010b). It is in the conceptual framework of critical realism that such projects should be scrutinised and weighed to determine their relevance and value. Another programme, The Green Goal programme, was implemented as legacy project at all stadiums and fan parks, where both a dry and wet waste-bin system was introduced for optimal recycling of dry materials and utilisation of wet waste for compost making. My '2010 Schools Adventure' campaign was implemented by the Organising Committee and Department of Education, Sports and Recreation and Arts and Culture to include 12 million learners and teachers. As part of this initiative, a Schools Football World Cup targeted 10,000 schools. All these projects were relatively small scale and lacked the coordination and reach to have a broader impact. No sustainable leagues were formed and this once-off initiative just whetted the appetite without any follow-up and development in the long run for either the players or the sport.

The 2010 FIFA World Cup Ticket Fund afforded 120,000 complimentary category 4 tickets (3.6 percent of the total inventory) as incentive to construction workers and children from impoverished communities (SRSA, 2010b). The potential impact of these initiatives has not been scientifically measured, as monitoring and evaluation practices mostly require empirical evidence and expenditure as proof of implementation. Such initiatives have the potential to become merely a memory, easily eroded by the realities of poverty and many hardships disenfranchised communities have to face daily.

The illusionary effect of nation building evaporated in outbreaks of xenophobia in local communities where competition is rife for access to resources needed for household survival (Kersting, 2007). In the differentiation between 'us' and 'others', especially if the external "others" are from other African countries, tolerance levels are low if there is increased competition for resources in impoverished communities (Makoba, 1999). Violence is directed towards migrant workers and asylum seekers from other African,countries who are often prepared to work for lower wages or successfully compete for professional occupations in different sectors of South African society. African foreigners have, since 2008, when sixty-two people were killed and more than 100,000 displaced due to xenophobic attacks, constantly been living in fear of mounting threats of mass xenophobic violence after the World Cup due to an expected shrinkage of job opportunities (Conway-Smith, 2010).

CONCLUSION

It is clear that the ownership of the 2010 FIFA World Cup is well-served by its brand name. The spectacle belonged to the FIFA brotherhood, along with new political recruits who stipulated the terms of engagement and the notions of a legacy, encapsulated by development initiatives through and within the sports fraternity. There were acts of resistance such as the staging of the Poor People's World Cup in which teams of forty impoverished Cape Town communities participated but many dissenting voices were silenced. The arrogant boasting that the World Cup was successful dominated the headlines and public forums, spreading the sublime euphoria created by the media for the FIFA World Cup.

The brotherhood is firmly entrenched in FIFA as a western capitalist ideology that created the forum for show-casing both pan-African unity and a tribal narrative, something that might be empowering for the Afro-centric elite, but simultaneously excludes and divides along regional and local 'fault lines' FIFA deftly conveys the illusion of equality, of standardised practices and application of rules (Warshaw, 2010).

When the 'circus leaves town', the impact should thus not only be assessed in terms of dubious priorities and overspending, exploitative practices, super profits, increased foreign debt and imports, the breaking of trickle-down promises, suspension of democratic freedoms, and repression of rising protests (Bond, 2010), but in terms of the long-term effects and strengthening of self-identity and pride, as imprinted on the collective consciousness of all concerned (Bures, 2010). An agenda for change should be informed by multi-stakeholder involvement and a clear understanding of what football means in the lives of diverse communities where it is embraced and given special meaning.

REFERENCES

Abahlali (2010), *Poor People's World Cup' Shows Exclusion of Poor in South Africa*, accessed 24 September 2010 at http://www.abahlali.org/node/7102.

Black, D. (2007), 'The Symbolic Politics of Sport Mega-events: 2010 in Comparative Perspective', *Politikon*, 34(3): 261–276.

Bond, P. (2010), *World Cup in South Africa: Six Red Cards for FIFA*, accessed 29 September 2010 at: http://links.org.au/node/1740.

Bures, F. (2010), *Interview with Steve Bloomfield: World Cup 2010 and 'Africa United'*, accessed 29 September 2010 at: http//www.worldhum.com/features/travel-interview-with-steve-bloomfield-world-cup-2010-africa-united-20100528.

Burnett, C. (2009), 'Engaging Sport-for-Development for Social Impact in the South African Context', *Sport in Society*, 12(9): 1192–1205.

Burnett, C. (2010), 'Sport-for-Development Approaches in the South African Context: A Case Study Analysis', *SA Journal for Research in Sport, Physical Education and Recreation*, 32(1): 29–43.

Burnett, C. & Hollander, W. J. (2011), *Evaluation and Impact Study of a Chance to Play*, unpublished report, Johannesburg: BH Impact Assessment Services.

Campbell, H. (2010a), *Pan-African Postcard. Jabulani: Celebration of Fractals and Africa's Humanity*, issue 488, accessed 24 September 2010 at: http://pambazuka.org/en/category/panafrican/65604.

Campbell, H. (2010b), *World Cup's Aftermath: Creating a Progressive Legacy*, issue 490, accessed 28 September 2010 at: http://www.pambazuka.org/en/category/panafrcian/65968.

Clark, C. (2010), *Interview with Guest Lecturer and Doctoral Student at the University of Johannesburg*, Johannesburg, 28 September 2010.

Clark, S. & Paechter, C. (2007), '"Why Can't Girls Play Football?" Gender Dynamics and the Playground', *Sport, Education and Society*, 12(3): 261–276.

Coalter, F. (2010), 'The Politics of Sport-for-Development: Limited Focus Programmes and Broad Gauge Problems?', *International Review for the Sociology of Sport*, 45(3): 295–314.

Conway-Smith, E. (2010), 'World Cup 2010: Fears of Xenophobic Backlash', *Sports*, 8 July, accessed 28 September 2010 at: http://www.globalpost.com/dispatch/Africa/100706/world-cup-2010-fears-xenophobic-backlash.

Cornelissen, J. (2004), *Corporate Communications: Theory and Practice*, London: Sage Publications.

Davies, P. (1991), *All Played Out—The Full Story of Italia '90*, London: Mandarin.

Delonno, P. (2010), 'World Cup 2010: The Legacy', *Business Report*, 30 July 2010, accepted 12 August 2010 at: http://www.busrep.co.za/index.php?/SectionId=56 6cfArticleleld=4102101.

Dimant, T. (2010), 'The Economy', in J. Kane-Berman (ed.), *South Africa Survey 2009/2010*, Johannesburg: South African Institute of Race Relations, pp. 77–180.

Donnelly, L., Grossmann, C. Y. & Harbour, T. (2010), 'The March of the White Elephants', *Mail & Guardian*, 30 July 2010, accessed 1 August 2010 at: http://www.mg.co.za/article/2010–07–19-the-march-of-white-elephants.

Grant Thornton South Africa (2010), *2010 FIFA World Cup Visitors Will Stay Longer and Spend More*, accessed 1 August 2010 at: http://www.gt.co.za/News/Press-releases/Strategic solutions/2010/2010eia.asp.

Grundlingh, A. (1998), 'From Redemption to Recidivism? Rugby and Change in South Africa During the 1995 Rugby World Cup and Its Aftermath', *Sporting Traditions*, 14(2): 67–86.

Isa, M. (2010), 'More Jobs Lost in Second Quarter', *Business Day*, 30 July 2010, accessed 1 August 2010 at: http://www.businessday.co.za/articles/Content.aspx?id=116159.

Kadlec, A. (2007), *Dewey's Critical Pragmatism*, Lanham, MD: Rowman and Littlefield.

Keim, M. (2003), *Nation-building at Play—Sport as a Tool for Social Integration in Post-Apartheid South Africa*, Aachen: Meyer and Meyer.

Kersting, N. (2007), 'Sport and National Identity: A Comparison of the 2006 and 2010 FIFA World Cups ^{TM}', *Politikon*, 34(3): 277–293.

Kidd, B. (2008), 'A New Social Movement: Sport for Development and Peace', *Sport in Society*, 11: 370–380.

LOC (Local Organizing Committee) 2010 FIFA World Cup (2010), *World Cup Legacy Reaches Grassroots*, Thursday 25 February, accessed 8 April 2010 at: http://www.fifa.com/worldcup/organisation/media/newsid=1173945.html#world+cup+legacy+reaches+grassroots.

Makoba, M.W. (ed.) (1999), *African Renaissance*, Cape Town: Mafube.

Maffesoli, M. (1996), *The Time of the Tribes: The Decline of Individualism in Mass Society*, London: Sage.

Mandela, N. (2000), 'Opening Address', *Laureus Sport for Good Foundation Awards*, Monaco.

Mann, M. (1986), *The Sources of Social Power, Volume 1: A History of Power from the Beginning to A.D. 1760*, Cambridge: Cambridge University Press.

McDonald, I. (2002), 'Critical Social Research and Political Intervention: Moralistic Versus Radical Approaches', in J. Sugden & E. Tomlinson (eds), *Power Games: A Critical Sociology of Sport*, London: Routledge, pp. 100–116.

McKinley, D. T. (2010), *South African Soccer: For the Love of the Game or for the Love of Money and Power,* accessed 29 September 2010 at: http://www.sacsis.org/za/site/article/509.

Ndaba, D. (2010), When the Sun Sets on the 2010 World Cup, Will the Host Cities Be Ready to Swat Their New Sporting Assets?, *Engineering News,* 30 July 2010, accessed 1 August 2010 at: http://www.engineringnews.co.za/article/when-the-sun-sets-on-the-2010-world-cup-will-the-host-cities-be-ready-to-sweat-their-new-sporting-assets-2010-ou-02.

Norris, P. (1999), *Cosmopolitans, Nationalists and Parocials,* paper presented at the fourth annual meeting of the Johan F. Kennedy Visions of Governance for the Twenty-First Century, Mount Washington Hotel, Bretton Woods, 11–14 July 1999.

South African Institute of Race Relations. (2010), 'Demographics: Provincial Profiles', *Fast Facts.* 8: 1–28.

SRSA (Sport and Recreation South Africa) (2010a), *"Ke Nako Africa', 10 June–11 July 2010',* Pretoria: Department of Sport and Recreation, South Africa.

SRSA (Sport and Recreation South Africa) (2010b), *The Legacy of the 2010 FIFA World Cup,* accepted 28 September 2010 at: http://www.sa2010.gov.za/node/2926.

Statistics South Africa. (2010), *Quarterly Labour Force Survey,* Quarter 2 (April to June), 2010, accessed 1 August 2010 at: http://www.businessday.co.za/articles/Continent.aspx:id=116159.

Stofile, M. A. (2007), *Opening Address on the Occasion of the 2010 National Communication Partnership Conference,* 15 August 2007, Sandton, Gauteng, South Africa.

Sugden, J. (2010), 'Critical Left-realism and Sport Interventions in Divided Societies'. *International Review for the Sociology of Sport,* 45(3): 258–272.

Sugden, J. & Tomlinson, A. (1999), 'Digging the Dirt and Staying Clean. Retrieving the Investigative Tradition for a Critical Sociology of Sport', *International Review for the Sociology of Sport,* 34(4): 385–397.

Sugden, J. & Tomlinson, A. (2007), 'Stories from Planet Football and Sports World'. Source Relations and Collusion in Sport Journalism, *Journalism Practice,* 1(1): 44–61.

Sylvester, J. & Harju, D. (2010), 'What's Left After the World Cup?', *ePoliticsSA,* 1: 2–22.

Ward, S. (1997), 'Being Objective About Objectivity: The Ironies of Standpoint Epistemological Critiques of Science', *Sociology,* 31(4): 73–91.

Warshaw, A. (2010), *Blatter Breaks Silence over Goal-line Technology,* accessed 28 September 2010 at: http://insideworldfootball.com/index.php?option=com_content&view=article&id=7869:blatter breaks silence over goal-line technology.

Wright, C. (2010), *2010 World Cup: the Winners and Losers,* accessed 28 September 2010 at: http:soccerlens.com/2010-world-cup-the-winners-and-losers/50294.

3 Constructing Peace and Fostering Social Integration

Sport and Play in Azerbaijan

Joel Rookwood

The dissolution of the Soviet Union in 1991 was preceded and followed by declarations of independence from various nations-elect previously subject to Russian governance. Although territorial divisions have remained stable in some areas, the Caucasus region, a geo-political region at the border of Europe and Asia, has proven relatively unstable (Matveeva, 1999). North Caucasus comprises nine semi-autonomous republics, all of which remain federal subjects of Russia. The three independent states of Georgia (including Abkhazia and South Ossetia), Azerbaijan (including Nagorno-Karabakh) and Armenia, form the South Caucasus. This area has been subject to notable societal problems and ongoing political and militaristic struggles in Chechnya (Dunlop & Menon, 2006), Dagestan (Wear & Kisriev, 2001) and Georgia (Peimani, 2009), among others:

> The collapse of the Soviet Union has given rise to a number of plural societies, the principal common feature of which has been their rapid, and seemingly irrevocable, descent along a trajectory of ethnic conflict, political separatism, and socioeconomic disintegration. Nowhere has this collapse had more tragic consequences than the Caucuses. (Wear & Kisriev, 2001: 105)

Azerbaijan and Armenia gained internationally recognised autonomous status during the post-1991 era. A legacy of political and militaristic antagonism between these two countries fostered strained relations, with divisions also evident along ethno-religious and socio-cultural lines (Yamskov, 1991). The fractious relationship between Armenians and Azerbaijanis has recently been dictated by territorial disputes, notably regarding Nagorno-Karabakh. The political and military control of this region has a complex history and remains a heavily disputed issue. Territorial clashes have involved ethnically motivated violence resulting in pogroms and the deaths of many citizens, whilst extensive civilian populations have been forcibly displaced and whose relocation has involved exposure to unharmonious and violent conditions in various fractured communities (Potier, 2001). The resultant humanitarian crises have inspired intervention from sections of the international community to help stabilise social order, reduce the reliance on organised violence and promote the social development of the victims of conflict. Some non-governmental organisations (NGOs) have devised and implemented services and programmes in order to facilitate peace and social development amongst these communities of internally displaced persons (IDPs). In some cases, this has involved the construction of houses and educational and leisure facilities and the creation of culturally focused sports-based initiatives. NGOs are increasingly developing sporting programmes as a means of encouraging segregated groups and individuals to congregate within shared space in order to partake in communal sporting activities. Football in particular has proven significant in this regard as a function of its perceived global popularity, uniformity and applicability in local contexts (Rookwood, 2009a).

There is evidence that involvement in sport and play can help participants develop social, moral, emotional, physical and cognitive competencies, particularly among youth. Positive physiological effects of participation in sport and physical activity have been noted in contemporary society, especially when combined with the provision of clean air and adequate nutrition. Such interaction can perform a preventive and rehabilitative function in relation to some diseases, including cardio-vascular diseases and can decrease the likelihood of unhealthy practices (Rankinen & Bouchard, 2002). It can also positively affect self-esteem, self-worth and social integration and help combat discrimination. Sports participation can moreover attract young people to become volunteers, increase measures of altruism and community orientation and provide opportunities for leadership development. In the context of peace promotion, sport has also been found to play an important rehabilitative role for those affected by conflict, crisis, discrimination and marginalisation (Sugden, 2007). In addition, it has been argued that being labelled an 'athlete' reflects positively on youth and that partaking in sport can alleviate deviant behaviour and promote academic achievement (Bailey, 2005). Furthermore, Hedstrom and Gould (2004) claim that the values and ethics promoted in sport can shape the moral character instilled in participants. However, some cautionary and critical perspectives have also been noted in this respect, and questions remain regarding the values of competitive sport and how they should be disseminated, the kinds of behaviour that should be promoted through sport, the criteria required for assessing the value of sporting interactions and the related impact (Vanden Auweele, Malcolm & Meulders, 2006). Some of these questions are considered in this contribution in the context of a social integration initiative staged in the Azerbaijani city of Mingachevir.

Development projects cannot be fully understood in isolation from related societal factors and causes of social change and research approaches (not to mention implemented initiatives) that fail to address this issue, whilst aiming to explore the complexities of the relationship between sport and development, are destined to collapse. This chapter therefore examines the political context and the plight of IDPs in Azerbaijan. Focusing on a case study from the northern city of Mingachevir, this work also explores the suitability and applicability of sport and play to contribute to the peaceful advancement of Azerbaijani society. Following a primary phase of housing construction, the project in question was a secondary assimilation phase involving the erection of an extensive 'play park' in the centre of the IDP-'village', as well as a youth football project staged in the city. World Vision was responsible for the first stage, creating houses for a community of approximately 10,000 IDPs and British volunteers representing Samaritan's Purse organised and managed the second stage. IDPs of various ages volunteered their support in constructing the park, which was to be shared by both the 'indigenous' community of Mingachevir and the IDPs from Nagorno-Karabakh. The value and impact of this park and its construction are examined in this chapter.

The football initiative was a value-based project that focused on technical elements and fun-based drills. British coaches were supported both practically and linguistically by local personnel. The coaching element emphasised several values aiming to promote fair play, mutual understanding and co-operation and facilitate conflict prevention and co-existence. For example, some of the coaching drills were implemented in ways that offered participants practical ways of solving problems presented to them. There was also a competitive element, as teams of mixed identities (i.e. those from Mingachevir and those from Nagorno-Karabakh) competed in a tournament at the end of the programme. This relied on a carefully organised registration process carried out in collaboration with community leaders. This approach provided participants with opportunities to illustrate the tactical, technical and moral lessons they had learned and importantly, also prevented a victory representing a triumph over 'the other', but instead encouraged inter-community cooperation. A league was subsequently established to promote and help sustain relationships.

Selected interview and observational data obtained during the project is examined in the remainder of this chapter. This reflects the perspectives of the 'indigenous' residents of Mingachevir, the IDPs from Nagorno-Karabakh and the British volunteers who constructed the play park and ran the football coaching programme. The Azerbaijani comments were translated into English 'on location', which is how they are presented here. Attitudes are explored in relation to the value of play and sport in contributing to the promotion of a peace culture in Azerbaijan. The extent to which the function and meaning of sport are considered dependent on the manner in which these programmes are constructed and experienced in this context, is also analysed. Opinion was further gauged with respect to the degree to which this approach was rooted in and responsive to, people's perspectives and needs and whether the initiative was contextual and culturally sensitive. This work also explores whether character and moral development can be transferred to participants and whether coaches succeeded in implementing specific teaching strategies to promote positive moral change. Finally, this work examines whether by orienting practices toward peace building, initiatives such as these can be framed as opportunities for restructuring collective identities in ways that promote peaceful unity and facilitate the cultural assimilation of Azerbaijan's IDPs and it identifies some of the lessons that can be learned for those wishing to run related projects in other areas.

THE VALUE OF SPORT AND PLAY IN MINGACHEVIR

The intended function of both the play park construction and the football coaching project was to assist the assimilation of IDPs into Mingachevir culture. In terms of the value of play and sport, such engagements have been established in order to intervene in politically sensitive contexts and in the aftermath of military conflicts, to facilitate reconciliation between opposing groups and to support the victims of warfare. It has also been suggested that in post-war communities and for those who have recently experienced conflict, sporting interactions can promote mutual understanding, friendship, solidarity and fair play (Rookwood, 2009a). In an Olympic context, the 'Peace Games', established in Congo in August 2006, were organised by the International Olympic Committee (IOC) in collaboration with the United Nations Mission in the Democratic Republic of Congo. Tournaments were staged in basketball, football and various longer distance running events, although the objective was not merely to increase athletic ability but also 'to promote a culture of peace and reconciliation [and to offer] the youth of the Democratic Republic of Congo an alternative to violence and hatred' (Wassong, 2006: 323). However, it is unclear how successful this venture was in terms of peace promotion and peace building and whether youth participants perceived or experienced the initiative as one providing genuine and lasting 'alternatives to violence'.

In Israel, the ongoing Football for Peace (F4P) project was established in 2001 in order to support co-existence between Jews and Arabs. This youth development educational initiative is underpinned by neutrality, being unaffiliated to any religious or political group. As a function of the widespread and passionate interest in football, youth engagement in the sport at a grassroots level has been found to positively influence inter-faith and ethnic cooperation and coexistence in Israel (Ben-Porat, 2006). The F4P- model involves value-based football coaching, whereby coaches identify and reinforce specific concrete behaviours attached to the values of neutrality, inclusion, respect, trust and responsibility, so that they may be taken beyond the football field (Stidder, 2007). This model has been critiqued from a number of angles, such as moral development, physical education, coaching and pedagogy, gender and equality, sociology and politics, visual methodology and social development (Lambert, 2007; Rookwood & Wassong, 2010).

The decision to construct a play park in a central location within the Mingachevir IDP housing community was inspired by a desire to encourage and support younger boys and girls in their process of cultural assimilation. This specific age group often experiences a sense of alienation from peace building and social development initiatives, perceiving themselves as the: 'demographic majority that sees itself as an outcast minority' (Sommers, 2003: 1). Their involvement in the process in Azerbaijan was not revolutionary, but neither could it be described as typical practice. Before exploring the value of the play park, however, it is necessary to consider the significance of 'play', which relates to a range of voluntary, intrinsically motivated activities normally associated with pleasure and enjoyment (Hughes, 2009). It can include amusing, pretend or imaginary interpersonal and intra-personal interactions. The rites of play are evident throughout nature and are perceived in people and animals and these are notable particularly in the cognitive development and socialisation of humans. Play often involves the use of props, tools, animals or toys in the context of learning and recreation. Some commentators argue that play is a frivolous and non-serious activity:

> Play is a free activity standing consciously outside 'ordinary' life as being 'not serious' but at the same time absorbing the player. It is an activity connected with no material interest, and no profit can be gained by it. It proceeds within its own proper boundaries of time and space according to fixed rules and in an orderly manner. It promotes the formation of social groupings that tend to surround themselves with secrecy and to stress the difference from the common world by disguise or other means. (Huizinga, 1950: 13)

Children who engage in playful activities often do so with a sense of absorption and engagement. Although some types of playful activity adopt a relaxed pace and sense of freedom, other forms are characterised by compulsion. Also, play can have intrinsic constraints, applied with the expression of such notions as 'you're not playing fairly'. Play can also serve as an activity for rehearsing real-life events. In this way exposure to appropriate playful activities can prove particularly beneficial for children and young people and by extension it can prove dangerous depending on the conditions. The IDP-play park constructed in Azerbaijan was approximately 40 square metres. The park provided a mixture of apparatus such as swings, slides and climbing frames. It was not fenced in or supervised and children from both the IDP-community and Mingachevir were free to enjoy it, as those responsible for them (parents/guardians) deemed acceptable.

The participants in this work included those who volunteered their services to community leaders, as well as the Azerbaijani community leaders and British volunteers. As far as local interviewees were concerned, all contact was made through the community leaders, who also translated comments made into English. I arranged the interviews with the British volunteers, all of whom offered their services in this respect at the outset of the project. If we look at the perceived significance of play in the context of this initiative, the respondents in this research offered similar contextualised views during the construction of the project. For example:

> You can see that the kids playing together is really positive. I mean, they have disagreements, but they make friends again. This is like life though. It's a good rehearsal in that way . . . They can express themselves here and learn to share, wait their turn and have fun. (British volunteer, interview)

Also, during the opening of the park, one of the parents made the following remark:

> You can see kids mixing with each other [from the two communities]. It's a really positive sign. If they continue like this, then this park will have a huge effect on life here. (indigenous parent, observation)

In terms of the impact of this play park, another Azerbaijani community leader stated:

> It is difficult to say the effect this park will have, but it will help bring normality and stability to these kids. Growing up in a war zone makes you violent. But you can see the kids play and they can act like kids here. Here they are free. (IDP community leader, interview)

Respondents suggested that one of the main strengths of this park was not simply its physical legacy, but also:

> You have let our boys help build it. And we have helped build it. We can say 'now we live here'. We have our homes but this beautiful [park] makes us feel we are here . . . This is very good that the children will grow up with these memories. (IDP community member, interview)

The play park was considered to adhere to and allow for the development of locally respected attributes. Its construction was also perceived to be responsive to and rooted in the experiential and subjective realities of the young people:

> For these kids who have only known war, being physical is important. But in the right way. This is good for them. (IDP parent, interview)

From the perspective of the British volunteers, the involvement of the local communities in constructing the play park was not ideal really. But it was important for them to feel involved. Often they were more of a pain but they felt proud to help. They're likely to take care of it now too knowing how hard it was to build and that it was their efforts. Plus they learned lots of physical skills. (British volunteer, observation)

The involvement of the community members was important to allow them to develop a sense of ownership and involvement. As Chester points out:

> At the heart of good social action is the participation of those in need. This means that time is more important than money in social involvement . . . because social involvement is about changing people, attitudes and structures rather than simply providing goods and services. This applies to projects but also individual relationships. (2004: 139).

The football project was considered a supplementary rather than foundational element of the development initiative. More than three hundred children, aged between 8 and 18, participated in the various coaching events. Even though the play park was constructed on 'IDP territory' on the outskirts of Mingachevir, and where the indigenous community was invited to share in the play park, the football project was staged in the city's principal sports stadium in central Mingachevir. Again, members of 'the other' community were invited onto this land to partake in the programme, as a form of reciprocation, with Samaritan's Purse covering the cost of both aspects of the initiative (including the hiring of land and equipment and the purchase and delivery of materials and apparatus). Many of the players went on to represent teams in a subsequently established competitive football league. The ethos of the coaching programme and the associated league was one of shared experience, mutual understanding, discipline, respect and fair play. Teaching strategies were employed in the attempt to promote a positive change in moral growth, although coaches noted the difficulty in this value-based approach:

> Some of the things we were saying weren't getting properly translated. And some things like discipline, the locals were ignoring. Maybe it's more our thing than theirs. Translation was an issue too . . . But often for the kids it was about winning and about playing and not acting in a certain way. (British volunteer, interview)

This clearly reflects a weakness in the approach adopted in this project.

As regards the intended practical implementation of the values, discipline was infused by encouraging players to participate according to the regulations and by insisting on certain kinds of behaviour, which were made a condition for participation. Fair play was emphasised through the reference to cheating and honesty within competitive activities and encouraging the reinforcement of appropriate conduct whilst correcting unsuitable behaviour. Respect involved offering both team-mates and opponents a positive reception before and after coaching sessions and matches, for example. In addition, tournaments were staged involving mixed teams (arranged by coaches). Local volunteers were trained as part of the coach education programme—each of whom was given responsibility for a team—which then competed in leagues established afterwards by local partners. The education programme involved working with the coaches and teaching them how to run the various technical drills implemented in the project.

The experiences in Azerbaijan testify that there are certain lessons that can be learned for those wishing to run similar projects in other regions. Ultimately, the meaning of these sporting interactions is dependent on the manner in which programmes are constructed and experienced. To some of the young people,

> football is just a game. Some didn't care about the rules and just wanted to play. But most respected the coaches and wanted to learn, and made themselves behave just so they could be involved. They were so excited at playing that they really got into the spirit of how to play and how to treat other people. The only issue is, will the coaches take this on when we've gone? And will the kids respect them as much? (British volunteer, interview)

PEACE BUILDING AND SOCIAL INTEGRATION

> We should take care, in inculcating patriotism into our boys and girls, that is a patriotism above the narrow sentiment which usually stops at one's country, and thus inspires jealousy and enmity in dealing with others . . . Our patriotism should be of the wider, nobler kind which recognises justice and reasonableness in the claims of others and which lead our country into comradeship with the other nations of the world. The first step to this end is to develop peace and goodwill within our borders, by training our youth of both sexes to its practice as their habit of life, so that the jealousies of town against town, class against class and sect against sect no longer exist; and then to extend this good feeling beyond our frontiers towards our neighbours. (Lord Baden-Powell)

The widespread disintegration of communities highlights the need for reconciliation in many fractured societies. However, to frame all social development needs as reconciliatory is to deny the requirements for domestic integration of internally (and often forcibly) displaced persons. Given the potential contribution to the stabilisation of social order, the process of supporting such groups could be considered a form of peace building. Murithi considers this construct to be 'effectively a political activity' (2009: 3), whereas Paris defines the term as 'action undertaken at the end of a civil conflict to consolidate peace and prevent a recurrence of fighting' (2004: 38). If its definitive designation as a civil construct appears unfounded, it could, however, be argued that the operative term in this statement is 'action'. Peace building should not be confined to ideas and rhetoric. Importantly, applied sporting and playful interactions amongst youthful populations can acquire varying levels of significance in different cultures and are subject to the nature of intersubjective experience and understanding. It is imperative that all mediums for social development are not merely accepted uncritically as 'positive'. However, this project serves as evidence of the suitability of such engagement, subject to certain conditions.

The play park fostered an expressive freedom through the allowance of opportunities for intra-personal playful interactions, typically, although not exclusively, amongst the youth population of Mingachevir. Both boys and girls were supported and encouraged in the assimilation process in an environment that provided a relaxed pace and sense of freedom, enabling them to become absorbed in unstructured and creative activities (with the notable exception of the somewhat frantic and crowded opening of the park). Short-term social projects spread over a fortnight, such as the football coaching programme, together with the extended league system and the more permanent play park in Mingachevir, offer different examples of micro-centered initiatives. The league was established by the local community leaders after the UK-staff had departed in order to give youths from the two communities a chance to socialize and learn together during weekends. However, it is the interconnectivity of these individual developmental processes and experiences that will dictate the overall significance, the wider contribution and ultimate impact of each.

Sporting interaction can provide both negative and positive experiences for participants, depending on their approach to, understanding of and engagement in these constructs. The role of the coach is to make these experiences as positive as possible. There is clear potential for sport to be manipulated in forms which encourage violence and hatred. However, the simplicity and clearly defined regulatory component of global sports such as football also allow for shared experiences of an expressive, physical, communal activity that can be largely unaffected by particular linguistic, cultural, political and ethnic affiliation and identity. Although the values of competitive sport can lead to gamesmanship, the manner in which the games were presented here encouraged a focus on the more 'constructive' element of the sport. Inevitably, there were some difficulties in disseminating these values within coaching sessions as previously stated. These were affected by the complexities involved in translation, which in some cases necessitated a trilingual system from English to Russian to Azerbaijani. Such convolution and potential misinterpretation provides those who are not involved in such projects with ammunition to attack their value. However, in defence of practitioners, it can be said that this often represents the reality of all such work, as projects of this nature often involve those divided by culture and language.

In addition, a key research question concerned value implementation and whether the selected values served to promote fair play, mutual understanding and cooperation, as well as facilitate conflict prevention and co-existence. The intention was for this to be built upon a developed understanding of the kinds of behaviour that should be promoted through sport, and the criteria required for assessing the value of the sporting interactions. On reflection, the values were considered by participants to primarily represent British rather than Azerbaijani culture and there were problems with both the design and the implementation of the project, such as transportation to and accommodation within Mingachevir, as well as the funding for the initiative. However, the mode of engagement was considered culturally reflective, with both football and the play park proving immensely popular, helping to foster relationships. Notably, however, the long-term responsibility of this aspect lies with the local trainers and participants. The community leaders were empowered through the coach education programme and are far better placed than any international personnel to interpret, modify and implement the values in a way that could be considered constructive. Importantly, this case study is not one in which development was merely imposed. The decision to build the play park and conduct the football programme was taken following detailed consultation with various community leaders. There was the sense in this case that it was welcomed. However, the approach adopted with these social projects is not one that borrows from the producer-consumer model in which 'aid' is merely distributed. Instead, the two communities of Mingachevir were actively encouraged to participate in ways which are more likely to produce sustained social development:

> Some forms of charitable intervention can leave people marginalized. They can reinforce a sense of powerlessness. Something is done *for* the poor. They remain passive. They are not becoming contributors to society. They become more dependent on others. So social involvement is more than presenting people with solutions. Good social involvement involves helping people to find their *own* solutions. (Chester, 2004: 138)

Proving the impact of sport and the extent to which its values guide the future action of participants is an intrinsic problem for such development initiatives. In highlighting the value and focus of the F4P initiative, Nujidat argues that 'Maybe the children who have experienced F4P will not grow up to be professional football players, but surely they will be better human citizens because of it' (2007: 154). However, as with this project, it is unclear whether the F4P-initiative produces 'better human citizens', as providing definitions and related frames of reference are problematic procedures. Play is similarly difficult to analyse with respect to its impact. In this case both elements would clearly benefit from longitudinal analysis and although this is beyond the scope of this work, it is important to address these issues. Only by revisiting the communities involved could a more detailed judgement be made as to whether the initiative has succeeded in restructuring collective identities that promoted unity and assimilation. In addition, it would be necessary to undertake further analysis in order to determine the extent to which the teaching strategies employed, promoted a lasting positive change in moral growth amongst the project participants and the degree to which playful and sporting interactions can positively affect the inculcation of character and moral development in Azerbaijan.

CONCLUSION

The recent conflicts in the Caucasus region could be considered a result of a consistent failure to take effective measures to bring stability, together with a lack of understanding of the roots of the respective problems and the causes of violence. Fallout from conflict has enveloped the region, with escalating violence nourished by deep social and economic pathologies (Phillips, 2007; Dunlop & Menon, 2006). The territorial, political and military control and associated disputes between Azerbaijan and Armenia, notably regarding Nagorno-Karabakh, have a long and complex history. These issues are not going to be solved by individual, micro-centered cases of social involvement in the various communities of the two countries, internationalised or otherwise. Indeed the consequences of community-based responses, irrespective of their locations, intentions or ramifications may appear insignificant in isolation. Ethnically-motivated violence and forced displacement are among the conditions that many victims of this conflict have been subjected to within the various fractured communities of Azerbaijan and Armenia. The humanitarian crises that these hostilities and conditions have produced further complicate the task of responding effectively, in the bid to contribute to peace-building. However, ingrained socio-political complexity is not a sufficient reason for apathy or inactivity. Of course, effective interethnic, race and community initiatives should be encouraged and it is important for academics to contribute by engaging in related analysis. However, it is also important for those who have been subject to, schooled in and programmed for conflict, to be included in social development activities within their own borders, amongst those of comparable identity and ethnicity. This case study testifies to the fact that the problems associated with the assimilation of IDPs amongst an 'indigenous' population, calls for initiatives that promote social integration on community levels and that if a wider sense of patriotism can be fostered, one that inspires amity rather than enmity at a micro level, this can be a foundation on which relations at a macro level can be developed.

Other social integration projects implemented in fractured communities, such as F4P in Israel, and STAR, a value-based coaching programme based in post-war Liberia, have been built on a model of social integration. Youths from 'opposing' groups (Jews and Arabs in Israel and non-child soldiers and ex-combatants in Liberia) have congregated in shared space to partake in sporting programmes aimed at promoting peace and building relationships (Rookwood & Palmer, 2011). However, other social involvement projects have helped foster development despite the decision not to include representatives of 'the other'. For example, the Beslan sports initiative, implemented close to North Ossetia's border with Chechnya a month after the 2004 terrorist attack perpetrated by Chechen rebels, did not allow for integration with those divided by the borders of North Ossetia, given the unwillingness and insecurity of the local people. However, according to the participants and beneficiaries, the unilateral approach did not render the project futile (Rookwood, 2009b). Similarly the decision to focus only on Azerbaijani citizens in this initiative might be considered a limited approach; however, domestic, post-conflict social integration is certainly an important process, as the experiences of those committed to supporting the assimilation of IDPs in various fractured communities around the world would testify (Schiff & Winters, 1998; Sutton, 2009; Omeje, 2009). Ultimately, the plight of refugees and the relationship between citizens of the two countries is beyond the scope of this paper and of this project, despite its contextual relevance. However, the positive outcomes of such ventures might encourage and inspire future international approaches.

This is not to suggest that this project or research was implemented without limitations; indeed the initiative and the work undertaken here are fraught with problems. Practical dilemmas relating to transport, culture, security and language. for example, were evident throughout. The presentation and use of translated interview data as 'unproblematic', for example, was a feature open to criticism, as was the use of the term 'indigenous' (to differentiate them from IDPs); however, with limited space available here, it is clearly preferable to focus on more significant aspects of the work. Finally, sporting interactions, whether in the context of community projects or elite international competitions, cannot and should not always be expected to improve relations or even instigate dialogue between previously warring factions. The perceived applicability, global appeal and pacifist potential of sport and leisure should not be used as a blanket criterion for employing sports-based activities in all circumstances. However, as with other countries, future projects between Azerbaijan and Armenia should be based on culturally relevant and politically sensitive and yet meaningfully engaging practice and sport should be included if its potential benefits to international relations are to outweigh the risks.

REFERENCES

Bailey, R. (2005), 'Evaluating the Relationship Between Physical Education', Sport and Social Inclusion', *Educational Review,* 57(1): 71–90.

Ben-Porat, A. (2006), 'Split Loyalty: Football-cum-nationality in Israel', *Soccer and Society,* 7(2–3): 262–277.

Chester, T. (2004), *Good News to the Poor: Sharing the Gospel Through Social Involvement,* Leicester: Inter-Varsity Press.

Dunlop, J. & Menon, R. (2006), 'Chaos in the North Caucasus and Russia's Future', *Survival,* 48(2): 97–114.

Hedstrom, R. & Gould, D. (2004), *Research in Youth Sports: Critical Issues Status,* East Lansing: Institute for the Study of Youth Sports, Michigan State University.

Hughes, F. P. (2009), *Children, Play and Development,* London: Sage.

Huizinga, J. (1950), *Homo Ludens: A Study of the Play Element in Culture,* Boston: Beacon Press.

Lambert, J. (2007), 'A Values-based Approach to Coaching Spot in Divided Societies—The Football for Peace Coaching Manual', in J. Sugden & J. Wallis (eds), *Football for Peace? The Challenges of Using Sport for Co-Existence in Israel,* Oxford: Meyer and Meyer, pp. 13–34.

Matveeva, A. (1999), *The North Caucuses: Russia's Fragile Borderland,* London: Royal Institute of Foreign Affairs.

Murithi, T. (2009), *The Ethics of Peacebuilding,* Edinburgh: Edinburgh University Press.

Nujidat, G. (2007), 'A View from the Israeli Sports Authority', in J. Sugden & J. Wallis (eds), *Football for Peace? The Challenges of Using Sport for Co-existence in Israel,* Oxford:
Meyer and Meyer (eds), pp. 141–154.

Omeje, K. (2009), 'Introduction: Discourses of the Liberian Civil War and the Imperatives of Peacebuilding', in K. Omeje (ed.), *War to Peace Transition: Conflict Intervention and Peacebuilding In Liberia,* Plymouth: University Press of America, pp. 3–18.

Paris, R. (2004), *At War's End: Building Peace After Civil Conflict,* Cambridge: Cambridge University Press.

Peimani, H. (2009), *Conflict and Security in Central Asia and the Caucuses,* Santa Barbara, CA: Greenwood Publishing Group.

Phillips, T. (2007), *Beslan—The Tragedy of School No. 1,* London: Granta Books.

Potier, T. (2001), *Conflict in Nagorno-Karabakh, Abkhazia and South Ossetia: A Legal Appraisa,* Kluwer Law International: The Hague.

Rankinen, T. & Bouchard, C. (2002), 'Dose-Response Issues Concerning the Relations Between Regular Physical Activity and Health', *Research Digest: Presidents Council on Fitness and Sports,* 3(18): 1–8.

Rookwood, J. (2009a), *Social Development in Post-conflict Communities: Building Peace Through Sport in Africa and the Middle East,* Saarbrücken: VDM Publishing House Ltd.

Rookwood, J. (2009b), 'Applying Olympic Values—Peace Promotion Through Sport in Russia and Bosnia and Herzegovina', *Journal of Olympic History,* 17(2): 22–33.

Rookwood, J. & Palmer, C. (2011), '"Invasion Games in War-torn Nations"—Can Football Help to Build Peace?', *Soccer and Society.* 12(1): 184–200.

Rookwood, J. & Wassong, S. (2010), 'NGOs—Using Sport to Promote Peace and Integration in Fractured Societies', in N. Ferguson (ed.), *Conflict and the Reconstruction of Civil Society,* Newcastle: Cambridge Scholars Publishing, pp. 32–50.

Schiff, M. & Winters, L. (1998), 'Regional Integration as Diplomacy', *World Bank Economic Review*, 12(2): 271–295.

Sommers, M. (2003), 'Urbanization, War and Africa's Youth at Risk: Towards Understanding and Addressing Future Challenges', Creative Associates International, Inc. accessed 16 January 2011 at:http://www.beps.net/publications/BEPS-UrbanizationWarYouthatRisk-.pdf.

Stidder, G. (2007), 'Maagan and the German Dimension', in J. Sugden & J. Wallis (eds), *Football for Peace? The Challenges of Using Sport for Co-existence in Israel*, Oxford: Meyer and Meyer, pp. 81–96.

Sugden, J. (2007), 'War Stops Peace!', in J. Sugden & J. Wallis (eds), *Football for Peace? The Challenges of Using Sport for Co-existence in Israel*, Oxford: Meyer and Meyer, pp. 172–175.

Sutton, P. (2009), *The Politics of Suffering: Indigenous Australia and the End of the Liberal Consensus*, Melbourne: Melbourne University Press.

Vanden Auweele, Y., Malcolm, C. & Meulders, B. (2006), *Sport and Development*, Leuven, Belgium: Lannoo Campus.

Wassong, S. (2006), 'Olympic Education: Fundamentals, Successes and Failures', in N. Crowther, R. Barney & M. Heine (eds), *Cultural Imperialism in Action— Critiques in the Global Olympic Trust. Eighth International Symposium for Olympic Research*, London, Ontario: International Centre for Olympic Studies, pp. 220–229.

Wear, R. & Kisriev, E. (2001), 'Ethnic Parity and Democratic Pluralism in Dagestan: A Consociational Approach', *Europe-Asia Studies*, 53 (1): 105–131.

Yamskov, A. (1991), 'Ethnic Conflict in the Transcausasus: The Case of Nagorno-Karabakh', *Theory and Society.* 20(5): 631–660.

4 Sport Plus and Socially Vulnerable Youth
Opening the Black Box

Reinhard Haudenhuyse and Marc Theeboom

SCIENCE OR FICTION

Sports have long been viewed as an opportunity to engage young people in a positive alternative, not just in terms of participation in sports activities, but across a range of issues including education, employment and training, community leadership and healthy lifestyles. From a policy maker's perspective, sports provide a convincing, highly visible and cost-effective tool for integrating socially vulnerable youth (Hartmann, 2001). More recently, this approach became known as 'sport plus', referring to specific and intentional augmentations to and adaptations of, sports programmes that aim at achieving broader outcomes (Coalter, 2010). Important to note in the conception of sport plus is the underlying notion that offering sport activities alone is not viewed as a sufficient condition for achieving wider outcomes beyond 'mere' participation. Instrumental views of sports are, however, not new. For example, there is a long history of viewing sports as part of a physical education curriculum to achieve a variety of outcomes relating to the individual or the wider community (Bailey et al., 2009). Yet popular opinion about sports, as creating something more beyond mere participation, have been referred to as deeply entrenched storylines (Houlihan, Bloyce & Smith, 2009), with a mythopoeïc character (Coalter, 2007). Houlihan et al. (2009) have stated that these storylines are not necessarily false, but their persistence and impact is not related to the quality or quantity of evidence available. Notwithstanding the lack of 'circumstantial evidence' for making the case for the wider role of sports (Long & Sanderson, 2001), public opinion about the moralising, character building and socialising potentialities of sports is still in favour of its proponents. However, according to De Botton (2004), public opinion is often the worst thinkable opinion and this because the ideas of the majority of the population on most subjects, such as sports for example, are based on a sequence of mistakes and misconceptions that have not been subjected to any rational investigation (De Botton, 2004). To take a very well-known example, we can see that the general assumptions on sports and health-related outcomes are not as clear-cut as we would like to believe (Murphy & Waddington, 1998). Over the years, these health-related functions have received an increasing amount of attention by policymakers and have produced a plethora of sports-based health interventions. Sports have been given a significant role in contributing to the development of healthier, happier and more productive societies. However, there is no evidence indicating a direct causal relationship between doing sports and health-related benefits (Coalter, 2005, Murphy & Waddington, 1998). Enrolling yourself into a sports club will not automatically generate health benefits or training effects, not even if you were to participate in activities on a daily basis. The assumed health-related benefits will only manifest themselves when the involvement in sports encompasses the following: exercise or physical activity daily or three times a week (i.e., frequency), with an average-to-vigorous intensity, (i.e., intensity, which can be expressed as a percentage of the maximum heart rate), for a duration of sixty minutes (i.e., time) and involving continuous, rhythmic, and aerobic movements of large muscle groups (i.e., type of activity) (Cavill, Kahlmeier & Racioppi, 2006). Such principles have been empirically established, following on a long line of (ongoing) health-related research studies in sports. The findings of these studies have practical implications for improving the performance level of elite athletes and developing broader positive health outcomes for the wider population. Working towards the facilitation of health-related outcomes, coaches and programme coordinators will need to systematically implement sports activities that are in accordance with these principles. Sports-based, health-enhancing interventions would furthermore need to look at the broader social context or habitat of the participant. For example, where and how does the participant live, what are the effects of the parents, of family members, the school's physical education teacher or peers on health-related attitudes, behaviours and outcomes? The underlying semantic is that a thorough understanding needs to be developed in relation to why a specific program, with a well-defined, tried methodology and within a specific context, worked (in terms of health improvements) for certain participants and why it did not work for others.

Turning back to the theme of this chapter, do socially vulnerable youth become less socially vulnerable by doing sports? Again, there is no evidence indicating a direct causal relationship between doing sports and social integration or any other beneficial social outcomes for that matter (Coalter, 2005, Long & Sanderson, 2001). In his paper on social inclusion, Bailey (2007) suggested it could be reasonable to assume that certain principles and conditions also need to be fulfilled in order for sports to generate social outcomes. Coalter (2003) indicated that frequency, intensity and adherence of participation would also have substantial implications for the development of social skills and the development of particular attitudes and values. It has been argued that coaches and programme coordinators who work with socially vulnerable youth within a sports context do not necessarily possess concrete principles for work and action that they can systematically integrate in their activities and programme designs. Lawson (2005) has formulated that knowledge and understanding in these domains are in short supply. The underlying causes for this knowledge gap are to be found in the fact that beliefs or storylines on the social beneficial outcomes that are attributed to sports participation are taken for granted. In light of this fact, Green (2008: 132) stated that 'the belief that sport builds character is so ingrained that neither providers nor participants feel it necessary to do anything more than to provide opportunities'. In other words, it is uncritically assumed that participation in itself will contribute to processes of (re-)integration and emancipation of socially vulnerable groups. Also, the complexity of attributing social outcomes to specific sports practices has been responsible for widening this knowledge gap. The puzzle is a bit more complex for social outcomes compared to health-related outcomes, because it is far more difficult to measure them than, for example, determining the difference in fat percentage or respiratory capacity of participants throughout a programme. This makes it a lot harder to establish an empirical basis from which actions can be propagated. However, there are no ready-made instruments that can measure the degree of social vulnerability throughout a programme. The inability to measure social effects has for a large part been responsible for questioning the wider social role of sports within society. But even if we would have such instruments, there is still the issue of how effects, which can be attributed to the programme, came to be. In other words, what are the underlying assumptions in viewing sports as influencing the social vulnerability of youth? To answer this question, we need a thorough understanding of the processes of social vulnerability as well as the strategies to act upon these processes. This means that the question we put forward at the beginning of this paragraph, namely 'do socially vulnerable youth become less vulnerable by doing sports?', needs to be rephrased into: 'how can socially vulnerable youth become less vulnerable by doing sports?'

SPORT PLUS LOGICS

Starting from the theory of social vulnerability (Vettenburg, 1998), we can roughly identify two fundamental logical bases that underpin any sports-based intervention targeted at those youth we could define as socially vulnerable. The first one is to make those youth less vulnerable, and by consequence more resilient, capable or resourceful in protecting themselves against potentially detrimental factors that could jeopardize their personal development trajectory and future perspectives. This 'agency' strategy has recently been re-baptised as 'positive youth development' (e.g., Holt, 2008; Larson, 2000). The second logic is to make the institutional structures and social arrangements that tend to keep those youth locked into their target groups less harmful. This logic of 'structure' has received far less attention in comparison with the first. This can be explained by the fact that targeted sports-based interventions for youth are unable to significantly impact broader social structural processes (Kelly, 2011).

Metaphorically speaking, we could clarify these logical bases by means of the example of trying to protect our children when they take their bikes to school. Following the first logic, we can make our children more aware of the dangers and teach them the necessary skills to 'survive' on their bikes in traffic. In the light of this logic, we start from the basic assumption that the child is not sufficiently equipped to 'survive on the road', due to personal factors that are inherently attributed to the child itself (i.e., agency). Following the second logic, we can make the environment less damaging or safer by, for example, improving the standard of the infrastructure (e.g., bicycle roads), implementing speed limits for other road users, improving procedures if accidents do happen and so on. Here, we start from the basic assumption that the environment is not adequately organised to guarantee that the child can safely drive his or her bike (i.e., structure). This metaphor also shows the importance of putting these logical bases (i.e., agency and structure) in perspective. It would seem absurd and highly inefficient to organise traffic-safety lessons for children without, for example, enforcing speed limits or providing bicycle paths and traffic signs and vice versa. This has implications for the way we wish to evaluate, but more importantly, understand sports-based interventions in this domain. In order to improve, practitioners and policy makers need to understand how their structures and processes enable or hinder certain outcomes.

In the following sections, we will look at what is already known concerning coaching and organising sport plus practices for socially vulnerable youth. Despite the fact that many good practices can be found, a systematic framework as well as guiding principles on the organisational and didactic methodology of successful initiatives are largely missing. We could hypothesise that certain social settings will be more favourable for the development of beneficial outcomes for socially vulnerable youth (e.g., positively influencing processes of social bonding), whereas others are less favourable.

COACHING SPORT PLUS

Although there are some indications that, when working with socially vulnerable youth within a given sports context towards particular social outcomes, a specific methodology is required (e.g., Theeboom, De Knop & Wylleman, 1993; Hellison, 2000; Coalter, 2003; Crabbé, 2007), it remains unclear what constitutes this specificity. Coalter and Taylor (2009) concluded that those sports programmes, which adopt a street/youth worker approach, which are more person centred than sports centred, more youth-work oriented than sports-coach driven, tend to be more effective in terms of creating added value through sports practices. The researchers continued by saying that such programmes allow more in-depth, intensive and extensive social relationships

(Coalter & Taylor, 2009). It is precisely this relational aspect that is viewed as the cornerstone of youth-work practices in general and specifically those targeted at socially vulnerable youth (Smith, 2003). Also, Theeboom et al. (1993) stated that youth workers are accustomed to dealing with youth problems and are as such in a good position to work with socially vulnerable youth within a sports setting. More generally, a good youth worker is perceived as one who shows appreciation and who supports and protects where and when necessary (De Winter & Noom, 2003). Some have gone even further by suggesting that it would be easier for the youth worker to learn sports coaching and organisational skills than it is for the sports coach to learn the social and pedagogical youth-work principles (Robins, 1990). However, Coussée, Roets and De Bie (2010) argued that youth-work practice remains something of a vague category. Research has mainly treated youth activities as a black box, with little consideration for the processes or experiences within an activity that would lead to broader positive changes (Hansen, Larson & Dworkin, 2003). Similar observations have been formulated regarding sports-based interventions (Coalter, 2007). In addition, it is often the case that youth workers lack the specific technical skills in sport for organising sports activities (Theeboom et al., 1993).

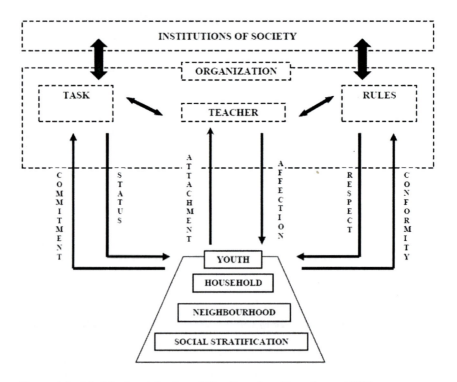

Figure 4.1   Model of social vulnerability (based on Vettenburg, 1998).

As we have stated earlier, social vulnerability is about interactional processes. In Figure 4.1 we can see a schematic overview of these interactional processes within the context of a school.

Central to the model are the bonding processes in relation to the teacher, the tasks and the rules that are situated within the context of an organisation (i.e., the school), which is in turn embedded in broader network of societal institutions (Figure 4.1). For a more detailed description of the different elements within the model, we refer to Vettenburg (1998). Although developed within a school context (Vettenburg, 1988), we can apply the model to social vulnerability in a sports setting. Instead of the teacher, the coach or sports leader takes a central role and the context in which the coach operates is the team (or group) and the sports/youth club or organisation. The task can be seen as the specific activities (e.g., sports exercises or games) that are being provided and the rules are the regulations that are used by the organisation. It is no coincidence that the teacher, or in our example the sports coach, has been given a central role in the model of social vulnerability (Figure 4.1). An international review of the literature on outcomes of physical education and school sports by Bailey and Dismore (2004) suggested that the actions and interactions of coaches and teachers significantly influence the extent to which young people experience the potentially positive aspects of sports. The model of social vulnerability allows us to look deeper into these actions and interactions when dealing with socially vulnerable youth within a sporting context. The coach is seen as the main actor in facilitating processes of conformity, attachment and commitment and by doing so creating opportunities for experiences of respect, affection and status within and also beyond, a given sports context (Figure 4.1). In the next sections, we will describe the authority model used, the motivational climate generated and the cultural capital of the coach and how these elements can be linked to the concept of social vulnerability.

Authority Relationship

Within a broader educational context, it has been indicated that an emancipatory authority relationship allows a more personal relationship with the 'student' and will be potentially less harming for socially vulnerable youth (Vettenburg, 1988). A distinction has been made between three types of authority relationships, namely a coercive power relationship, a manipulative authority relationship and an emancipatory authority relationship (Vettenburg & Van Kerckvoorde, 1982). Vettenburg and Van Kerckvoorde (1982) were able to establish a connection between the level of moral development of youth and the authority approach used within an educational setting. The lowest stages of moral development were found in classrooms where the teacher used a coercive power approach, whereas the highest stages of moral development were found in classrooms where the teacher used an emancipatory authority approach (Vettenburg & Van Kerckvoorde,

1982). Drawing on her data, Vettenburg (1988) found that youth who had a high degree of social vulnerability were less likely to have progressed in their level of moral development. However, this in no way means that we can conclude that socially vulnerable youth are morally inadequate (Kelly, 2011). The established relationship between general moral development and social vulnerability does not allow us to make such conclusions. Conceptions that attitudinal and behavioural changes through sports practices will lead to youth becoming less vulnerable are the foundation of misguided and ineffective practices that operate within a vacuum of oversimplification. What we can say is that an inappropriate pedagogical approach, in which the coach does not use an emancipatory authority model, needs to be seen as a factor that can potentially aggravate processes of social vulnerability. An appropriate pedagogical approach would then need to encompass offering optimal development opportunities for all, putting the participant first instead of the rules, encouraging authentic decision and responsibility sharing with tangible outcomes for the participants and providing tailored support when needed. In short, a coach should have authority without being authoritative and should strive towards emancipation of the participants, instead of demanding an uncritical compliance of the participants in a particular rule-based setting. Given the dearth of personal and social development opportunities and defective relationships, such an approach would be even more important when working with socially vulnerable youth.

Motivational Climate

Reference has also been made to the motivational climate as influencing the experiences of participants and programme outcomes. A distinction has been made between mastery and performance in motivational climate (Ames, 1992). In a motivational climate generating mastery, participants take themselves as a point of reference when comparing their performances. In contrast, in a motivational climate generating performance, students take their fellow participants as a point of reference to compare their own performances. Within a sports setting, several researchers have found that a motivational climate of mastery resulted in higher levels of enjoyment and perceptions of success, a higher appreciation of self-competence, higher levels of moral functioning and pro-social attitudes towards team mates, better performances and execution of techniques, higher levels of intrinsic motivation to play sports and an improved ability to deal with failure and learn from it (Theeboom, De Knop & Weiss, 1995; Cechinni et al., 2001; Tod & Hodge, 2001; Barkoukis, Tsorbatzoudis & Grouios, 2008: Boardley & Kavussanu, 2009). Coaches would then need to structure situations in ways that bring success and avoid placing participants in situations prematurely where they are likely to fail often (Bandura, 1995). This is in line with Whitehead and Corbin's (1997) perception of a 'good coach' as someone who can keep comparison in perspective, is proficient in giving appropriate feedback, which includes technical information on how to improve, is able to be adaptive, patient and sympathetic in his teaching and can encourage the development of self-praise which contributes to development of an internalised self-reward system. These qualities are viewed to be even more important when working with socially vulnerable youths in a sports setting (Coalter, Allison & Taylor, 2000; Andrews & Andrews, 2003). Feeling successful is important for everybody, young and old. Yet, it has been suggested that facilitating feelings of success, would be even more important for people whom we could define as socially vulnerable (West & Crompton, 2001; Andrews & Andrews, 2003:). Socially vulnerable young people, more than their non-vulnerable peers, are seen as being confronted with feelings of incompetence, failure, rejection and a lower self-esteem (Andrews & Andrews, 2003: Vettenburg, 1998). In this perspective, it would be very important for a coach or youth worker to create a climate in which socially vulnerable youth have a higher chance of experiencing feelings of success. On the other hand, facilitating experiences of success, for example by increasing feelings of self-esteem, will not by definition contribute to a more positive social trajectory. One can, for example, experience a high degree of self-esteem in robbing someone and getting away with it. Likewise, decreasing feelings of self-esteem will not by definition have a negative effect on the personal social trajectory of youth (Coalter & Taylor, 2010). Bandura (1995) further warns against the facilitation of quick and easy feelings of success. This is because when people experience only easy success they will come to expect quick results and will easily be discouraged by failure. Future research should focus on how differences in perceived motivational climate and the experiences of youths can have an impact on influencing processes of social vulnerability within a given sports settings. The literature has already provided us with tools for facilitating or manipulating mastery- or performance-oriented motivational climates within a certain sports setting (Theeboom et al., 1995; Barkoukis et al., 2008) and subsequently assess the perceived climate by those participating (see Newton, Duda & Yin, 2000: Smith, Cumming & Smoll, 2008).

Cultural Capital

Next to the authority relationship and the motivational climate generated, the perceived similarities of the coach are also viewed as having a big impact in influencing bonding and socialisation processes (Bandura, 1995). This is even more so when working with socially vulnerable youth (Coalter, 2007). Crabbé (2007) has referred to these similarities as the shared 'cultural capital' of coaches in relation to participants. However, one's cultural capital is not interchangeable because it is largely determined by, among others, the place where one lives, one's upbringing and education, and one's home situation. Nonetheless, a coach can actively create an understanding and appreciation of the cultural capital of the participants when his or her own cultural capital is distinctively different.

In the following section we will look at some organisational implications when working with socially vulnerable youths. A long-held distinction has been made between traditional and alternative community sports provision systems (Theeboom, Haudenhuyse & De Knop, 2010). Often, alternative sports practices are, in comparison with their traditional counterparts, more explicitly associated with broader societal outcomes for specific target groups. Furthermore, traditional mainstream sports provision systems are often viewed as not being effective and suitable for engaging socially vulnerable groups (Sugden & Yiannakis, 1982).

ORGANISING SPORT PLUS

Next to coaching, a difference in approach is also seen in the way that sports-based practices for vulnerable groups need to be organised (Martineck & Hellison, 1997: Skille & Waddington, 2006; Theeboom, Truyens & Haudenhuyse, 2008). Furthermore, there is a broad consensus that if sport is to contribute to achieving broader individual and societal outcomes, it needs to be part of an embedded project in which sports are not viewed as the only strategic aim (Coalter; 2003; Sandford, Armour & Warmington, 2006; Nichols, 2007). Studies focusing on the specific organisational modalities for socially vulnerable youths within a sports setting still remain scarce. In a study on the anti-social behaviour and the degree of organised sports participation among adolescents, Mahoney and Stattin (2000) found that it was the structure and context of the activities rather than the activity itself that determined whether the outcomes were positive or negative in terms of adolescent development. Evidence suggests that interventions need to be consciously and systematically organised to maximise the possibilities for achieving beneficial outcomes. In this perspective, it is not sport as such that can produce beneficial outcomes for certain groups, but rather certain types of organisational setting and coaching practices (Andrews & Andrews, 2003; Papacharisis et al., 2005; Theeboom, De Knop & Wylleman, 2008). Looking at U.K. and U.S.-based sport inclusion programmes for youths, Green (2008) concluded that the programmes that seem to be the most effective are those that do not look like traditional sports programmes. It has been implied that by downplaying the organisation and structure of sports activities, coaches can create more positive experiences for youths (Strean, 2010). In such a minimally organised setting, young participants are given more autonomy and freedom to direct the activities themselves, which is seen as positively contributing to their development and wellbeing. It is also considered the case that the un-optional, unstructured and informal nature of such practices makes them attractive and consequently more accessible, to socially vulnerable young people (Tiffany & Pring, 2008). The lack of structure is precisely what distinguished such alternative practices from other mainstream, rule-based practices, such as the school, which had created negative experiences for these youths in the first place. Some researchers have even argued that the way sports are traditionally provided and practiced might be the reason for generating or at least amplifying mechanisms of inclusion as well as exclusion (Andrews & Andrews, 2003; Collins & Kay, 2004; Elling & Claringbould, 2005). This should be a reason for researchers and practitioners to critically examine the dominant values and attitudes within traditional sports settings and how they affect the experiences of those participating in them. However, this does not necessarily mean that 'traditional' organised sports provision models will, by definition, lead to processes of exclusion or aggravate social vulnerability. In a study on alternative sports provision schemes targeting inner city youths at-risk (i.e., the open sport hall, Norway), Skille and Waddington (2006) discovered that the high level of informality and flexibility actually facilitated the development of traditional and hegemonic patterns of gender relations. The direct outcome of this non-traditional sports provision system was that girls and young, 'less able' boys were largely being excluded from the self-organised activities (Skille & Waddington, 2006). The researchers saw the lack of adult control as the main culprit. In line with this, activities comprised primarily of peer participants, compared to those involving family members or conventional adults, are viewed as having a less positive effect on social bonding processes for socially vulnerable youths (Wong, 2005). Looking at the activities in Swedish youth centres, Mahoney, Stattin and Lord (2004) found that the degree of involvement of youths in unstructured activities was conducive to the development of anti-social behaviour. The authors put the aggregation of 'anti-social' peers and young people with poor relationships to their parents and the school forward as the explanation of these findings (Mahoney et al., 2004). However, it has to be noted that the distinction between 'traditional' and 'alternative' sports schemes is not always clear-cut and well-defined in the above-mentioned studies. What are the distinctive features of a traditional and an alternative organised sports club and how are these related to wider social outcomes? Coalter (2005) has perhaps made a more tangible dichotomy when he refers to 'necessary' and 'sufficient' conditions. Necessary conditions are those that need to be fulfilled in order that socially vulnerable youths become involved in sports and stay involved. The sufficient conditions, on the other hand, can be understood as the conditions which maximise the potential wider outcomes in terms of social vulnerability. Such conditions could be studied across different programmes or interventions, irrespective of their perceived traditional or alternative characteristics. When evaluating programmes, Weiss (1998) stated that the focus should be on components of programmes instead of on the totality of programmes. According to this philosophy, we should start by looking at families of necessary and sufficient mechanisms within such programmes working towards specific mutual outcomes for socially vulnerable youths, whatever their ascribed typology, category or policy domain. This implies that in order to understand the underlying processes which are believed to generate positive social outcomes, we need to deconstruct or de-contextualise sports practices for socially vulnerable youths. Such an approach will be more manageable for practitioners and policymakers. Weiss (1998) remarked that evaluation at the level of components, instead of at the level of the totality of programmes, would furthermore create less defensive and unreceptive attitudes towards evaluators in the field, because programmes as a whole could not then be labelled as 'good' or 'bad'.

CONTEXTUALISING SPORTS

Some would argue for a radical contextualisation of 'sport' in sports-based social interventions (Coalter, 2008). This is seen as allowing a more thorough understanding of the social processes and mechanisms that might lead to desired outcomes for some participants or some organisations in certain circumstances (Coalter, 2010). An increasing number of social researchers have started to focus on contextual organisational components, in which social interventions are ideally seen as taking place in order to create beneficial outcomes for the youth involved (see Carnegie Council, 1995: Witt & Crompton, 1997; Lerner, Fisher & Weinberg, 2000; Benson, 2002: National Research Council and Institute Medicine, 2002). If integrated, the identified components of these proposed generic frameworks are more likely to facilitate positive developmental outcomes for youth. For example, components such as physical and psychological safety, appropriate structures, supportive relationships, opportunities for belonging, positive social norms, support for feeling useful, opportunities for skill-building and the integration of family, school and community efforts have been put forward by the National Research Council and Institute of Medicine (2002) as cornerstones of any intervention or project that aims to generate socially beneficial outcomes for youth. We have yet to understand how such frameworks and components would shape the way sports initiatives for socially vulnerable youths need to organise their activities in order to generate added value for those involved. And more specifically, what influence these components might have on the different bonding processes within the model of social vulnerability (Figure.4.1). What also needs to be scrutinised, is the interplay of such factors with a specific sports context (e.g., team/individual, competitive/recreational, contact/non-contact) and the characteristics of the participants involved (e.g., girls/boys, age, background, attitudes towards the programme, sports-related skills, ambitions and motivations). For example, in relation to the characteristics of the participants, Weiss (1998: 134) has stated that 'the characteristics of the group become the environment that mediates the program for each participant'. This indicates the importance of taking such—potentially damaging (Dishion, McCord & Poulin, 1999; Mahoney et al., 2004)—group influences into account when looking at the contextual features of social intervention for socially vulnerable youths. A key question in relation to contextualising sports practices for vulnerable youths remains, however: what is the specific added value, if any, of a specific sport discipline? Is the added value limited to the fact that different sports disciplines will attract different youths (i.e. necessary conditions) or are there other inherent features of specific sport disciplines that could help to generate the sufficient conditions in which socially vulnerable youths could become less vulnerable?

CONCLUDING REMARKS

In relation to working with socially vulnerable youth, Theeboom et al. (1993) argued that knowledge of the specific situation of youth, combined with good organisational ability in sports and didactic skills, would ensure some success in organising programmes that could create added value beyond mere participation. We would also suggest that developing practitioner knowledge of the wider processes of social vulnerability could help achieve this goal. Armed with such an understanding, sports practitioners could be in a better position to develop strategies to challenge processes of vulnerability. At the level of coaching, the emancipatory authority relationship, the motivational climate created and the shared cultural capital of the coach, were described as key elements in working towards broader outcomes for socially vulnerable youth. On the other hand, we have seen that sports, irrespective of the mode of delivery, traditional or alternative, can produce both positive and negative experiences for those involved. More than the mode of delivery, the context in which sports are 'consumed' seems to play a fundamental role in terms of generating broader social outcomes for vulnerable youths. We put 'consumed' here between brackets, because youths involved in sports practices should not only be viewed as mere consumers, but also as creators of their own sports experiences (Smith, 1982). As such, youth are not only made responsible for the delivery of the activities, but also encouraged to think and act upon the circumstances that give rise to their increased social vulnerability, rather than merely learning how to cope with their vulnerability (Tiffany & Pring, 2008). This requires a clear understanding of the wider processes of social vulnerability—such as discriminatory practices, cultural exclusion and institutional racism—on behalf of those engaged with youth.

In order to enhance opportunities for sport to act as an agent of personal and social change, one needs to 'add things to it' (Spaaij, 2009). This statement implies that providing sports activities alone does not offer sufficient conditions in which broader outcomes for socially vulnerable youth can be generated. However, our understanding of what the 'added things' are and what specifically this 'it' needs to be is rather limited. The current knowledge base of sports-based social interventions targeted at socially vulnerable youth, is largely built on positivistic research that predominantly uses an agency approach. Studies focusing on teaching feelings of social responsibility (Hellison, 2003), for example, youth leadership (Martinek & Hellison, 2009; Gould & Voelker, 2010), enhancing self-esteem (Coalter & Taylor, 2010), coaching life skills (Gould, Collins, Lauer & Chung, 2006; Papacharisis et al., 2005) or promoting positive youth development (Holt, 2008), will fail to increase our understanding of how sports practices can influence processes of social vulnerability. Such approaches could be categorised under what Lawson (2005) has called 'narrow empowerment', indicating the failure of going beyond the individual level. Sports practices focusing on an agency approach risk legitimising a reductive analysis of complex processes, by highlighting individual deficits and de-emphasising structural inequalities (Kelly, 2011). Coalter & Taylor (2010) have strongly opposed and illustrated the inadequacies of deficit model approaches that are based on the assumption that deprived communities produce deficient youth. The narrow over-emphasis on agency and the downplaying of structural mechanisms will result in keeping the very youth for whom such intervention are conceptualised socially vulnerable. At best such interventions will succeed in not reinforcing processes of social vulnerability within a specific sports setting. On its own, this is still a valuable but not sufficient outcome. There is a scarcity of research using interpretative and constructionist approaches that would provide us with access to personal perspectives of the lived experience and social interaction of socially vulnerable youth involved in organised sports settings.

Using social vulnerability as an analytical and empirical framework, we can focus on how bonding processes develop (or not) in relation to the sporting tasks, the coach and the rules within specific organisational settings for certain youth (Figure 4.1). These processes can be studied throughout different practices for socially vulnerable youth in relation to the specific outcomes. For example, how does the choice of the specific sports activities and the way they are being offered, have an influence on the processes of commitment and status of socially vulnerable youth? How do the specific background characteristics of the coach (e.g., place of residence, training, ethnicity), or the way in which the coach interacts with the participants, have an effect on processes of affection and attachment, and how does the enforcement of rules influence processes of respect and conformity (Figure 4.1)? Additionally, we need to look at the broader sporting context in which such processes unfold, for example, the composition of the group or the features of the localities where the activities are run. Background factors (i.e., household, neighbourhood and social stratification) of the participants themselves also need to be taken into account and should not merely be treated as confounding variables (i.e., covariates). Furthermore, we need to understand how these processes transfer to other contexts such as the school, the job market or other. As already indicated, if sport is to contribute to achieving broader individual and societal outcomes, it needs to be part of an embedded project in which sports are not viewed as the sole strategic aim. But herein lies, somewhat paradoxically, the danger of undermining the potential of sport *plus* practices targeted at socially vulnerable groups. It should not be expected, nor seen as desirable, that sport *plus* practises solve the problems a society (re-)produces. Re-framing sport *plus* practises in conformity with the requirements of the educational system, the labour market and society at large has disempowering effects on both those working with vulnerable youth and young people themselves (Coosseé et al., 2010) by disregarding broader societal structures that make young people vulnerable and undermining the inherent potential value of such practices for youth. If sport is to be part of a broader and more integrated intervention in the lives of socially vulnerable youth, it should have a clear position and acknowledged autonomy in relation to other societal institutions.

Most importantly, we need to evaluate how and to what extent certain processes have instigated broader outcomes for socially vulnerable youth. As already mentioned, to date we do not possess instruments that can ascertain the degree of social vulnerability. The focus of evaluation should be on the necessary and sufficient mechanisms within sports practices (Weiss, 1998) and how those mechanisms have contributed to making socially vulnerable youth less so.

We need to be vigilant, however, that a radical contextualisation of sport practices targeted at socially vulnerable youth will not lead to downplaying the characteristics that are inherent in specific sports disciplines and settings. We could end up with a lot of things to add without something substantial to be added to. We do not, in saying this, wish to de-emphasize the importance of the contextual factors that can facilitate certain bonding processes for socially vulnerable youth. The underlying motivation of those who strongly advocate a contextualisation of sport plus practices can be understood through the concerns about the blind 'evangelic' beliefs in the power of sports (Coalter, 2010). As we have indicated earlier, this blind belief has been responsible for creating a knowledge gap in our understanding of sports-based social interventions for socially vulnerable youth. By using the theory of social vulnerability as an analytical framework for studying and understanding sport plus practices for socially vulnerable youth, we can begin to narrow this gap.

REFERENCES

Ames, C. (1992), 'Achievement Goals and the Classroom Motivational Climate', in J. Meece & D. Schunk (eds), *Students' Perceptions in the Classroom: Causes and Consequences*, Hillsdale, NJ: Erlbaum.

Andrews, J. & Andrews, G. (2003), 'Life in a Secure Unit: The Rehabilitation of Young People Through the Use of Sport', *Social Science and Medicine*, 56: 531–550.

Bailey, R. (2007), 'Youth Sport and Social Inclusion', in N. Holt (ed.), *Positive Youth Development Through Sport*, London: Routledge.

Bailey, R. & Dismore, H. (2004), *Sport in Education: Project Report*, 4th International Conference of Ministers and Senior Officials Responsible for Physical Education and Sport (MINEPS IV), Athens, Greece, 6–8 December 2004.

Bailey, R., Armour, K., Kirk, D., Jess, M., Pickup, I. & Sandford, R. (2009), 'The Educational Benefits Claimed for Physical Education and School Sport: An Academic Review', *Research Papers in Education*, 24(1): 1–27.

Bandura, A. (1995), *Self-Efficacy in Changing Societies*, Cambridge: Cambridge University Press.

Barkoukis, V., Tsorbatzoudis, H. & Grouios, G. (2008), 'Manipulation of Motivational Climate in Physical Education: Effects of a Seven-month Intervention', *European Physical Education Review*, 14(3): 367–387.

Benson, P. (2002), 'Adolescent Development in Social and Community Context: A Program of Research', *New Direction for Youth Development*, 95: 123–147.

Boardley, I. & Kavussanu, M. (2009), 'The Influence of Social Variables and Moral Disengagement on Prosocial and Antisocial Behaviours in Field Hockey and Netball', *Journal of Sports Sciences*, 27(8): 843–854.

Carnegie Council (1995), *Great Transition: Preparing Adolescents for a New Century*, New York: Carnegie Corporation.

Cavill, N., Kahlmeier, S. & Racioppi, F. (2006), *Physical Activity and Health in Europe: Evidence for Action*. Copenhagen: World Health Organization, Europe.

Cecchini, J., Gonzalez, C., Carmona, A., Arruza, J., Escarti, A. & Balagué, G. (2001), 'The Influence of the Physical Education Teacher on Intrinsic Motivation, Self-Confidence, Anxiety, and Pre- and Post-competition Mood States, *European Journal of Sport Science*, 1(4): 1–12.

Coalter, F. (2003), 'The Social Role of Sport: Opportunities and Challenges (Paper 3)', in S. Campbell & B. Simmonds (eds), *Sport, Active Recreation and Social Inclusion*, London: Smith Institute.

Coalter, F. (2005), *The Social Benefits of Sports. An Overview to Inform the Community Planning Process*, Sport Scotland Research Report no. 98, Edinburgh.

Coalter, F. (2007), *A Wider Social Role for Sport: Who's Keeping the Score?*, London: Routledge.

Coalter, F. (2008), 'Sport-in-development: Development for and Through Sport', in M. Nicholson and R. Hoye (eds), *Sport and Social Capital*, Oxford: Elsevier.

Coalter, F. (2010), 'The Politics of Sport-for-development: Limited Focus Programmes and Broad Gauge Problems?, *International Review for the Sociology of Sport*, 45(3): 295–314.

Coalter, F. & Taylor, J. (2009), *Sport and Conflict: A Report on Monitoring and Evaluation*, prepared for Comic Relief.

Coalter, F. & Taylor, J. (2010), *Sport-for-development Impact Study. A Research Initiative Funded by Comic Relief and UK Sport and Managed by International Development Through Sport*. Department of Sports Studies University of Stirling, Stirling.

Coalter, F., Allison, M. & Taylor, J. (2000), *The Role of Sport in Regenerating Deprived Urban Areas*, Edinburgh: The Scottish Office.

Collins, M. & Kay, T. (2004), *Sport and Social Exclusion*, London: Routledge.

Cousseé, F., Roets, G. & De Bie, M. (2010), 'Empowering the Powerful: Challenging Hidden Processes of Marginalization in Youth Work Policy and Practice in Belgium', *Critical Social Policy*, 29(3): 421.

Crabbé, T. (2007), 'Reaching the "Hard to Reach": Engagement, Relationships Building and Social Control in Sport Based Social Inclusion Work', *International Journal of Sport Management and Marketing*, 2(1/2): 27–40.

De Botton, A. (2004), *Status Anxiety*, London: Hamish Hamilton.

De Winter, M. & Noom, M. (2003), 'Someone Who Treats Me as an Ordinary Human Being . . . Homeless Youth Examine the Quality of Professional Care', *British Journal for Social Work*, 33(3): 325–337.

Dishion, T., McCord, J. & Poulin, F. (1999), 'When Interventions Harm: Peer-Groups and Problem Behaviour', *American Psychologist*, 57(9): 755–764.

Elling, A. & Claringbould, I. (2005), 'Mechanisms of Inclusion and Exclusion in the Dutch Sports Landscape: Who Can and Wants to Belong?', *Sociology of Sport Journal*, 22(4): 498–517.

Gould, D. & Voelker, D. (2010), 'Youth Sport Leadership Development: Leveraging the Sports Captaincy Experience', *Journal of Sport Psychology in Action*, 1(1): 1–14.

Gould, D., Collins, K., Lauer, L. & Chung, Y. (2006), 'Coaching Life Skills: A Working Model', *Sport and Exercise Psychology Review*, 2 (1).

Green, C. (2008), 'Sport as an Agent for Social and Personal Change', in V. Girginov (ed.), *Management of Sports Development*, Butterworth-Heinemann.

Hansen, D., Larson, R. & Dworkin, J. (2003), What Adolescents Learn in Organized Youth Activities: A Survey of Self-reported Developmental Experiences', *Journal of Research on Adolescence*, 13(1): 25–55.

Hartmann, D. (2001), Notes on Midnight Basketball and the Cultural Politics of Recreation, Race, and At-risk Urban Youth, *Journal of Sport & Social Issues*, 25(4): 339–371.

Hellison, D. (2000), 'Physical Activity Programs for Underserved Youth', *Journal of Science and Medicine in Sport*, 3(3): 238–242.

Hellison, D. (2003), *Teaching Responsibility Through Physical Activity*, Human Kinetics.

Holt, N. (2008), *Positive Youth Development Through Sport*, London: Routledge.

Houlihan, B., Bloyce, D. & Smith, A. (2009), 'Developing the Research Agenda in Sport Policy', *International Journal of Sport Policy*, 1(1): 1–12.

Kelly, L (2011), 'Social Inclusion Through Sports Based Interventions?', *Critical Social Policy*, 31(1).

Larson, R. (2000), 'Towards a Psychology of Positive Youth Development', *American Psychologist*, 55(1): 170–183.

Lawson, A. (2005), 'Empowering People, Facilitating Community Development, and Contributing to Sustainable Development: The Social Work of Sport, Exercise, and Physical Education Programs', *Sport, Education and Society*, 10(1): 135–160.

Lerner, R., Fisher, C. & Weinberg, R. (2000), 'Toward a Science for and of the People: Promoting Civil Society Through the Application of Developmental Science', *Child Development*, 71(1): 11–20.

Long, J. & Sanderson, I. (2001), 'The Social Benefits of Sport: Where's the Proof?', in C. Gratton & I. Henry (eds), *Sport in the City*, London: Routledge.

Mahoney, J. & Stattin, H. (2000), 'Leisure Activities and Adolescent Antisocial Behaviour: The Role of Structure and Social Context', *Journal of Adolescence*, 23(2): 113–127.

Mahoney, J., Stattin, H. & Lord, H. (2004), 'Unstructured Youth Recreation Centre Participation and Antisocial Behaviour Development: Selection Influences and the Moderating Role of Antisocial Peers', *International Journal of Behavioral Development*, 28(6): 553–560.

Martineck, T. & Hellison, D. (1997), 'Fostering Resiliency in Underserved Youth Through Physical Activity', *Quest*, 49(1): 34–49.

Martinek, T. & Hellison, D. (2009), *Youth Leadership in Sport and Physical Education*, New York: Palgrave Macmillan.

Murphy, P. & Waddington, I. (1998), 'Sport for All: Some Public Health Policy Issues and Problems', *Critical Public Health*, 8(3): 193–205.

National Research Council and Institute of Medicine (2002), 'Community Programs to Promote Youth Development. Committee on Community Level Programs for Youth', in J. Eccles & J. Gootman (eds), *Board on Children, Youth and Families, Division of Behavioural and Social Sciences and Education*, Washington, DC: National Academy Press.

Newton, M., Duda, J. & Yin, Z. (2000) 'Examination of the Psychometric Properties of the Perceived Motivational Climate in Sport Questionnaire—2 in a Sample of Female Athletes, *Journal of Sport Sciences*, 18(4): 275–290.

Nichols, G. (2007), *Sport and Crime Reduction: The Role of Sports in Tackling Youth Crime*, London: Routledge.

Papacharisis, V., Goudas, M., Danish, S. & Theodorakis, Y. (2005), 'The Effectiveness of Teaching Life Skills Program in a Sport Context', *Journal of Applied Sport Psychology*, 17(3): 247–254.

Robins, D. (1990), *Sport as Prevention: The Role of Sport in Crime Prevention Programmes Aimed at Young People*, Oxford: University of Oxford, Centre for Criminological Research.

Sandford, R., Armour, K. & Warmington, P. (2006), 'Re-engaging Disaffected Youth Through Physical Activity Programmes, *British Educational Research Journal*, 32(2): 251–271.

#Skille, E. A. & Waddington, I. (2006), 'Alternative Sport Programmes and Social Inclusion in Norway', *European Physical Education Review*, 12(3): 251–271.

Smith, M. (1982), *Creators Not Consumers. Rediscovering Social Education* (2nd edn.), Leicester: National Association of Youth Clubs.

Smith, M. (2003), 'From Youth Work to Youth Development. The New Government Framework for English Youth Services', *Youth and Policy*, 79, accessed 6 July 2011 at: http://www.infed.org/archives/jeffs_and_smith/smith_youth_work_to_youth_development.htm.

Smith, R., Cumming, S. & Smoll, F. (2008), 'Development and Validation of the Motivational Climate Scale for Youth Sports', *Journal of Applied Sport Psychology*, 20(1): 116–136.

Spaaij, R. (2009), 'Sport as a Vehicle for Social Mobility and Regulation of Disadvantaged Urban Youth: Lessons from Rotterdam', *International Review for the Sociology of Sport*, 44: 2–3.

Strean, W. (2010), 'Remembering Instructors: Play, Pain and Pedagogy', *Qualitative Research in Sport and Exercise*, 1(3): 210–220.

Sugden, J. & Yiannakis, A. (1982), 'Sport and Juvenile Delinquency: A Theoretical Base', *Journal of Sport and Social Issues*, 6(1): 22–30.

Theeboom, M., De Knop, P. & Weiss, M. (1995), 'Motivational Climate, Psychological Responses, and Motor Skill Development in Children's Sport: A Field Based Intervention Study', *Journal of Sport & Exercise Psychology*, 17(3): 294–311.

Theeboom, M., De Knop, P. & Wylleman, P. (1993), 'Underprivileged Youth: a Forgotten Target Group Within a Sports Policy?', in W. Duquet, P. De Knop & L. Bollaert (eds), *Youth Sport: A Social Approach*, Brussel: VUBPRESS.

Theeboom, M., De Knop, P. & Wylleman, P. (2008), 'Martial Arts and Socially Vulnerable Youth: An Analysis of Flemish Initiatives', *Sport, Education and Society*, 13(3): 301–318.

Theeboom, M., Haudenhuyse, R. & De Knop, P. (2010), 'Community Sports Development for Socially Deprived Groups: A Wider Role for the Commercial Sports Sector? A Look at the Flemish Situation', *Sport in Society*, 13(9): 1392–1410.

Theeboom, M., Truyens, J. & Haudenhuyse, R. (2008), 'Sport and Socially Deprived Youth in Flanders (Belgium)', *Sport & Culture & Society*, University of Ljubljana.

Tiffany, G. & Pring, R. (2008), 'Lessons from Detached Youth Work: Democratic Education', *Nuffield Review of 14–19 Education and Training, England and Wales*, Issues Paper 11.

Tod, D. & Hodge, K. (2001), 'Moral Reasoning and Achievement Motivation in Sport: A Qualitative Inquiry', *Journal of Sport Behaviour*, 24(3): 307–327.

Vettenburg, N. (1988), *Schoolervaringen, delinquentie en maatschappelijke kwetsbaarheid: een theoretisch en empririsch onderzoek in het beroepsonderwijs* (*'Experiences at School, Delinquency and Social Vulnerability: A Theoretical and Empirical Study in Vocational Education'*), K.U. Leuven, Onderzoeksgroep Jeugdcriminologie.

Vettenburg, N. (1998), 'Juvenile Delinquency and the Cultural Characteristics of the Family', *International Journal of Adolescent Medicine and Health*, 3: 193–209.

Vettenburg, N. & Van Kerckvoorde, J. (1982), 'De leerkracht-leerling relatie in de praktijk. Relaties in het onderwijs' ('The Student-Teacher Relationship in Practice. Relations in Education'), *Impuls*, 5: 192–198.

Weiss, C. (1998), *Evaluation: Methods for Studying Programs and Policies* (2nd edn.), New Jersey: Prentice-Hall.

West, S. & Crompton, J. (2001), 'Programs That Work: A Review of the Impact of Adventure Programs on At-risk Youth', *Journal of Park and Recreation Administration*, 19(2): 113–140.

Whitehead, J. & Corbin, C. (1997), 'Self-esteem in Children and Youth: The Role of Sport and Physical Education', in K. R. Fox (ed), *The Physical Self: From Motivation to Well-being*, Champaign IL: Human Kinetics.

Witt, P. & Crompton, J. (1997), 'The Protective Factors Framework: A Key to Programming for Benefits and Evaluating for Results', *Journal of Park and Recreation Administration*, 15(3): 1–18.

Wong, S. (2005), 'The Effects of Adolescent Activities on Delinquency: A Differential Involvement Approach', *Journal of Youth and Adolescence*, 34(4): 321–333.

5 'We Are a Very, Very Homogenous Group'
Promoting and Managing Social Diversity in Sports?

Bettina Rulofs

This article focuses on the question of how social inclusion of diverse social groups in sport can be achieved and how social cohesion can be realised in sports clubs in times of increasing social conflicts and processes of social disintegration.

The inclusion of diverse social groups in sport has been one of the major goals of organised sport in Germany as well as other European countries. The motto 'sport for all' was the title of several campaigns during the last few decades. These campaigns in Germany have mainly focused on specific aspects of social diversity (e.g., gender, immigrants, people with disabilities), whilst an overall and integral strategy of promoting social diversity and cohesion in sport was neglected. Recently, the concept of 'managing diversity' has been put on the agenda of sports organisations in an attempt to convey such an integral instrument for the, until then, distinct campaigns of social inclusion. Diversity management originated in the fields of economics and business. It aims at the inclusion of diverse social groups in organisations and at the same time, it focuses on implementing a culture of appreciation of social diversity.

At a first glance, there is a wide range of reasons for using systematic management of diversity in sport. First of all, sports clubs have undergone a radical change in the age structure of their members. The former sports club as a place mainly for young people has now matured into an organisation that attracts a wide range of age groups, including the elderly. This development is of vital importance if sports organisations want to face the challenge of demographic change (cf. Breuer & Haase, 2007; Steinbach & Hartmann, 2007: 238). The number of women and girls participating in sport has increased immensely during the last decades. Thus sports clubs are well-advised to change some of their male-dominated traditions and learn to meet the interests of women and girls. Furthermore, ethnic diversity has increased in sport due to processes of migration and globalisation. For example, the proportion of 'foreign players' is 42 percent in the five big European Soccer Leagues (Great Britain, Spain, Italy, Germany and France) (cf. Poli & Ravenel, 2008: 10).

In short, sports clubs nowadays face more social diversity than they used to, which goes hand-in-hand with the necessity of managing the different habits and life situations of diverse groups and consequently the social conflicts which are sometimes connected to the above.

At the same time, the public appraisal and financial support of sport by political parties and welfare systems is dependent on whether sports clubs are able and willing to open themselves up to all. Against these backgrounds it is obvious that sports organisations should implement systematic concepts for the promotion and management of social diversity.

But which specific conditions and requirements need to be considered when trying to develop diversity management in sports organisations? Following sociological as well as sport-specific approaches in this field, this contribution will propose approaches to diversity management in sport. In order to do this, this chapter first focuses on sociological approaches which deal with the question of how sports clubs learn to change, because implementing diversity management in sport goes together with changing traditional structures and procedures in sport. Following this, the chapter will consider the conditions and necessary changes on the structural level of sports organisations and on the level of groups and individuals. Finally the first findings of an ongoing study with coaches in Germany will be presented regarding the question as to how they manage diversity in their teams. This shows that there are different ways of dealing with diversity in sport and that the success of diversity management is strongly associated with the particular setting and context of a sports group.

CONDITIONS FOR IMPROVING SOCIAL INCLUSION IN SPORTS ORGANISATIONS

Looking at sports clubs as the most common entity of organised sport in Germany and many other European countries, it should be recognised that sports clubs are usually slow and reluctant to confront new situations (cf. Thiel & Meier, 2004; Meier & Thiel, 2006). Innovative people who are dedicated to new ideas are often confronted with the lethargy of structures in sports clubs when the traditional ways of the club are questioned. Although this may be disappointing for the processing of new developments, it is better for the functional continuity of club structures. Otherwise they might have felt forced to embrace every new movement appearing in their surroundings and been in danger of losing their original concept and guiding principles—even if those might be vague (as is often the case with volunteer organisations) (cf. Thiel & Meier, 2004: 120; Meier & Thiel, 2006: 181).

With respect to processes of social inclusion this slowness or even dismissive attitude of sports clubs becomes crucial. Based on empirical studies in sports clubs, the Dutch sociologists Knoppers and Anthonissen (2006) have revealed that managers of clubs tend to refuse changes when new member groups (e.g., women, ethnic minorities) appear. They would rather apply strategies of homogenising the members' interests (according to the traditional interests of club members) and try to avoid any conflict that might result from the new members' interests. Following the advice of popular business literature, sports managers often stick to their belief that a club needs a 'corporate identity' and that it can only function effectively when each member supports this corporate identity. Under these circumstances it becomes very difficult for new social groups and their individual identities to gain acceptance.

Generally, sports clubs do not announce an official exclusion of certain groups of people. Following the principle of equality they are formally open to everyone. Yet often there are informal processes of exclusion at work which are subtle and therefore difficult to decode. Mostly, it is the given culture of a club, the developed routines, habits and practices that are crucial to the question of whether newcomers are able to develop a sense of belonging to a sports group or not (cf. Doherty & Chelladurai, 1999; Elling & Claringbould, 2005: 508ff; Seiberth & Thiel, 2007: 7ff).

To sum up, there seems to be a set of conditions that makes social inclusion in sports clubs difficult. This is, first of all, the fundamental reluctance of sports clubs to face any new developments, in combination with the tendency of club managers to homogenise their members' interests. Finally, informal processes might lead to the exclusion of so-called foreign people.

In view of this, the question arises of how a change in the direction of social inclusion is possible. It is helpful to use approaches from organisational sociology and organisational learning in this case.

Any major change in an organisation needs a long-term process of learning that affects the organisation as a whole. This is especially the case for processes of social inclusion (cf. Hansen & Müller, 2003: 26ff). As far as sports clubs are concerned, most of them have a long history of dealing with a predominantly homogenous group of members, namely young people, mostly boys and men from the middle classes. This means that sports clubs have developed a well-functioning system of routines which fit into the lifestyle and requirements of this specific group. Now that new groups are entering the field of sport, clubs are required to forget their past experiences and former routines which suited their traditions (cf. Willke, 2005: 118). Only by neglecting these conventions will opportunities for the newcomers arise. Usually this process is not easy, maybe even painful for the organisation, because some of the important achievements in the past have to be given up. Therefore, in many cases there may be resistance to the new situation. To 'overcome this resistance to change' is the main task in the process of diversity management (cf. Cunningham, 2007: 306ff). It is even more difficult to overcome this resistance when there is subtle antagonism seething under the surface as is often the case in organisations, due to the fact that members are not aware of their old routines. In such situations the members of an organisation would first of all have to become aware of the established procedures. They would need an active examination of the club's culture and identity in order to find possibilities of acknowledging the change (cf. Meier & Thiel, 2006: 187ff).

Literature about organisational learning proposes that a learning process is only successful when both sides of an organisation, its members as well as the body of the organisation itself (with its structures and guidelines), develop their knowledge in a reciprocal process (cf. Willke, 2005: 119). For the system of sport this means that it is not only the individual actors (trainers, athletes, functionaries) who have to learn how to deal with diversity, the organisation itself has to implement the knowledge for promoting social inclusion. In Europe many sports organisations at a national level have published guidelines for sport for all and this is an important step towards providing a structural framework. Yet the question remains how these normative objectives can be transferred from the national head of sports systems into their respective member organisations, down to the level of sports clubs and their individual members.

Taking into account that sports clubs are slow and sometimes reluctant to change (even when this change is initiated by the national organisation), it is self-evident that they will only engage in social diversity if they are able to see diversity as a development that is fitting for the organisation's identity and aims.

A closer look at diversity management is now necessary in order to analyse its possible applicability to sport.

DIVERSITY MANAGEMENT: DEFINITION, GOALS AND APPROACHES TOWARDS SPORT

Diversity management was originally conceived for large American companies which followed the U.S. politics of 'affirmative action'. Meanwhile diversity management has become established in Europe as well (e.g., Ford, Lufthansa, BP), and it is no longer limited to the economic sector. Nowadays non-profit organisations (e.g., universities, hospitals, NGOs) have also committed themselves to the idea of promoting diversity (cf. Süß, 2007: 440; Stuber, 2009: 97ff). In Germany, for example, over 600 organisations from the economic as well as public/welfare system have signed the so-called charter of diversity which obliges them to provide an environment free of prejudice and discrimination. The charter aims to include people from differing backgrounds, no matter what age, gender, ethnic or religious background, sexual identity, ability, social status etc. (cf. www.diversity-charter.org). The German Sports Federation as the head of all sports clubs in Germany has also signed the charter of diversity.

With the various types of diversity in mind, it is relevant to refer to 'differences among people that are likely to affect their acceptance, work performance, satisfaction, or progress in an organization' (Hays-Thomas,

2004: 112). According to this definition, the differences between people cannot be viewed as unchangeable or even natural. Instead, they are the result of processes of social construction which lead to different chances and positions in social hierarchy. Of course, gender, age, ethnicity, (dis) ability, and so on are the most common types of diversity which most programmes focus on. Yet there are other differences that might become essential for the acceptance of individuals in a certain organization (e.g., the length of membership) (cf. Gardenswartz & Rowe, 1995).

In sport the physical ability of a person certainly is one of the most important categories for competition as well as processes of social positioning. Thus basic distinctions have to be drawn between the dimensions of diversity in the field of sport: age, gender and (dis)ability are mostly related to the body and its physical performance and therefore it becomes a difficult task to decipher the social construction of these categories. In most of the cases religion, ethnicity, class and sexual identity are referred to as cultural or social differences.

Generally, diversity management is defined as a strategy to manage people in an organization in such a way 'that the potential advantages of diversity are maximized while its potential disadvantages are minimized' (Cox, 1993: 11). This definition is based on the concept that diverse groups are able to produce a high level of creativity as long as the possible conflicts which may arise from the differences between people are managed (e.g., Cox, 1993).

In view of this, the goals of diversity management can be centered on two perspectives (cf. Becker, 2006: 11):

1. In organisations with homogenous members, diversity management primarily aims at an opening for social diversity; this means that the conditions for the inclusion of underrepresented groups have to be provided;
2. In organisations with heterogeneous members, it aims at implementing a culture of appreciation of differences in such a way that the members' various talents are utilized for the organization's goals; this also implies that social conflicts have to be coped with.

Regarding these two perspectives, it is obvious that diversity management is about balancing suspense: increasing the diversity within a system and at the same time dealing with the dissimilarities (cf. Judy, 2005).

Meanwhile many different approaches towards diversity management have been developed (cf. Engel, 2007: 97). When analysing these different approaches, a change in the conceptualisation of diversity management becomes evident. Up until the late 1990s the focus of diversity programmes was on affirmative action for underprivileged groups which, viewed critically, led to an exaggeration of differences. Nowadays, diversity management focuses on a profound change of the culture of an organisation.

Developing a culture of appreciating differences is the main goal of diversity management. The German diversity expert Stuber (2009: 82) emphasizes that diversity management aims at convincing organisations that their core goals can be achieved more effectively with than without diversity. Viewed in such an optimistic way, diversity can be a valuable potential asset of an organisation (cf. Stuber, 2009: 15ff).

The main question which arises from this is whether and in what way sports organisations (e.g. sports teams, clubs and associations), can recognize social diversity as valuable. Pragmatically speaking, it is obvious that there are limits to diversity in given situations. Take for example a sports club that has a long and successful tradition in competitive team sports (e.g., soccer, basketball) for boys and young men. It might well be asking too much of that club to open its doors to all kinds of social groups (e.g., girls, the elderly). Diversity management must therefore be considered with a view to the particular situation of an organisation and in particular to its main objectives.

In general, the main objective of a sports club is to meet its members' interests (cf. Horch, 1992; Braun, 2003: 48). Because the interests of members always vary (even if they stem from the same social group), diversity management could help to raise sensitivity towards different interests and to convey ideal opportunities for the individual members. Thus the members' satisfaction and the identification with the sports club could be improved.

Yet there are of course other objectives in sports clubs as well as variations in the goals between the individual organisations. In some settings for instance, 'success in sport' might be the main perspective and in others 'developing social contacts' or 'health promotion' are the aims. These different perspectives are decisive factors for the question of how far social diversity can be recognized as a valuable element in a sports club.

To summarise, one could say that the concept of diversity management seems to fit the necessities of organised sport regarding social inclusion. However, each sports club must be examined carefully to see to what extent social diversity can be recognized as a valuable element and what specific measures have to be taken in order to promote diversity in this given context.

So far approaches towards diversity management in sport are rare. With his book *Diversity in Sports Organizations*, the American scientist Cunningham (2007) proposed a comprehensive work which is also instructive for European sport, although the particularities of volunteer sports clubs are not sufficiently considered. According to Cunningham and following the principles of organisational learning (see above), diversity management needs at least two levels of implementation: the structural level of organisations and the level of groups and their members in sport. In what follows, these two levels are described separately though of course the different levels complement one another.

DIVERSITY MANAGEMENT AT THE STRUCTURAL
LEVEL OF ORGANISATIONS IN SPORT

Considering the German and other European sports systems, the national bodies of sport, the associations for different sports and the sports clubs are considered at this level of action.

Diversity strategies can work top-down as well as bottom-up. Ideally, the executive committees at the top announce the main goal of diversity management (e.g., by offering a guideline for diversity). At the same time the organisation should provide a chance for its members at the bottom to express their experiences with diversity (cf. Cunningham, 2007: 310; Stuber 2009: 146ff). As mentioned above, social diversity is already the focus of national executive committees in European sport who have adopted official guidelines for social inclusion. The people at the bottom of sports clubs hierarchies, however, mostly have not yet had the opportunity to express their view of the chances and problems social diversity brings. This is a significant shortcoming which delays the progress of diversity management in sport. In order to fill that gap of knowledge, empirical studies will have to focus on analysing the members of sports organisations and their respective attitudes and experiences with diversity in sport.

Generally, there are a wide range of measures which may promote social diversity from the top down. For example, establishing reward systems and change teams or implementing diversity training into the systems of education in sport (e.g., for coaches and functionaries) (cf. Cunningham, 2007: 309ff). However, with the particular conditions of sports organisations in mind, one aspect is essential above all: sports organisations must be able to consider social diversity as a valuable commodity fitting into the organisation's identity. Following this idea there is a need for instruments which help sports organisations to identify their status quo of social diversity (cf. Stuber, 2009: 144ff). This diversity analysis in sports organisations has to find answers to the following questions:

- *Analysis of culture and identity*: What is the traditional culture and the identity of the sports organisation? What are its main goals?
- *Analysis of social composition*: Which social groups are represented in the organisation, which are underrepresented? Who are the newcomers, who are the old members?
- *Analysis of power relations*: Who is in power? Which social groups are underrepresented in the executive committees?
- *Analysis of social cohesion*: Do the members feel accepted by the organisation? Are the members committing themselves? What kinds of conflicts are reported by the members?
- *Analysis of measures*: Did the organisation take any measures for promoting social diversity so far? What are the successes and problems?

- *Analysis of chances for diversity*: How far does social diversity fit into the club's identity? How can social diversity support the core goals?

Only by answering these (or similar) questions can a sports association judge its particular status quo on diversity. In this way it is possible to develop an adequate diversity strategy which meets the specific situation and character of the organisation.

In Germany the national head of youth organisations in sport (Deutsche Sportjugend) has developed a comparable tool for its member organisations. This 'intercultural checklist' includes a questionnaire with specific items concerning cultural diversity. It serves as a first means for sports associations to reflect on their situation. Yet it is restricted to ethnic diversity and neglects other dimensions.

DIVERSITY MANAGEMENT AT THE LEVEL OF GROUPS AND MEMBERS IN SPORT

At this level of action ,the various groups in sport and their members are the chief focus, for example, the teams with their coaches and athletes or the sports classes in clubs with their instructors and practitioners.

For the management of diversity at this level the people in key-positions, namely the coaches and instructors, are essential. They are in direct and continuous contact with the club members in sport. They experience the members' interests and attitudes towards diversity regularly and they are of the utmost importance for any development in sport (cf. Mrazek & Rittner, 1992: 11).

Studies concerning the social competencies of coaches in sport reveal that social and cultural diversity in a sports team is one of the most difficult challenges for a coach. Coaches estimate differences in their team, and establishing social cohesion, as one of the most demanding tasks (cf. Borggrefe, Thiel & Cachay, 2006: 171ff). This is probably associated with their belief that a homogenous group of athletes is more successful than a heterogeneous group.

Cunningham (2007) points out that diversity management in sports teams aims at valuing the differences within a team as a benefit. As was mentioned above, this optimistic perspective on the possible chances of diversity may not occur in every setting in sport.

In order to find out more about the conditions, chances and problems of managing diversity in sports groups research, interviews were conducted with coaches and instructors in sport. The nineteen interviewees of the ongoing study were derived from different settings in sport (such as team and individual sports, high performance and recreational sports). The interviews reveal a great variety of ways of dealing with diversity in sport. At a first glance the interviews reveal that the social competencies of the coaches and their personal attitude towards diversity are highly important. Besides these features of the personality of the coach, it is noticeable that there are further conditions for the success of diversity management. This success is measured according to the two central perspectives of diversity management (see above):

1. Opening up to social diversity;
2. Implementing a culture which appreciates differences.

Whether sports groups are able to meet both perspectives seems to depend not only on the coaches' personal competencies, but also on the respective setting and context of the group. Up until now, three different types of settings are identified which seem to be distinctive in the management of diversity, as explained below.

A. The study sample so far includes only one coach who seems to be successful with respect to both perspectives of diversity management. He coaches a team which is diverse in many respects. The team includes athletes between 6 and 85 years, male and female, from different social classes, different religious and ethnic groups, hetero- and homosexuals, most of them are healthy, but some have physical handicaps. The coach describes his team as 'a very, very homogenous group' and he refers to a very strong social cohesion, a strong sense of belonging within the group.

Strikingly, this group practises an elite sport, namely high-diving and the team practices five times a week at a regional high performance centre. According to the coach, the management of diversity is easy in this team, because they engage in an individual sport. Each member of the group needs and gets individual treatment. The different physical abilities of the young and old, the male and female and the able and disabled members seem to be of no importance because in competitions the individuals start in different categories, each of them trying to bring out their best.

In the coaches' opinion the athletes appreciate the differences between the members of the group, they profit from the different experiences and life situations and the coach even labels the group as 'a big family'.

Obviously the setting of this particular group, acting in an individual sport at a high performance level, supports the positive outcome of diversity management.

B. The second type includes team sports, e.g. soccer. The members of the group are quite diverse as regards their social status and cultural backgrounds. But looking at the body-related dimension of diversity there are no variations: all of them are adolescent boys of good health. The core goal of this group, namely to be successful in team sports, does not allow diversity in the physical dimension. According to the coaches, the cultural diversity of the team is a benefit. They point out that the different life situations of the boys shape different characters and according to the coaches: 'it is of the utmost importance for a team sport to have different characters in the team'. Conflicts seem to be rare and as the coaches point out, this is due to the attitude of the boys: 'They want to win the game and for winning it doesn't matter which social class or ethnic group you belong to.'

In sum, the particular setting of these groups, to fight as a team in competitive sports, allows for the recognition of social and cultural diversity as a potential asset.

C. Other groups are characterized by a high level of diversity. However, according to the coaches, establishing social cohesion within these groups is almost impossible. This refers to sports classes in leisure or health sports such as dancing, swimming or fitness. These classes attract a great diversity of people, male and female, from different age-ranges and from differing social, ethnic and religious backgrounds. Here the coaches comment on social divisions within the groups. Processes of social exclusion are at work, people being divided into an 'in-group' and an 'out-group'. One interviewee, who teaches dancing-classes in a sports club, points out: 'The people in my class are not able to socialize with each other. The differences are just too large. There is this mechanic who cannot talk to the mathematician. They don't have the same topics of conversation, so they separate from each other.'

With respect to diversity management the problem of these groups is the lack of a mutual aim. Each of them wants to improve their own individual physical performance. Some of them want to develop social contacts. However, they look for friends who belong to the same social group. Therefore this particular setting in recreational and individual sports makes it difficult to view diversity as a benefit.

In conclusion, in order to develop diversity management in sport more attention needs to be paid to the different settings of groups, each with their particular conditions for viewing diversity as a benefit in relation to their respective goals.

CONCLUDING REMARKS

Sports organisations in Europe are challenged by the increasing diversity of their participants over the last years. The implementation of diversity management may help sports organisations to meet these challenges. Diversity management aims at developing a culture of appreciating differences. This culture should help organisations to open themselves up for diversity and to treat diversity as an advantage.

It is not sufficient to announce diversity management as a normative objective at the top level of a sports organization. For the development of diversity management in sport it is essential to reflect on the particular conditions of the clubs and groups at the bottom. Sports clubs are usually reluctant to change. In order to prepare them seriously and carefully for diversity management they need instruments that help them to analyse their status quo with respect to diversity. Clubs are only able to develop an adequate diversity strategy if they get a precise picture of the given diversity situation in their club and if they get an idea of the possible contributions of diversity to the club's goals. It is one of the main tasks in the future to organise such a support for the clubs.

As regards the sports teams and classes at the bottom of the sports system, their coaches are of the utmost importance for progress in diversity management. Certainly, there is a need for training their social competencies in diversity management. However, it is also important to notice that the success of diversity management in sport depends on particular settings and associated conditions. Coaches and functionaries have to learn about these differing conditions for diversity management.

'Diversity is an Opportunity!'—this is the title of the 'charter of diversity' which was adopted by the German Sports Federation. In order to pass on this idea to the sports clubs and groups at the lowest levels of organised sport, a better understanding of their particular situations is necessary and more support for the implementation of diversity strategies should be offered. Diversity management—as it is conceived in this paper—could help to achieve this aim.

REFERENCES

Becker, M. (2006), Wissenschaftstheoretische Grundlagen des Diversity Managements', in M. Becker & A. Seidel (eds), *Diversity Management—Unternehmens- und Personalpolitik der Vielfalt*, Stuttgart: Schäffer-Poeschel Verlag, pp. 3–48.

Borggrefe, C., Thiel, A. & Cachay, K. (2006), *Sozialkompetenz von Trainerinnen und Trainern im Spitzensport* (Berichte und Materialien des Bundesinstituts für Sportwissenschaft, Bd. 5), Köln: Sport & Buch Strauß.

Braun, S. (2003), Freiwillige Vereinigungen zwischen Staat, Markt und Privatsphäre. Konzepte, Kontroversen und Perspektiven', in J. Baur & S. Braun (eds), *Integrationsleistungen von Sportvereinen als Freiwilligenorganizationen*, Aachen: Meyer & Meyer, pp. 43–87.

Breuer, C. & Haase, A. (2007), Sportvereine und demographischer Wandel', in C. Breuer (ed.), *Sportentwicklungsbericht 2005/2006—Analyse zur Situation der Sportvereine in Deutschland*, Köln: Sportverlag Strauß, pp. 60–84.

Cox, T. (1993), 'Cultural Diversity in Organizations' *Academy of Management Executive*, 2: 34–47.

Cunningham, G. B. (2007), *Diversity in Sports Organizations*, Scottsdale: Arizona: Holcomb Hathaway.

Doherty, A. J. & Chelladurai, P. (1999), 'Managing Cultural Diversity in Sport Organizations: A Theoretical Perspective', *Journal of Sport Management*, 13: 280–297.

Elling, A. & Claringbould, I. (2005), 'Mechanisms of Inclusion and Exclusion in the Dutch Sports Landscape: Who Can and Wants to Belong?', *Sociology of Sport Journal*, 22: 498–515.

Engel, R. (2007), 'Die Vielfalt der Diversity Management Ansätze. Geschichte, praktische Anwendungen in Organisationen und zukünftige Herausforderungen in Europa', in I. Koall, V. Bruchhagen & F. Höher (eds), *Diversity Outlooks. Managing Diversity zwischen Ethik, Profit und Antidiskriminierung*, Münster: LIT, pp. 97–110.

Gardenswartz, L. & Rowe, A. (1995), *Diversity Teams at Work*, Burr Ridge, IL: Irwin Professional Pub.

Hansen, K. & Müller, U. (2003), 'Aspekte der Globalisierung, Geschlecht und Organisationsreform', in E. Belinszki, K. Hansen & U. Müller (eds), *Diversity Management*, Münster: LIT Verlag, pp. 9–60.

Hays-Thomas, R. (2004), 'Why Now? The Contemporary Focus on Managing Diversity', in M. S. Stockdale & F. J. Crobsy (eds), *The Psychology and Management of Workplace Diversity*, Malden: Blackwell, pp. 3–30.

Horch, H.-D. (1992), *Geld, Macht und Engagement in freiwilligen Vereinigungen—Grundlagen einer Wirtschaftssoziologie von Non-Profit-Organisationen*, Berlin: Duncker & Humblot.

Judy, M. (2005), 'Unterschiede machen', in G. Hartmann & M. Judy (eds), *Unterschiede machen. Managing Gender und Diversity in Organisationen und Gesellschaft*, Wien: Edition Volkshochschule, pp. 57–81.

Knoppers, A. & Anthonissen, A. (2006), *'Making Sense of Diversity in Organizing Sport'*, Aachen: Meyer & Meyer.

Meier, H. & Thiel, A. (2006), ' "Starke Kulturen"—Sportvereine im Spannungsfeld zwischen struktureller Veränderung und Existenzsicherung', in M. Krüger & B. Schulze (eds), *Fußball in Geschichte und Gesellschaft. Tagung der dvs-Sektionen Sportgeschichte und Sportsoziologie vom 29.09.-01.10.2004 in Münster*, Hamburg: Czwalina Verlag, pp. 181–189.

Mrazek, J. & Rittner, V. (1992), *Übungsleiter und Trainer im Sportverein. Band I: Die Personen und die Gruppen*, Schorndorf: Hofmann.

Poli, R. & Ravenel, L. (2008), *Annual Review of the European Football Players' Market*, accessed 3 October 2010 at: de.fifa.com/mm/document/afdeveloping/courses/65/76/83/annual_review_2008_extract_ok.pdf.

Seiberth, K. & Thiel, A. (2007), 'Fremd im Sport? Barrieren der Integration von Menschen mit Migrationshintergrund in Sportorganisationen', in R. Johler, A. Thiel, J. Schmid & R. Treptow (eds), *Europa und seine Fremden. Die Gestaltung kultureller Vielfalt als Herausforderung*, Bielefeld: transcript, pp. 197–213.

Steinbach, D. & Hartmann, S. (2007), 'Demographischer Wandel und organisierter Sport. Projektionen der Mitgliederentwicklung des DOSB für den Zeitraum bis 2030', *Sport und Gesellschaft*, 4.

6 Discourses on Integration and Interaction in a Martial Arts Club

Lian Malai Madsen

A recurrent theme in the public debate in contemporary Western Europe concerns the cultural differences between ethnic minorities and majority populations. In the Danish version of this debate, media presentations and political contributions regarding cultural diversity often involve stereotypical images of minority youth as a societal problem. According to the dominant discursive constructions by the media and politicians, the solution to problems related to minority youth (such as educational underachievement or participation in criminal gang activities) is better integration. In addition, it is a widespread assumption among Danish politicians and practitioners in leisure associations that participation in organised recreational activities and sports clubs strengthens integration of culturally or socially marginalised youth into society (e.g. Anderson, 2003; 2005; 2006; Boeskov & Ilkjær, 2005; Agergaard, 2008; Madsen, 2008). This ethnographic and interactive study of identity work among children and adolescents in a martial arts club in Copenhagen (Madsen, 2008) contributes insights of relevance to a discussion of such assumptions.

Matters of linguistic behaviour are central to discourses on cultural differences and integration. According to the dominant public and political perceptions of integration, cultural and linguistic minorities are required to learn the majority language and adapt to majority cultural practices to be considered well-integrated (Jørgensen, 2010: 108). Children and adolescents in general, but in particular children and adolescents from a minority background, are expected to acquire certain linguistic and social types of behaviour in order to be successfully socialised as good democratic citizens (e.g. Kristiansen, 2003). In this chapter, I discuss the understanding of integration processes reflected in sports-political initiatives and discourses in Denmark. My discussion is based on the observed conduct of the young members of a martial arts club. I argue for the importance of not merely assuming that membership of a sports club will by itself lead to integration and social cohesion, but that the different conditions for participation in sports activities need to be taken into account, as well as the local social status relations within the community of the club. Furthermore, I illustrate that linguistic practice plays a significant part in integration processes at a micro-level. In this way, my work brings into focus how a sociolinguistic perspective, considering micro-sociological aspects, can fruitfully supplement research within the sociology of sports. After presenting my data and my approach, I discuss a type of discourse on diversity that has been particularly influential within the integration debate in Denmark. I point to general problematic aspects of the sports-political integration initiatives reflecting this type of dominant discourse. After this, I present my ethnographic analysis of the social status relations and orientation in relation to sports disciplines within the club. Finally, before my concluding discussion, I present an example of how social processes that can be characterised as integration processes, are carried out at a micro-level in interactions among the young club members.

DATA AND APPROACH

The data I discuss were collected for a study of identity work and language use among children and youth in a martial arts club in Copenhagen (Madsen, 2008). From August 2004 to June 2005, I observed and collected data from sixteen children and adolescents in a Taekwondo club with highly diverse members. During the fieldwork period, the participants in my study formed five different friendship groups, two girl groups (girls 1: 11–12 years old and girls 2: 14–15 years old) and three boy groups (boys 1: 10–11 years old, boys 2: 12–13 years old and boys 3: 14–15 years old). The data consist of field notes, largely unstructured, qualitative interviews with the groups and individuals, video-recorded group conversations, and participants' self-recordings (audio only).

My research is driven by an interest in how social differentiation and identity categories make sense for the young members of the club. I have approached my data with an emphasis on what actually occurs in the data, how social categories are made relevant through linguistic acts and how my findings resemble, or differ from, phenomena dealt with in existing research and theoretical accounts. In addition, I am concerned with how the conduct of the young club members relates to, reproduces, reinterprets or resists influential ideas about cultural diversity and youth in contemporary Danish society. I employ the approach of interactional sociolinguistics, which has developed from the tradition of linguistic anthropology (Gumperz, 1972; 1982; Kulick, 1992; Rampton, 1995; 2006; Ochs, 1996). Within this approach, it is emphasised that social categories and structures are produced and reproduced in everyday life. Therefore, the starting point is the lived and local realities and these are related to larger-scale socio-cultural processes. Ethnography is a central element of interactional sociolinguistics and a major strength of the approach is the combination of the analytical frameworks provided by linguistics and the reflexive sensitivity required in ethnography. My starting point is the ethnographic and linguistic micro-analysis of situated interactions among the 16 young members of the Taekwondo club and I relate the analyses of the situational negotiations of social meaning to broader processes of social stereotyping and dominant ideas manifest in so-called discourses. The discourses I relate my study to specifically concern a pervasive emphasis on ethnic and cultural differences, integration as adaption and the persistent understanding of particular youth groups as non-majority.

DISCOURSES ON INTEGRATION

The notion of integration has been prominent in Danish public debate since the mid 1990s (Olwig & Pærregaard, 2007: 18). In 2002, the government (still in power in 2011) even established a distinct Ministry of Integration. The Web page of the Ministry of Integration makes clear that this ministry deals with the development of immigrants and refugees towards becoming successful members of Danish society. From the written information and the links on the page, we can see that this involves participation in language courses, cultural courses, employment, education and tax paying (see www. nyidanmark.dk). Yet, in the general debate, as well as in much research on integration, it is rather unclear what exactly the concept of integration refers to (Ejrnæs, 2002). By far the most dominant discourse in Danish media, and subject of current policy making, is an ethnocentric discourse on diversity (Yilmaz, 1999: 180–181; Rennison, 2009: 120–158). This ethnocentric discourse emphasizes values related to culture and the view of integration within this discourse is assimilationist. Ethnic minorities are regarded as either 'un-adapted strangers' or 'disciplined strangers' if they are well-integrated (Rennison, 2009: 153) and the goal of integration is to reach mono-cultural coherence through assimilation of cultural minorities into the majority culture. This ethnocentric discourse on integration is not an exclusively Danish phenomenon, but is characteristic of public debate and policy making in a range of Western European countries (e.g., Blommaert & Verschueren, 1998; Yilmaz, 1999; Jaspers, 2005; Extra, Spotti, & Van Avermaet, 2009). A significant aspect of the public and political integration debate is an assumed connection between participation in organised leisure activities and successful participation in society in general.

Recent work within the sociology of sports has documented that it is a common assumption within sports as well as sports studies that participation in organised recreational activities and sports clubs contributes to the integration of minority and socially marginalised youth into society (e.g., Anderson, 2003; 2005; 2006; Boeskov & Ilkjær, 2005; Agergaard, 2008). The idea of sports activities potentially leading to social inclusion and more general societal benefits is widespread and international (e.g. Bailey, 2007; Hedstrom & Gould, 2004). However, what appears particularly salient in Danish public discourse is that the lack of participation in organised leisure activities in the form of club membership which would involve contact with adults, is considered symptomatic of problems with societal integration (Rambøll & Andersen, 2010: 32). One aspect of this idea is illustrated by the category '*foreningsløse børn*' (club-less children) which figures in the statistics signifying social problems (Anderson, 2005: 168).

It is characteristic of the Taekwondo club in particular that the educational aspects and societal benefits of the sports activities are emphasised and valued. This is the case on an organisational level as well as among the young practitioners. A focus on elite development and competition is a central part of the club's identity, but at the same time the club frequently participates in local sports-political initiatives focusing on integration (for detailed discussion see Madsen, 2008: chapter 1). In addition, several of the members of the club hold the understanding that the competences and values achieved through Taekwondo and the ideological aspects of the sport, lead to some form of social mobilisation when transferred to other areas of life. An example of this is presented here by the chief children's instructor:

> well there've been many cases where you can say partly there've been some cases who balanced on the border of becoming some terrible criminals whom then through the Taekwondo sport through finding some friends here in the club or somebody they can look up to and being able to come here in the club and belong here and even though they have done some shit then they've gotten some chances and been helped by the club right like a kind of family and then they've straightened up. (interview with chief children's instructor, my translation)

The children's instructor describes the means of development from 'borderline criminals' to 'straightened up' as a combination of the Taekwondo sport and the belonging to a family-like community in the club. Yet there are no interview reports on how these developments supposedly occur and how the belonging is achieved.

The Ministry of Integration has launched a number of initiatives focusing on the integration of ethnic minorities through participation in sports clubs (the club participates in the initiative Get2Sport, see www.get2sport.dk). My observations in the Taekwondo club certainly suggest that the idea of integration through sports is well-supported among the sports practitioners. However, my study in the martial arts club points to aspects worth discussing further in relation to the understanding of integration as it is represented in such sports-political initiatives. The integration projects typically aim at increasing the number of members (and sometimes instructors) with ethnic minority backgrounds in the clubs. These projects rarely take into consideration how exactly membership of a club leads to 'a community based on shared values and interest across ethnic, social, and political borders' (http://www.nyidanmark.dk/dadk/Integration/puljer/puljebeskrivelser/det_frivil-lige_integrationsarbejde_og_deltagelse_i_idraets_og_foreningslivet). It is assumed that participants are accepted into the community of a club based merely on shared interests. Conditions for participation, community-based power relations and processes of inclusion and exclusion within the community are entirely overlooked. In addition, it is characteristic that ways of orienting oneself in relation to sporting skills as well as the relationship between sports skills and hierarchies of social status in a given sports club, are disregarded. Finally and in tune with the general Danish integration debate, ethnicity and cultural differences are foregrounded as relevant to problems of integration. Political, sports-related integration initiatives overwhelmingly focus on ethnic and cultural minorities gaining knowledge of and adapting to majority cultural practices.

My ethnographic and linguistic study informs the discussion of such common assumptions about membership of a sports club by looking into the details of the social processes actually occurring among the young martial arts practitioners. The study of social practices in the club points to the importance of taking into consideration the community-constructed social hierarchies and the local processes of inclusion and exclusion. In the club, the local processes of inclusion and exclusion are not merely related to aspects of ethnicities and a much more complex picture appears when you attend to the subtlety of practices as they occur. Hence, an interactive sociolinguistic perspective, taking into account the linguistic constructions and sequences of interaction, in combination with an analytical focus on a sports club as a social community, makes visible how formal membership of a sports club involves a variety of different participant positions. These positions are constructed, ascribed and negotiated among the members and they are associated with different social values allowing varying degrees of influence within the sports club.

IDENTITY-POSITIONINGS IN THE CLUB

The positioning of individuals in a larger social community can be studied through an ethnographic observation of the regular practices of the participants. During the time I spent in the Taekwondo club, I observed certain patterns of behaviour in the five groups of friends focused on in my study. It became clear that a significant point of orientation within the social community of the club was the different ways of relating to the sports activities. Some participants engaged in practices related to the competitive dimension of the sport, whereas others predominantly engaged in social practices around the sport activity and were less focused on the competitive skills used in the sports discipline itself. This insight led me to carry out a systematic analysis of my ethnographic observations (including information gathered from interviews). The analysis therefore takes into account the young club member's orientation towards the sports discipline, as well as the local power relations and differences in social status between the

Table 6.1 Characteristic Practices Related to Membership Status and Taekwondo Orientation of Groups

Group	Related to membership status	Related to Taekwondo orientation
Boys 3	· spent the most time in the club · consider the club a 'second home' · referred to by 10 other participants · often referred to as coolest, most popular members · interacted with many other (mostly male) members	· very talented and ambitious fighters · only (and very often) attended fighting practice and competitions · serious attitude to Taekwondo often practiced on own initiative outside training sessions · occasionally participated in social activities · frequently discussed fights and competitions · emphasised sports skills, ambitions, the fun of winning fights as well as friendships as reason for membership
Boys 2	· spent a lot of time in the club · hung out in several different rooms · referred to by 6 other participants interacted with many other (male) members	· did not often attend fighting practice, but occasionally participated in competition · spent time in the club outside sessions on social activities rather than practice · always participated in social activities · rarely discussed competition-related topics · emphasised fun qualities of the sport and friendships as reason for membership
Boys 1	· spent quite a lot of time in the club · mostly stayed in café or training hall · only referred to by 3 participants · did not interact with many other members	· did not attend fighting practice or participate in competition (only one of the members, once) · spent time in the club outside sessions on social activities rather than practice · sometimes participated in social activities · a few times discussed competition-related topics · emphasised sports skills as well as friendships as reason for membership
Girls 2	· did not spend much time in the club outside training sessions, but sometimes in the café · referred to by 3 participants · rarely interacted with other young members (often with adults)	· often participated (or in one of the girls' case used to participate) in fighting practice and competitions · rarely practiced outside training sessions · occasionally participated in social activities

Continued

Table 6.1   Continued

Group	Related to membership status	Related to Taekwondo orientation
Girls 2		· frequently discussed fights and competitions · emphasised the fun of fighting as reason for membership
Girls 1	· did not spend much time in the club · never spent time in the café, but stayed in changing room and training hall · not referred to by any other club members · never interacted with members outside the girls' class	· never participated in fighting practice or competitions · spent time in the club outside sessions on social activities rather than practice · participated in social activities around the girls' class · never discussed fights and competitions · emphasised cosy fellowship with girlfriends as important motivation for membership

young members. The characteristic practices of the groups related to membership status and Taekwondo orientation are summed up in Table 6.1, where information on the participants' accounts of their motivation for being members of the club is also inserted.

The social practices the participants engage in over time make up their positioning in relation to other club members. Through the practices they signal affiliation or distance in relation to values and categories salient within the club (and often also on a larger social scale, for instance affiliation with streetwise hip-hop culture is more widespread). In this way participants position themselves, on the one hand, within the social community, and, on the other hand, others position them based on their conduct. Social positioning within a social community is crucial to processes of integration. Whether integration is understood as complete assimilation into a majority community or as some level of adaption by all participants involved, it is difficult to imagine any productive change in the conduct of an individual in relation to an encounter with a particular community, if this individual is marginally positioned in relation to this community. Wenger's (1998) learning theory of 'communities of practice' approaches these issues.

A community of practice refers to a collective of people engaging in a framework of doing something. It is defined by participation, through mutual engagement, in a joint enterprise and through time and the development of a shared repertoire of resources (Wenger, 1998: 73). This definition covers a sports club community very well. Wenger (1998: 167) lists four main forms of participating in communities of practice: full participation (insider), full non-participation (outsider), peripherality and marginality. Both peripheral and marginal participation involve a combination of participation and non-participation. The difference between the two forms of participation is related to potential development through time, namely to the participation trajectory. Non-participation for peripheral participants is *enabling* and an opportunity for learning. It is the position of newcomers to a community of practice and it entails the possibility of becoming full participants. We can imagine this form of trajectory as fruitful for integration. Conversely, marginal participants are restricted by non-participation. Marginality refers to long-standing members kept in a marginal position. Identity formation is influenced by the mix of participation and non-participation in the communities of practice we encounter. The mix of participation and non-participation, according to Wenger (1998: 167), reflects the power of individuals and communities to define and influence relations with the rest of the world. Identity formation has to do with our degree of investment in communities, but also our ability to shape the meanings defining these communities.

On the basis of the social practices characteristic of each group (illustrated in Table 6.1), it is possible to carry out an analysis that includes aspects of Wenger's theory of communities of practice. I have placed each group in the two-dimensional illustration in Figure 6.1 according to their typical form of participation as well as their primary orientation in relation to the sports discipline (as competition or social fellowship). The horizontal axis represents a continuum between orientation towards casual social participation at one end and orientation towards competition at the other end. In relation to the practices within the Taekwondo club, a strong degree of orientation towards competition is signified by, for example, frequent participation in fighting practice, expression of competitive ambitions, participation in competitions and frequent reference to these aspects of Taekwondo during interactions. Orientation towards casual social participation is signified by the opposite: no participation in the fighting practice and the competitions, no reference to these aspects during interactions. Instead, members with this orientation are characterised by frequent participation in social activities and expressions of friendship and social fellowship as the main motivation for their participation in the community of practice. The vertical axis represents the member's participation status in the community of practice, as a continuum between central members (approaching Wenger's full participation) and marginal members. Central membership is characterised by a central positioning within the social networks of the club and a high status within the social hierarchy. Marginal membership is characterised by the opposite. In principle, central membership can be obtained through both social and Taekwondo-bound professional activities. Of course, this figure is a rather rough analytical abstraction of complex combinations of practices with individual variations. Nevertheless, the positioning of the groups sheds light on aspects of the relation between membership status and Taekwondo orientation. Therefore, it provides an interesting foundation for the discussion of the social significance of various aspects of identity in the community of practice.

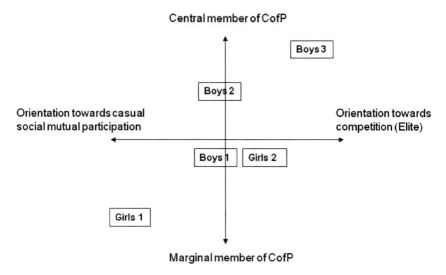

Figure 6.1   Identity positioning of the groups.

The oldest boys among the participants (boys 3) are positioned as very central members of the community of practice with a strong orientation towards competition. The younger boys (boys 2) are positioned as central members oriented slightly more towards casual social participation than competition. The positioning of the youngest boys (boys 1) with respect to Taekwondo orientation is similar to the positioning of boys 2, but they are positioned as more marginal members of the community of practice. The oldest girls among the participants (girls 2) are likewise positioned as rather marginal members, but they are oriented more towards competition than casual social participation. Finally, the youngest girls (girls 1) are positioned as the most marginal members with a strong orientation towards casual social participation. Figure 6.1 suggests that membership status in this community of practice relates to a combination of specific Taekwondo orientation, gender, and age. The participants in the most central social positions are the oldest among the young members, they are male, and they are oriented strongly towards competition. The participants in the most marginal social positions are the youngest of the female participants and they are not oriented towards competition at all. Yet central membership status does not correlate in a straightforward manner to any of these categories individually. The girls in group 2 are older, as well as more oriented towards competition, than boys 2, yet they are positioned as more marginal members.

MICRO-INTEGRATION IN INTERACTION

We have seen how the employment of Wenger's (1998) concept of community of practice as an analytical unit brings into focus the need for much more nuanced considerations of what it means to participate in a sports club. It is necessary to take into account what the conditions for participation are and how community specific power relations may play a central part in relation to a sports club's potential as a site for socialising processes that enhance cohesion. I shall now turn to an example of a sequence of interactions where social processes that might be described as entailing socio-cultural integration did take place on a micro-level. Extract 1 is an example of interactive behaviour typical of the oldest boys participating in my study. It is an exchange of utterances between Murat and Ilias of 34 minutes of self-recording made on their way back to Copenhagen on the train after a regional elite fighter practice session of the youth talent team. Murat carries the mp3-recorder. Salim, who is another talented team member (but not a participant in my study otherwise), is present as well. Just before this sequence, Salim has mentioned that he did a test exam in school earlier that day.

Extract 1: Term test

1	Murat:	jeg fi jeg var til prøve terminsprøve engelsk mundtlig jeg
2		fik elleve (.) i dag.
	Murat:	*I go I went to a test term test English oral I got eleven. (.)*
	today.	
3	Ilias:	VED DU HVAD JEG VAR I jeg var i i terminsprøve fransk og
4		jeg fik ti
	Ilias:	*DO YOU KNOW WHAT I WAS IN I was in in term*
	test	*French and I got ten*
5	Murat:	jeg fik elleve
	Murat:	*I got eleven*

Murat after this continuously repeats 'ten, eleven, ten, eleven' until Ilias and Salim tell him to be quiet (in a less polite manner 'shut your arse').

In these three utterances, Murat and Ilias explicitly claim linguistic competence by referring to or brag about recently achieved results of tests in foreign languages taught in Danish schools. In line 1–2 Murat tells the interlocutors that he received the mark eleven in a term test in English. Murat's utterance could be understood as merely offering information about the experience of the test, but Ilias's counter information (line 3–4) in a loud voice suggests that he reacts to Murat's utterance as bragging. The sequential connection, the loud volume in Ilias' turn, and the comparative repetition of the test results (by Murat) that follow, frame the contributions and thereby the contributors, in a competitive relationship. Both Murat and Ilias use a number of non-standard features associated with a late modern, urban youth style of Danish (Madsen, 2008). These include pronunciation without the Danish 'stød' in words like 'terminsprøve', 'engelsk', 'fransk' and 'ti'. The boys also leave out the preposition in 'terminsprøve engelsk' (term test English), and 'terminsprøve fransk' (term test French).

Furthermore, Ilias uses the preposition 'i' (in) in a non-standard manner ('i terminsprøve', in term test). Finally, they both employ a pronunciation at the level of utterance with a characteristic prosody (see Pharao & Foget Hansen, 2006).

Thus, Murat and Ilias appear to be engaged in a situational (rather playful) fight over status. The fight takes place during an interaction in an out-of-school context and could be described as carried out through claims of school-related linguistic capital. The linguistic practice employed by the boys in this sequence, however, is not a practice typically appreciated in educational contexts. Their linguistic practice is characterised by the use of features associated with a late modern, urban youth style. This style does not stereotypically connote academic success. The style could be said to represent informality, non-standard vernacular and peer-socialising and in this sense contrasts with formal, mainstream-appreciated and elititist societal connotations (see Madsen, 2008). The use of the style in combination with academically ambitious practices by the boys thus results in a renegotiation of the dominant norms of societal and school-related success being equated with standard linguistic practices. The boys manage situated identity constructions as successful, but common students.

Extract 1, is, of course, only a single and short example, but it is highly characteristic of the behaviour of this group of boys. Sequences such as extract 1 illustrate at least two central points in relation to discourses on integration:

1. Negotiation of social status relations is central even in interactions among close friends. This underlines the significance of status relations for participation in social communities and hence, for processes of integration.

2. Processes of integration are not merely a co-presence of diverse groups of individuals. Processes of integration involve micro acts that bring about and integrate relations of different cultural frames (also on a socio-symbolic level).

That the boys in their peer interactions demonstrate a capability for navigating between the normative demands of peer culture as well as majority cultural elite expectations can of course not be directly attributed to their participation in a sports club (for instance we find similar episodes in data from boys practicing hip-hop music; see Stæhr, 2010; Madsen, 2011). Still, it is likely that the leisure environment perhaps provides a less restricted social space than, for instance, a school context and thereby leisure contexts might be considered particularly fruitful sites for these kinds of identity practices entailing micro-integration.

CONCLUDING DISCUSSION

In this chapter I have argued that assumptions of participation in sports clubs as fruitful for integration are characteristic of public discourse, political initiatives on integration, as well as among practitioners in sports clubs. The dominating view of integration in current public discourse and policy in Denmark is assimilationist and this understanding appears reflected to some extent in the sports-political initiatives aimed at integration. This does not necessarily mean that practitioners in sports clubs participating in integration projects employ an assimilationist notion of integration in their work (we saw an example of belonging presented by an instructor as 'like a family'). Nevertheless, it is characteristic at a political level, as well as among practitioners in sports clubs, that there is a lack of reflection on how integration processes are supposed to occur in club communities. The data I have discussed add two significant points to discussions of integration through sports. Firstly, the observed conduct of the young members nuances the dominant understanding of integration within ethnocentric discourse. Secondly, the study in the martial arts club underlines the importance of considering local processes of social inclusion and exclusion in a sports club. This second point is of particular relevance to political initiatives, practitioners in sports clubs as well as sports studies concerned with socialising and educational aspects of sports.

With respect to the first point, the analyses of the interactive data presented in this paper make clear that ideas of social integration, as they are presented in dominant stereotypical discourses, cannot account for what happens among the young club members. As we have seen, young minority boys, within the framework of the recreational social site of a sports club, refer to degrees of academic success. Furthermore, the boys frequently employ non-standard linguistic resources in combination with the school-related interactive activities. They thereby challenge stereotypical assumptions about an opposition between successful academic and successful urban, streetwise, masculine youth identities. Social integration in the sense that it is practiced interactively among the boys does not merely involve adaptation to dominant measures of societal success, but involves bringing together different norms, values and practices. The young speakers successfully manage norms of academic success and socio-symbolic values among peers. They master integrated identity constructions of themselves as good students, skilled martial arts practitioners and cool young urban boys of a high social status in the club community.

With respect to the second point, I have demonstrated how formal membership in a sports club involves a variety of different participant positions and how the different positions are associated with different social credits allowing varying degrees of influence within the community of practice. The study in the martial arts club points to the importance of taking into account community-constructed power hierarchies. In the club (as we saw in Figure 6.1), there is a great difference between participating as an 11-—year-old girl practicing in the girls class and practicing as a 15-year-old boy in the elite fighting team. Although all of the participants in the study were long-standing members, those who did not engage in competition fighting and in particular the girls, remained marginal participants. The analysis of the social practices of the young club members underlines the fact that considering a sports club as a potential socialising and unifying community requires more detailed accounts of the local processes of integration within the community of practice of the club as well as the social negotiations involved in these processes.

REFERENCES

Agergaard, S. (2008), *Unges idrætsdeltagelse og integration i idrætsforeninger i Århus, Vest*, Copenhagen: Idrættens analyseinstitut.
Anderson, S. (2003), *Civilizing Children: Children's Sports and Civil Sociality in Copenhagen,Denmark*, PhD dissertation, Institute for Anthropology, Copenhagen.
Anderson, S. (2005), ' "Vi kender hinanden alle sammen hvor vi så end er fra" At leve lokalt gennem global sport i København', in K. F. Olwig, L. Gilliam & K. Valentin (eds), *Lokale liv fjerne forbindelser. Studier af børn, unge og migration*, Copenhagen: Hans Reitzel, pp. 153–174.
Anderson, S. (2006), 'Storbymennesker. Tilflyttere og lokale i københavnske kampsportsklubber', in M. Rytter & M. Holm Pedersen (eds), *Den stille integration. Nye fortællinger om at høre til i Danmark*, Copenhagen: C.A. Reitzel, pp. 63–91.
Bailey, R. (2007), 'Youth Sport and Social Inclusion', in N. Holt (ed.), *Positive Youth Development Through Sport'*, London: Routledge, pp. 85–97.
Blommaert, J. & Verschueren, J. (1998), *Debating Diversity: Analysing the Discourse of Tolerance*, London: Routledge.
Boeskov, S. & Ilkjær, T. (2005), *Integration og det frivillige foreningsliv. En undersøgelse af barrierer og løsninger i relation til foreningsdeltagelse hos unge med anden etnisk baggrund*, Copenhagen: Department of Sports Studies, University of Copenhagen.
Ejrnæs, M. (2002), *Etniske minoriteters tilpasning til livet i Danmark—forholdet mellem majoritetssamfund og etniske minoriteter*, AMID Working Paper Series 18/2002.
Extra, G., Spotti, M. & Van Avermaet, P. (2009), *Language Testing, Migration and Citizenship: Cross National Perspectives on Integration Regimes*, London: Continuum.
Gumperz, J. (1972), 'Introduction', in J. Gumperz & D. Hymes (eds), *Directions in Sociolinguistics: The Ethnography of Communication*, London: Blackwell, pp. 1–25.
Gumperz, J. (1982), *Discourse Strategies*, Cambridge: Cambridge University Press.
Hedstrom, R. & Gould, D. (2004), *Research in Youth Sports: Critical Issues Status*, Michigan: Michigan State University.
Jaspers, J. (2005), 'Linguistic Sabotage in a Context of Monolingualism and Standardization', *Working Papers in Urban Language and Literacies*, 28.

Jørgensen, J. N. (2010), *Languaging. Nine Years of Poly-Lingual Development of Young Turkish-Danish Grade School Students*, Copenhagen: Danish School of Education, University of Aarhus.

Kristiansen, T. (2003), 'Language Attitudes and Language Politics in Denmark', in *International Journal of the Sociology of Language*, 159: 57–71.

Kulick, D. (1992), *Language Shift and Cultural Reproduction: Socialization, Self, and Syncretism in a Papua New Guinean Village*, Cambridge: Cambridge University Press.

Madsen, L. M. (2008), *Fighters and Outsiders. Linguistic Practices, Social Identities, and Social Relationships Among Urban Youth in a Martial Arts Club*, Copenhagen: University of Copenhagen.

Madsen, L. M. (2011), 'Interactional Renegotiations of Educational Discourses in Recreational Learning Contexts', in *Linguistics ad Education* 22(1): 53–67.

Ochs, E. (1996), 'Linguistic Resources for Socialising Humanity', in J. Gumperz & S. Levinson (eds), *Rethinking Linguistic Relativity*, Cambridge: Cambridge University Press, pp. 438–469.

Olwig, K. F. & Pærregaard, K. (eds) (2007), *Integration. Antropologiske perspektive*, Copenhagen: Museum Tusculanums Forlag.

Pharao, N. & Foget Hansen, G. (2006), 'Prosodic Aspects of the Copenhagen Multiethnolect', in *Nordic Prosody, Proceedings of the IXth Conference, Lund 2004*, Frankfurt/Berlin/New York: Peter Lang, pp. 87–96.

Rambøll Management Consulting & Calmar Andersen, S. (2010), *Mehmet og modkulturen. En undersøgelse af drenge med etnisk minoritetsbaggrund*, Copenhagen: Rambøll.

Rampton, B. (1995), *Crossing. Language and Ethnicity Among Adolescents*, London: Longman.

Rampton, B. (2006), *Language in Late Modernity. Interaction in an Urban School*, Cambridge: Cambridge University Press.

Rennison, B. W. (2009), *Kampen om integrationen: Diskurser om etnisk mangfoldighedsledelse*, Copenhagen: Hans Reitzel.

Stæhr, A. (2010), *Rappen reddede os. Et studie af senmoderne storbydrenges identitetsarbejde i fritids- og skolemiljøer*, Copenhagen: University of Copenhagen.

Wenger, E. (1998), *Communities of Practice. Learning, Meaning and Identity*, Cambridge: Cambridge University Press.

Yilmaz, F. (1999), 'Konstruktionen af de etniske minoriteter: Eliten, medierne og 'etnificering' af den danske debat', *Politica*, 31(2): 2–24.

7 What Is the Development in Sport-for-Development?

Fred Coalter

THE UNITED NATIONS, SPORT AND PLAYING ON EVERYBODY'S TEAM

In November 2003 the General Assembly of the United Nations adopted a resolution affirming its commitment to sport as a means to promote education, health, development and peace. Following this, the United Nations declared 2005 to be the Year of Sport and Physical Education, explaining: 'the United Nations is turning to the world of sport for help in the work for peace and the effort to achieve the Millennium Development Goals' (United Nations, 2005a). These goals included universal primary education, promoting gender equality and empowering women, combating HIV/AIDS and addressing issues of environmental sustainability. The wide-ranging contribution expected of sport is stated clearly (United Nations, 2005b):

> The world of sport presents a natural partnership for the United Nations' system. By its very nature sport is about participation. It is about inclusion and citizenship. Sport brings individuals and communities together, highlighting commonalities and bridging cultural or ethnic divides. Sport provides a forum to learn skills such as discipline, confidence and leadership and it teaches core principles such as tolerance, cooperation and respect. Sport teaches the value of effort and how to manage victory, as well as defeat.

Many of these statements of desired outcomes are derived from traditional and widespread ideologies of 'sport'—the development of discipline, confidence, tolerance and respect—although robust evidence for such claims is very limited (Coalter, 2007). In addition to a relatively weak generic evidence base, in the emerging policy area of sport-for-development we are also faced with a widespread lack of evidence for the effectiveness of some of the core claims (Kruse, 2006; UNICEF, 2006). In part, this reflects the recent establishment of many of the organisations and programmes and the widespread lack of expertise and resources to undertake monitoring and evaluation of aid-dependent organisations, which often have insufficient funds to deliver their core programmes. However, it also reflects the widespread failure to specify precisely the nature of the desired outcomes and to develop measurable indicators. In turn this reflects what Kruse (2006: 8) has referred to as 'an intuitive certainty. . . . that there is a positive link between sport and development'. These beliefs, apparently shared by many funders and sport-for-development organisations are reinforced by the fact that the rhetorical label of sport-for-development 'is intriguingly vague and open for several interpretations'. Or, to paraphrase Pawson (2006), many of the claims made by sport-for-development evangelists are 'ill-defined interventions with hard to follow outcomes'. Kruse's comments raise a number of issues for policy makers and practitioners which will be addressed in this chapter:

- How are such programmes supposed to work? What is the presumed programme theory underpinning such claims?
- What assumptions do we make about participants? How and in what ways are they in need of 'development'? What is meant by this term?
- Is change uni-directional? Will participation in sport-for-development programmes always lead to positive outcomes?
- More generally, what is the relationship between a highly individualised definition of 'development' and a more general process of development?

CONCEPTUAL ENTREPRENEURS

Such questions are rarely asked because of the sports evangelism which dominates much of the rhetoric in sport-for-development. This evangelical belief in the transformational power of sport and its contribution to ill-defined 'development' are aided by the 'mythopoeic' nature of sport. Mythopoeic concepts tend to be ones whose demarcation criteria are not specific and this can be applied to the way an over-generalised notion of 'sport' is frequently used in policy debates. Such mythopoeic concepts are based on popular and idealistic ideas which are produced largely outside of sociological analysis and which 'isolates a particular relationship between variables to the exclusion of others and without a sound basis for doing so' (Glasner, 1977: 2–3). Such myths contain elements of truth, but elements which become reified and distorted and 'represent' rather than reflect reality, standing for supposed, but largely unexamined, impacts and processes. The strength of such myths lies in their 'ability to evoke vague and generalised images' (Glasner, 1977: 1). For example, the mythopoeic nature of sport can partly be illustrated by the fact that it is a rich source for a wide variety of metaphors—'playing the game, level playing fields, it's not cricket, first past the post, getting to first base, throwing in the towel, being on a winning team'—which seem to represent a social and moral universe.

We are often treated to stories ('case studies') of personal deliverance and hope for the future. The proponents of sport-for-development are similar to Hewitt's (1998), 'conceptual entrepreneurs', those who promote ideas about the solution of individual problems by concentrating on simple solutions and single concepts (in Hewitt's case it is self-esteem, a concept frequently used in sport-for-development discourse).

BEYOND THE BLACK BOX

This mixture of evangelism and conceptual entrepreneurialism leads to a view of sport as a sort of magic box, or in Scriven's (1994) terms, a black box, whose contents and processes are taken for granted; 'sport works' much like a medical treatment model and its workings (medicine) are taken for granted and unsupported generalisations are offered about 'sport's' contribution to 'development'. For example, the assumption of much sport-for-development rhetoric seems to be that participation in 'sport' contributes to the development of a range of individual impacts For example,

- Physical fitness and improved health;
- Improved mental health and psychological well-being, leading to the reduction of anxiety and stress;
- Personality development via improved self-conception, physical and global self-esteem/ confidence, self-confidence and an increased locus of control;
- Socio-psychological benefits such as empathy, integrity, tolerance, co-operation, trustworthiness and the development of social skills.

Such impacts are viewed as almost automatic. Further, the social significance of these, largely individual, impacts is presumed to be that they lead to changes in attitudes and especially, behaviour (e.g., reduced criminality; improved educational performance) (Coalter, 2002; 2006).

However, the collective noun 'sport' disguises more than it reveals; for example, what is the relationship between American football and diving, or swimming and boxing? Sport is a collective noun which encompasses a wide range of experiences and relationships. For example, there are individual, partner and team sports; there are sports based on the development of cognitive and spatial skills and those based on motor skills; there are contact and non-contact sports and there are sports based on criterion and norm evaluations. In this regard the President's Council on Physical Fitness and Sports (2006: 4) refers to

> the importance of not lumping all sports or sport participants together. For several reasons, broad generalizations about "sports" are unlikely to be helpful. For one, the rule structures of the various sports promote

different types of social interaction. The developmental stimuli provided by a boxing match are likely to differ from those of a golf tournament. In addition, each sport tends to have its own subculture and implicit moral norms. The culture of rugby is quite different from that of competitive swimming. There are also differences based on age and competitive level. Major League baseball and Little League provide quite different social experiences. Even within a single sport area and developmental level, individual sport teams are different because each team develops its own unique moral microculture through the influence of particular coaches, athletes, fans, parents, and programs. Moreover, even within a single team, participants' own appraisals of the experience may vary substantially.

Such comments illustrate the limitations of speaking about 'sport' in the abstract and raise the significant issue of sufficient conditions; the type of sports and the conditions under which the potential to achieve the desired outcomes are maximised for identifiable social groups. Svoboda (1994) argues that presumed positive outcomes are 'only a possibility' and a direct linear relationship between simple participation and impact cannot be assumed. Coalter, Allison, and Taylor (2000: 85), in a wide-ranging review of the social and economic impacts of sport, concluded that there was 'a widespread lack of empirical research on outcomes, and more importantly, the mechanisms and processes via which they are achieved (especially in 'real life' situations)'. Patriksson (1995: 128) states the challenge as follows:

> The point is that sport has the potential both to improve and inhibit an individual's personal growth. The futility of arguing whether sport is good or bad has been observed by several authors. Sport, like most activities, is not a priori good or bad, but has the potential of producing both positive and negative outcomes. Questions like 'what conditions are necessary for sport to have beneficial outcomes?' must be asked more often.

Or, as Papacharisis, Goudas, Danish, and Theodorakis (2005: 247) argue, 'there is nothing about . . . sport itself that is magical. . . . It is the experience of sport that may facilitate the result'.

Such perspectives illustrate the need to adopt a clear box approach to the understanding and evaluation of programmes and require us to shift our focus from a concern with necessary conditions (i.e., increasing participation in 'sport') to sufficient conditions (i.e., the type of sports—e.g. individual/partner/team, contact and non-contact, motor/cognitive skills—and the various conditions under which the potential to achieve the desired outcomes are maximised for identifiable social groups). From such a perspective we are not concerned with some abstract collective noun, 'sport', but with the actual processes and experiences offered to participants. Following Pawson (2006) and his realist perspective, we are concerned not with families of programmes (i.e., sport-for-development) but families of mechanisms, what are the relationships and experiences which might lead to change and 'development'? In this regard, Pawson (2006) contends that 'mechanisms are the engines of explanation' and the basis for generalisation—'what type of experience works for what type of participant in what type of context?' Coakley (2004: 99) sums up the distinction between necessary and sufficient conditions by arguing that 'sports are sites for socialisation experiences, not causes of socialisation outcomes'.

PROGRAMME THEORY

For this reason we need to think much more systematically about 'sport' and one way of addressing these issues is via programme theory. A programme theory seeks to identify the components, mechanisms, relationships and sequences of causes and effects which are presumed to lead to desired outcomes (Weiss, 1997). As illustrated by Figure 7.1, we need to address systematically our assumptions about how participation in a sports programme leads to certain intermediate effects, which then result in certain intermediate outcomes and, in certain cases, contribute to strategic outcomes. If we understand such processes then this understanding can contribute to the design and implementation of more effective programmes.

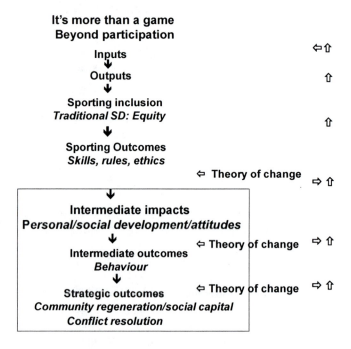

Figure 7.1   The individual and social impacts of sport: a logic model.

Some of the advantages of a programme theory approach include:

- It emphasizes the essential distinction between necessary conditions and sufficient conditions, the processes and experiences necessary to maximise the potential to achieve desired outcomes;
- It assists in the formulation of theoretically coherent, realistic and precise outcomes related to programme processes and participants;
- It enables the identification of critical success factors;
- It provides the basis for formative, rather than summative (i.e., outcome), evaluation and contributes to the improvement of interventions;
- By exploring potentially generic mechanisms, it can provide a basis for generalisation which can inform future programme design.

The utility of programme theory is best summed up by the World Bank (2004: 10), which argues that the approach allows an in-depth understanding of the working of

> a program or activity—the 'program theory' or 'program logic'. In particular it need not assume simple linear cause-and-effect relationships. . . . By mapping out the determining or causal factors judged important for success, and how they might interact, it can then be decided which steps should be monitored as the progress develops, to see how well they are in fact borne out. This allows the critical success factors to be identified.

MOTIVATIONAL CLIMATES AND PERCEIVED SELF-EFFICACY

One example of this approach would be to consider the relative impact of differing motivational climates. For example, Biddle (2006) identifies two broad possible forms of motivational climate in sports programmes. One is based on an ethos of mastery in which individual effort and improvement are recognised and supported; everyone has an equal and important role in the programme and learning is based on cooperation. Another approach is to emphasize performance and competition, resulting in unequal recognition (good and bad players), with mistakes being punished and rivalry between team members encouraged. Clearly such motivational climates are based on different social relationships, provide different learning experiences and present different world views.

Further, the issue of motivational climates and how and what type of learning occurs is related closely to the development of self-efficacy. Although rarely articulated systematically, the notion of self-efficacy could be deemed to be central to any concept of development and is closely related to the concept of resilience. For example, Pajares (2002: 1) argues that self-efficacy beliefs touch virtually every aspect of people's lives—whether they think productively, self-debilitatingly, pessimistically or optimistically; how well they motivate themselves and persevere in the face of adversities; their vulnerability to stress and depression and the life choices they make.

As self-efficacy is central to notions of individual development, it is clear that serious consideration needs to be given as to how it can be developed via particular types of programme and motivational climate. As Bandura (1994: 2) argues, 'successful efficacy builders structure situations . . . in ways that bring success and avoid placing people in situations prematurely where they are likely to fail often'. In this regard Pajares (2002: 7) argues that

> just as positive persuasions may work to encourage and empower, negative persuasion can work to defeat and weaken self-efficacy beliefs. In fact, it is usually easier to weaken self-efficacy beliefs through negative appraisals than to strengthen such beliefs through positive encouragement.

In addition to issues relating to the social climate of programmes, social cognitive theory proposes that learning occurs via observation and imitation and this relates to a feature common to many, although by no means all, sport-for-development programmes: role models. It is proposed that learning is most likely to occur when there is a lack of social distance and a perceived similarity between the teacher and the learner (this may be especially important for females in cultures with few public female role models) and when there is a self-efficacy expectation on the part of the learner (i.e., she/he is capable of developing the skill/completing the task). This is strengthened by perceived similarities with the teacher—if she can do it then so can I—what Bandura (1994) refers to as 'vicarious experience' and there is an outcome expectancy that the performance of the activity will have desirable outcomes, which can be affirmed and reinforced by the social climate of the programme. These examples clearly indicate the importance of understanding programme theory, the various processes, relationships and mechanisms which need to be considered in the design of programmes.

Another example relates to the claims of sport-for-development programmes to contribute to the reduction of HIV/AIDS. There is little systematic discussion as to how sports participation can contribute to changed sexual behaviour, other than as a vehicle for the dissemination of relevant knowledge. The approach to this can broadly be divided into a traditional didactic approach, in which sport is used as 'fly paper' to attract young people to AIDS education programmes that they otherwise would not attend. The second, more sophisticated, approach is via the use of symbolic games integrated into sports programmes (http://www.kickingaidsout.net). However, the basic underlying theory seems to be the rather simple, but unwarranted, assumption (Grunseit & Aggleton, 1998), that increased knowledge and understanding will lead to changed sexual behaviour. There is limited research as to the effectiveness of either approach, but that which does exist is not encouraging (Kruse, 2006; Botcheva & Huffman, 2004).

However, it is possible to develop a slightly more sophisticated programme theory (Weiss, 1997), which seems to be implicit in some programmes and which would provide the basis for a process-led approach to monitoring and evaluation. I must emphasize that this 'programme theory' (Figure 7.2) is somewhat basic and based almost wholly on fieldwork observations and discussions, but it serves to illustrate the generic point about needing to construct the assumptions and theories of behavioural change which inform programmes. There is no claim that this is definitive or effective or that the programmes are targeted at relevant high-risk groups. For example, Pisani (2008) argues that many such programmes are not targeted at relevant high risks groups (e.g., sex workers; intravenous drug users), often for ideological, political or moral reasons.

The logic outlined in Figure 7.2 (each stage of which can be monitored and evaluated) is that the process of developing practical sporting skills (via effort and practice) may lead to the increase in a sense of self-efficacy. In addition, by operating within an ethical framework, it is assumed that participants will develop a certain degree of moral reasoning via an emphasis on sporting and ethical attitudes (e.g., respecting opponents; the need for fair play and obeying rules; collective responsibility). Within this context

Develop sporting skills
⇩
Develop sporting/ethical attitudes
⇩
Develop self-efficacy/confidence
⇩
HIV/AIDS information
⇩
Gender equity attitudes/behaviour
⇩
Self-esteem/self-worth
⇩
Reduced risk-taking sexual behaviour

...maybe

Figure 7.2 A speculative logic model of sports-based HIV/AIDS education and sexual behaviour change.

of the developing individual, information about health and HIV/AIDS is provided and the approach adopted, either via traditional didactic methods or via a more symbolic and integrated approach, may be significant. There may also be an assumption that those involved in sport and concerned about fitness may be more receptive to health messages and are developing an awareness that they can take some control over their fitness and health. This information is communicated within the context of an emphasis on gender equity and respect. This entails both increasing young women's self-confidence (often via peer leadership roles) and changing young men's attitudes to young women, frequently by playing the same game (soccer). The issue of gender relations, power and respect are regarded by many as central to addressing the issues of HIV/AIDS, especially communicated via the role model approach of peer leadership (Kruse, 2006). These various intermediate effects may also lead to an increase in self-esteem and feelings of self-worth, although this is a much misused and misunderstood concept (see Fox, 1992; Emler, 2001; Baumeister et al., 2003; Coalter, 2007), which needs care in both measurement and interpretation.

Consequently, this hypothetical programme-theory, or theory of change, suggests that it is a combination of increased self-efficacy, the understanding of relevant information, changed gender attitudes and improved self-worth which may lead to a reduction in risky sexual behaviour, an outcome which is exceptionally difficult to measure. Nevertheless, if the programme theory is regarded as plausible and the programme is delivered consistently as theoretically intended (not an easy task in the circumstances in which many such organisations operate), then it provides a plausible basis for assuming that it has maximised the possibility of achieving the desired outcomes of safer sexual behaviour (even if this cannot be measured directly).

One thing to note about these various examples is that we have departed substantially from any simple assertions about 'sport'-for-development. Following Pawson, Greenhalgh, Harvey, and Walshe (2004: 5), we have illustrated that 'interventions are chains which are long and thickly populated—interventions carry not one, but several implicit mechanisms of action'.

THE VALIDITY OF THE DEFICIT MODEL

Having illustrated the need for and value of a programme theory approach, we now turn to another frequently unexamined aspect of sport-for-development programmes : the nature of the participants and their supposed 'developmental needs'. Much of this seems to be based on a crude environmental determinism which assumes that deprived environments produce 'deficient' people (although these deficiencies are rarely defined, but implied by the supposedly positive impact of sports). However, data from work that I have undertaken in Africa and India raise significant questions about such assumptions.

We have already commented on the importance of self-efficacy to notions of learning and personal development and Figures 7.3 and 7.4 illustrate data from both The Kids' League, a programme in Gulu, northern Uganda, for internally displaced young people and Magic Bus Voyagers a programme based mostly in Dharavi, the Mumbai slum featured in the film *Slum Dog Millionaire.* These are data collected via self-completion questionnaires prior to full participation in the sport-for-development programmes. In this a Likert scale measuring self-efficacy was included and each respondent was allocated a score. The key issue illustrated by Figures 7.3 and 7.4 is that there is a broad distribution of self-evaluation; these groups are not homogeneous and do not systematically view themselves as having low self-efficacy.

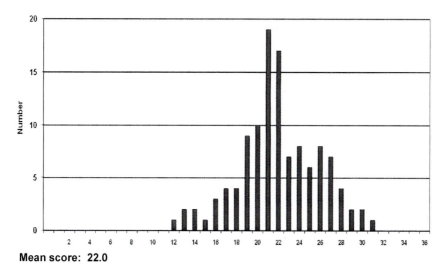

Mean score: 22.0

Figure 7.3 The Kids' League perceived self-efficacy; data before.

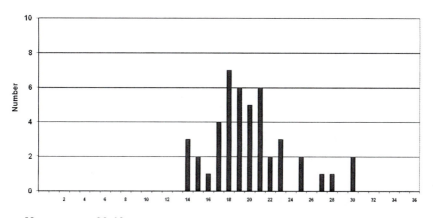

Mean score: 20.13

Figure 7.4 Magic Bus Voyagers perceived self-efficacy; data before

One might say that these are relatively normal groups of young people—some have relatively high self-evaluations, some clearly have low evaluations and most are somewhere in the middle. Although not included in this chapter, the data for self-esteem indicate that the majority of the young people fall within what is regarded as a normal distribution of self-evaluation. Perhaps these data should not be such a surprise, although they do raise significant issues about easy generalisations about 'development needs'. First, participation in such programmes is voluntary, and those who choose to take part are likely to have a reasonable degree of perceived self-efficacy, the confidence to participate. Second, as several members of the organisations argued, the day-to-day struggle for survival and the economic and familial responsibilities often assumed by these young people mean that they are required to develop relatively high levels of perceived self-efficacy and resilience simply to survive. Or as one put it—'you would not survive here for a day Fred'.

Whatever the reason, the data indicate that, although these respondents come from very deprived communities, they can be viewed as a relatively normal selection of young people and certainly not uniformly 'deficient' in terms of their own self-evaluations. Even though perceived self-efficacy is a subjective judgement and may have a weak relationship to objective facts, such beliefs nevertheless inform people's actions and behaviour and must be taken seriously.

PROGRAMME IMPACTS ARE NOT UNIFORM

Just as the young people cannot be regarded as uniformly deficient, the impact of participation in the programme was varied and certainly not uni-directional (Figures 7.5 and 7.6). The first thing to notice is that there were very high levels of adjustment of scores between the two surveys ; 93 percent of the Magic Bus sample changed their evaluation scores and 91 percent in the Kids' League did. Second, such adjustments included both increases and decreases in self-evaluations, a more complex set of impacts than is assumed in much sport-for-development rhetoric.

Key to reading scattergrams (Figures 7.5 and 7.6)

Before score below average and then increased	Before score above average and then increased
Before score below average and then decreased	Before score above average and then decreased

In the Kids' League, two-thirds (67 percent) increased their self-evaluation, with a quarter (26 percent) recording a decline. Among Magic Bus participants the impact of the programme was spread more evenly, with half (49 percent) increasing their perceived self-efficacy and 44 percent decreasing.

In other words, the diverse groups of participants were affected in a variety of ways and this varied between programmes. However, the key thing to notice is the clear tendency for those with scores at or below the

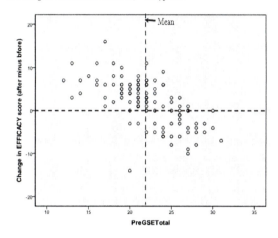

Figure 7.5 The Kids' League self-efficacy: data after.

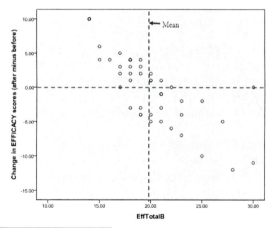

Figure 7.6 Magic Bus Voyagers self-efficacy: data after.

average to increase their score and for those with scores above the average to decrease their scores. Although there were project-specific variations, the overall picture is that many of those with the weakest self-evaluations improved their score. This indicates that those with lower self-efficacy have, in the right circumstances, the most to gain—as would be expected on the basis of previous research (Fox, 1992). However, we should also note that many of those with initially higher than average self-evaluations adjusted their assessments downward. This could reflect a more realistic evaluation of their abilities based on their experiences in the programme, both in terms of their own skills and in relation to other participants. In such circumstances such adjustments should not be regarded as negative.

WHAT DOES THIS TELL US?

Such data raise significant questions about the implicit environmental determinism which assumes that deprived communities automatically produce deficient young people. The young people were not a homogeneous group and there was a range of self-evaluations with many having quite strong self-belief in their own efficacy (and strong self-esteem). To ignore this as a result of an unquestioned deficit model contains obvious dangers.

Second, as with all forms of social intervention, causation is contingent, reflects a range of participants, circumstances, relationships and interactions and no outcomes are guaranteed. In this regard Pawson et al. (2004: 7) states that

> It is through the workings of entire systems of social relationships that any changes in behaviours . . . are effected . . . Rarely if ever is the 'same' programme equally effective in all circumstances because of the influence of contextual factors.

Although this seems axiomatic, it is something which is largely ignored in the evangelistic assertions of the sport-for-development movement. Although the data indicate general tendencies, the variations between the programmes indicate that, not surprisingly, there is no simple and predictable 'sport-for-development' effect. As in all forms of social intervention, the nature and extent of impacts are largely contingent and vary between programme types, participants and cultural contexts. In this regard we need to acknowledge not only that participants and the experience of sport differ substantially between programmes, but also that many sport-development programmes offer much more than sport; educational programmes, cultural activities, educational programmes. In many circumstances it might be better to consider the impact of membership of sport-for-development organisations and their 'entire system of social relationships', rather than simply talk of 'sport'. Such data illustrates the limitations of our ability to generalise about sport-for-development and emphasize the need to understand better the nature of differing programme processes and participant experiences.

'DEVELOPMENT' AND DISPLACEMENT OF SCOPE?

The above data and arguments raise significant questions about implicit environmental determinism and the validity of a simple deficit model of individuals and communities; a view that deprived communities produce deficient young people whose deficiencies can be addressed and at least ameliorated via sport-for-development. There is a clear need for more systematic debate and discussion about such assumptions and the precise meaning of 'development' in such programmes. However, there is an even greater question relating to the model of 'development' underpinning such rhetoric and this raises significant questions about 'displacement of scope' (Wagner, 1964) in which micro-level effects are, wrongly, generalised to the macro-level.

Even if participation in a sport-for-development programme leads to an increase in the self-efficacy of the participants, self-esteem or other areas of social skills, how does this relate to 'development'? As such subjective measures are often context-specific, will these new psychological and social skills 'go beyond the touchline' and impact on other areas of life? Are participants failing at school and, if so, is this because of poor self-efficacy or self-esteem? Will any improvement as a result of participating in the programme lead to improved educational performance? Will this improved performance enable individuals to obtain scarce jobs or create employment where it does not exist? How is this clearly neo-liberal individual approach to micro-level development (Kidd, 2008) related to development at the wider meso levels of community and macro levels of economy?

The increased profile of sport-for-development can be explained by a number of factors. For example, Kidd (2008: 374) suggests that this new emphasis was enabled by the collapse of the Soviet Union and the triumph of western liberalism, which led to 'a new focus on entrepreneurship as a strategy of social development, creating new openings for the creation of non-governmental organisations and private foundations'. There was also an accompanying shift in the aid paradigm, from an emphasis on economic capital investment to investing in human capital (Renard, 2006) and the publication of the Millenium Development Goals placed emphasis on more personal issues of social inclusion; strengthening education, improving community, safety and social cohesion, helping girls and women and youth at risk, and addressing issues of public health (Kidd, 2008). The latter included HIV/AIDS, which was to provide the sport-and-development movement with a major opportunity, becoming a central component of many programmes. However, all these strands led to fragmented and sometimes opportunistic, development with little systematic discussion of precisely what (or if) sport-for-development contributed to 'development'.

Of course sport-for-development is not alone here. For example, in relation to HIV/AIDS programmes, Pisani (2008: 288) argues that

> You almost never have to show you've prevented any infections. You can be judged a success for just doing what you said you were going to do, like train some nurses . . . or give leaflets to 400 out of the nation's 160,000 drug injectors.

However, more worryingly, Pisani (2008: 300) argues that many of these programmes were based on false assumptions and the systematic ignoring of (morally or politically) uncomfortable evidence. Further, the interconnected networks of self-interested organisations meant that 'doing honest analysis that would lead to programme improvement is a glorious way to be hated by just about everyone'. That this might also be the case in sport-for-development is indicated by Johann Koss's (President of Right to Play) statement at the 2003 Next Step conference that 'we invite people to do research into things like sport and development, sport and peace. We need to prove what we say that we do.' Like many policy advocates or evangelists, Koss views the outcomes of research as being pre-given; performing the function of proving success and thereby supporting further influence and investment. Sport-for-development needs more than this.

It is suggested above that there is an urgent need to address the programme assumptions and the methodological individualism that underpin much thinking about sport-for-development. The nature and relevance of impacts and outcomes need to be questioned and a recognition given to the fact that actions and choices take place within the material, economic and cultural realities within which the 'empowered' live. Else we are in danger of simply conforming to Weiss's (1997: 105) description of many well-meaning social interventions:

> We mount limited-focus programs to cope with broad-gauge problems. We devote limited resources to long-standing and stubborn problems. Above all we concentrate attention on changing the attitudes and behaviour of target groups without concomitant attention to the institutional structures and social arrangements that tend to keep them 'target groups'.

REFERENCES

Bandura, A. (1994), 'Self-efficacy', in V. S. Ramachaudran (ed.), *Encyclopedia of Human Behavior* (Vol. 4: 71–81), New York: Academic Press, (Reprinted in H. Friedman [ed.], Encyclopedia of Mental Health, San Diego: Academic Press, 1998).

Baumeister, R., Campbell, J., Krueger, J. & Vohs, K. (2003), 'Does High Self-Esteem Cause Better Performance, Interpersonal Success, Happiness or Healthier Lifestyles?', *Psychological Science in the Public Interest*, 4(1): 1–44.

Biddle, S. (2006), 'Defining and Measuring Indicators of Psycho-social Well-Being in Youth Sport and Physical Activity', in Y. Vanden Auweele, C. Malcolm & B. Meulders (eds), *Sports and Development*, Leuven: Lannoo Campus, pp. 163–184.

Botcheva, L. & Huffman, M.D. (2004), *Grassroot Soccer Foundation HIV/AIDS Education Program: An Intervention in Zimbabwe*, White River Junction, VT: Grassroot Soccer Foundation.

Coakley, J. (2004), *Sport in Society: Issues and Controversies* (8th edn), Boston: McGraw Hill.

Coalter, F. (2002), *Sport and Community Development: A Manual*, Research Report, 86, Edinburgh: sportscotland.

Coalter, F. (2006), *Sport-in-Development: A Monitoring and Evaluation Manual*, London: UK Sport.

Coalter, F. (2007), *A Wider Social Role for Sport: Who's Keeping the Score?*, London: Routledge.

Coalter, F., Allison, M. & Taylor, J. (2000), *The Role of Sport in Regenerating Deprived Urban Areas*, Edinburgh: Scottish Executive.

Emler, N. (2001), *Self-Esteem: The Costs and Causes of Low Self-Worth*, York: Joseph Rowntree Foundation.

Fox, K. R. (1992), 'Physical Education and the Development of Self-Esteem in Children', in N. Armstrong (ed.), *New Directions in Physical Education*, vol. 2, Towards a National Curriculum, Leeds: Human Kinetics.

Glasner, P. E. (1977), *The Sociology of Secularisation*, London: Routledge & Kegan Paul.

Grunseit, A. & Aggleton, P. (1998), 'Lessons Learned: An Update on the Published Literature Concerning the Impact of HIV and Sexuality Education for Young People', *Health Education*, 98(2): 45–54.

Hewitt, J. (1998), *The Myth of Self-Esteem*, New York: St Martin's Press.

Kruse, S. E. (2006), 'Review of Kicking AIDS Out: Is Sport an Effective Tool in the Fight Against HIV/AIDS?', Draft report to NORAD.

Kidd, B. (2008), 'A New Social Movement: Sport for Development and Peace', *Sport in Society*, 11(4): 370–380.

Pajares, F. (2002), 'Overview of Social Cognitive Theory and of Self-efficacy', accessed 9 March 2012 at: http://www.emory.edu/EDUCATION/mfp/eff.html.

Papacharisis, V., Goudas, M., Danish, S. J. & Theodorakis, Y. (2005), 'The Effectiveness of Teaching a Life Skills Program in a Sport Context', *Journal of Applied Sports Psychology*, 17: 247–254.

Patriksson, M. (1995), 'Scientific Review Part 2', in *The Significance of Sport for Society—Health, Socialisation, Economy: A Scientific Review*, prepared for the 8th Conference of European Ministers responsible for Sport, Lisbon, 17–18 May 1995, Strasbourg: Council of Europe Press.

Pawson, R. (2006), *Evidence-Based Policy: A Realist Perspective*, London: Sage.

Pawson, R., Greenhalgh, T., Harvey, G. & Walshe, K. (2004), 'Realist Synthesis: An Introduction', *ESRC Research Methods Programme*, University of Manchester RMP Methods, Paper 2.

Pisani, E. (2008), *The Wisdom of Whores: Bureaucrats, Brothels and the Business of AIDS*, London: Granta Books.

President's Council on Physical Fitness and Sports (2006), 'Sports and Character Development', *Research Digest Series*, 7/1, Washington, DC: President's Council on Physical Fitness and Sports.

Renard, R. (2006), 'The Cracks in the New Aid Paradigm', Discussion paper, Institute of Development Policy and Management, Antwerp, Belgium.

Scriven, M. (1994), 'The Fine Line Between Evaluation and Explanation', *Evaluation Practice*, 15: 75–77.

Svoboda, B. (1994), *Sport and Physical Activity as a Socialisation Environment, Scientific Review Part 1*, Strasbourg: Council of Europe, Committee for the Development of Sport (CDDS).

UNICEF (2006), *Monitoring and Evaluation for Sport-based Programming for Development: Sport Recreation and Play, Workshop Report.* UNICEF, New York: UNICEF.

United Nations (2005a), *Sport as a Tool for Development and Peace: Towards Achieving the Millennium Development Goals. Report from the United Nations Inter-Agency Task Force on Sport for Development and Peace*, Geneva: United Nations.

United Nations (2005b), *Business Plan International Year of Sport and Physical Education*, New York: United Nations.

Wagner, H. L. (1964), 'Displacement of Scope: A Problem of the Relationship Between Small-Scale and Large-Scale Sociological Theories', *The American Journal of Sociology*, 69(6): 571–584.

Weiss, C. H. (1997), 'How Can Theory-Based Evaluation Make Greater Headway?', *Evaluation Review*, 21(4): 501–524.

World Bank (2004), *Monitoring and Evaluation: Some Tools, Methods and Approaches*, Washington, DC: World Bank.

Part II

Sports Corporations at Play

Doing Business in Sports—Who's Added Value?

8   Sports Governance
Between the Obsession with Rules and Regulation and the Aversion to Being Ruled and Regulated

Hans Bruyninckx

When political scientists investigate the world of sports (which they rarely do), they do so using the typical concepts that drive their disciplinary approaches when investigating social reality (Senn, 1999; Güldenpfennig, 2003; Bruyninckx & Scheerder, 2009; Tokarski, Petry, Groll & Mittag, 2009). This means that issues of 'sports governance' (i.e., practices that steer sports activities in a socially desirable direction) are framed in terms of power, legitimacy, the formulation of policy measures, the creation of rules and norms, the role of the state or international governmental institutions, the distinction between public and private spheres of authority, the distribution of costs and benefits as a consequence of policy interventions, and so on. The world of sports is not approached through the dominant focus on competition, results, medals, records and other 'fun' parts of the reality of sporting events. This is rather different from the approaches to sports policy used by traditional sports scientists whose framework of reference is in general limited to a more particularistic approach to sports (Güldenpfennig, 2003).

In general, political scientists have devoted very little attention to the world of sports. Several reasons can be mentioned to explain this. A first reason is probably that political scientists have long focused on so-called 'high politics' (war and conflict), on formal institutions such as political parties or parliaments or thematically on traditional socio-economic spheres of policy making such as social policy, health or educational policies. Newer themes such as the politics of culture, environmental issues, gender politics and sports politics have only been added to the research agenda of mainstream political scientists relatively recently (Tokarski, Petry & Jesse, 2006; Tokarski et al., 2009). The fact that research careers were (until recently) not easily made in these 'peripheral' domains of political science certainly also played a role.

A main reason, however, might be the fact that the world of sports and the world of government have largely been separate or more precisely, have been perceived as separate. The sports world has for the most part managed to stay out of the regulatory hands of state institutions (Tokarski et al., 2009). This is certainly the case in Western democracies and at the international level (Bruyninckx, 2009).[1] Sports policy, especially internationally, is by and large a fairly recent phenomenon and has attracted limited attention from policy scientists (Scheerder, van Tuycom & Vermeersch, 2007; Bruyninckx & Scheerder, 2009; Tokarski et al., 2009). The world of sports has predominantly managed to live by its own set of rules and regulations and has for a long time objected to state intervention at the national and certainly the international level (Bruyninckx, 2009).

It is important to point out that we approach the subject essentially from the perspective of the relationship between political institutions at the state or international level and sports federations at the national, regional or international level. In essence, therefore, we are discussing the relationships between the state and formally organised professional sports bodies. By making this choice, we make the argument more economical, knowing full well that this leaves out the reality of non-organised and non-professional sports. This is by no means a normative choice, just a pragmatic one (Scheerder et al., 2007).

As obsessed as it is with its own rules (of the game), its own legal systems, its own economic rationality, just as strong has been the objection, or aversion, of the world of sports to be subjected to more public rules and intervention. In this contribution, we wish to explain why that is the case, taking a theory-of-governance based approach. We will argue that few of the preconditions for functional governance practices are strongly present in the world of professional sports and (international) sports federations. In part two the concept of governance will be introduced; in the next part we will discuss the origins of governance in sports and in part four we will uncover the 'competition' between the world of sports and public interests when it comes to public intervention and regulation. Next we will analyse the reactions by the sports world to attempts to exert more public authority over professional sports and major events and we will end this chapter by discussing some of the criticisms on the current practices of sports governance.

GOVERNANCE AS A CONCEPT TO APPROACH THE SPORTS WORLD

The concept of governance is increasingly used for a number of social, economic and political practices in several spheres of social life, including policy making, regulation, the setting of rules, norms and standards or more broadly when it comes to the study of exercising authority. It is mostly used or understood as a substitute for or an addition to, more traditional notions of government.

The origins of the concept are both normative and descriptive. During the 1980s and 1990s traditional state government was critically evaluated as being ineffective and inefficient, slow and reactive, ill-adapted to a fast-changing world and society, top-down and hence non-participatory, based on traditional and old-fashioned instruments (legal, economic and communicative) (Spaargaren, Mol & Bruyninckx, 2006). This negative evaluation suggested that a better form of steering, norm setting and exercising of authority in our (late-)modern society was both necessary and possible (Bruyninckx & Scheerder, 2009).

The core elements of governance thinking can be summarised as follows. Instead of being state-driven and top-down, governance was supposed to be multi-actor and multi-level (Spaargaren et al., 2006). Besides the state, market actors (companies, investors, banks) and civil society actors (non-governmental organisations, scientists, etc.) are conceptualised as being central to the steering of society. This poses a first problem in the case of sports. It is rather difficult to identify sports federations or professional sports clubs as being either a market actor or as a civil society actor (Tokarski et al., 2009: 43). Although they refuse or object to being labelled as (purely) economic or market actors, it is rather obvious that commercial interests are a major preoccupation, not to say the core business, of major sports organisations (e.g., the International Olympic Committee, IOC, or the International Federation of Football Association, FIFA). It is, on the other hand, just as absurd to accept the notion that they are non-governmental organisations. The multi-level character refers to the increased importance of the international (and European Union) level as well as to the importance of sub-state levels of authority. Here matching is often the problem. As we will mention later, the organisation of sports is mostly different from political multi-level organisation, thus making the matching of normative frameworks and governance arrangements rather difficult (Young, 2008). The governance literature also often refers to 'innovative policy approaches', including voluntary agreements, bench mark approaches, etc. In addition, participatory and more horizontal approaches to rule and norm formulation are suggested. All of this allows pitching governance as having the opposite characteristics from those of government. It has an explicitly positive connotation. It is flexible and adaptive and therefore more effective and efficient, fast and pro-active, participatory and bottom-up or networked (Spaargaren et al., 2006; Bruyninckx & Scheerder, 2009).

A more descriptive or empirical strand of literature refers to the new forms of governance, or so-called governance regimes or arrangements, which have emerged in recent times. Examples include voluntary agreements in environmental politics, codes of conduct for multinational companies such as the UN Global Compact, new financial governance agreements following the financial crisis, and the like. Increasingly this type of arrangement is emerging in sports. Codes of conduct on racism or environmental standards for large events are but two examples.

Three main approaches that are of use for us emerge from the literature on governance (Arts, Leroy & van Tatenhove, 2006; Tokarski et al., 2006; 2009; Bruyninckx & Scheerder, 2009).

- A first form is 'governance as steering'. The emphasis is on the capacity of new arrangements and forms to steer or manage specific societal practices in order to reach social and political goals. Much attention is going into efficiency and effectiveness or in other words, performance.
- A second interpretation is more focused on the process of rule and norm setting and highlights its networked nature. Networked governance or participatory governance, is compared to traditional top-down state-centred forms. The process as such becomes the focal point in this approach.
- A third notion refers to 'good governance', a term often used in the context of international (governmental) organizations such as the International Monetary Fund or the World Bank. It refers to qualities such as legitimacy, transparency, clear legal and ethical frameworks, etc. It sets a sort of normative benchmark by which to judge governance practices.

In the subsequent parts of this chapter we will apply these general notions of governance to the world of sports. But first we will briefly explain the origins of calls and arguments for more public intervention and rule-setting in sports.

THE ORIGINS OF SPORTS GOVERNANCE

In general the sports world has operated under very specific conditions when it comes to public rules and regulations.

First, sports federations and organisations have traditionally known a large degree of autonomy and in that sense were subject to almost complete self-governance or private governance (Tokarski et al., 2006; 2009; Geeraert, Scheerder & Bruyninckx, 2012). Public authorities at the national level and even less so at the international level, had very little impact on the organisation of the sports world. Professional activities were regarded as taking place in a separate sphere, detached from the normal rules and regulations of society. Yet, within this sphere of private authority, sports institutions had many state-like institutional characteristics that resembled the traditional, statist, top-down system of government (Bruyninckx, 2009). In that sense, there was nothing democratic, participatory or even legitimate about the organisational form of sports federations and organisations. Many sports organisations operate under a sort of constitution and have an executive committee while mostly lacking a legislative branch (i.e., a forum for participation and legitimate decision making), thus operating de facto as an authoritarian system setting rules and regulations. Even the most typical of state characteristics, namely sovereignty—referring to the fact that there is no power above the state—is claimed by the largest and most dominant sports organisations. The IOC literally talks about 'sovereignty' within the Olympic venues during the games (Bruyninckx, 2009). The same de facto claim of sovereignty is made by FIFA in relation to the World Cup premises. Most sports federations also have a legal system, including an internal compliance and sanctions system. Typical for the reality of sports is that this system operates completely detached from, or parallel to, the normal public government system (e.g., the legal court system), which applies to most other sectors of society. This high degree of autonomy has, in other words, allowed the world of sports to function according to its own priorities, largely unchallenged by public institutions.

A second characteristic is that the sports world is extremely rule-driven. Obviously, a first level of rules are derived from the nature of the game itself: scoring, what is allowed and what not, timing, etc. That these rules don't always coincide with broader societal conventions is clear. Football players, for example, can deliberately use violence with the intention of injuring each other, without much fear of a criminal charge being brought under the normal legal system. At a second level, sports federations set rules about the economic organisation of sport competitions. They can choose monopolies (National Football League, NFL; Union of European Football Associations, UEFA Champions League), set contract rules (television contracts), have internal tax systems (taxes on team budgets in the National Basketball Association, NBA), design solidarity mechanisms (the draft system in the NFL and the NBA), and so on. Moreover, the connection between the rules of the game and the economic reality of the sport is abundantly obvious. The discussion about the 'golden goal' had less to do with the sport than with certainty for sponsors about television advertisements. Sports federations also have their own proper medical system of rules. Most often reference is made to doping practices, but other medical practices are regulated as well. The NBA for example has clear rules on when players are on the 'injured list', while the Women's Tennis Association (WTA) and the Association of Tennis Professionals (ATP) oblige players to use the tournament physiotherapist when injured during the game. In addition, sports federations (and even individual teams) have their own behavioural rules, not only during the game, but also when players are in the public sphere. Some sports teams prevent their players from practicing certain activities (e.g. skiing) in their spare time, because it would damage the interest of the team (or the teams' investors). Even some of the most private and personal choices, for example regarding medical treatment or the players' sex life, can be regulated. The tension between the personal freedom to move around and the right to privacy on the one hand and the rules regarding doping on the other, the whereabouts system, also illustrates this. In other words, the sports world is driven by, and often obsessed with rules. This obsession is probably nowhere more evident than in American professional (and even college) sports, or in the organisational form of the Olympic Games and FIFA football world and regional championships.

The combination of these two characteristics leads to a strong feeling and practice of 'exceptionalism' for sports which we would probably not accept from other forms of social activity and organisation. Working in the sports world does not fall under the normal labour laws (clubs 'own' players); contracts are not normal contracts; competition laws don't seem to apply (monopolies and cartels are the standard operating procedures in some sports); criminal activities committed during sports competitions are not treated as such (e.g., deliberate violence by players against other players or even by fans in stadiums is considered internal business). Yet, in the last fifteen years this 'exceptionalism' has become an element of public debate and has been under attack. The question logically arises as to what drives these moves towards more public intervention in the sports world?

One element is certainly the rapid, massive and global commercialisation of sport. It is fair to say that for professional sports, the commercial character has become the most defining element and driving force (Simson & Jennings, 1992; Barney, Wenn & Martyn, 2002; Pound, 2004; Bruyninckx, 2009). Rules of the game (e.g., the 'golden goal' principle that was suspended), location strategies for large events (access to new markets), wages (strongly linked to the commercial and advertising value of players) and in the end, success in competition are to a large extent determined by commercial and financial interests. The fact that public authority has shown an increased interest in regulating certain aspects of (professional) sports is related to some key elements of the commercialisation of sports. A first element concerns the rules of the sports market. Within the EU, the common market principle, based on the free movement of goods and services and a set of strict and overarching rules on market organisation (competition, monopoly, regulatory competences, etc.), exist. The fact that the sports world (and football more specifically) has largely escaped these rules has become a point of serious debate within the EU in the last 10 years (Scheerder et al., 2007; Tokarski et al., 2009). In the United States, anti-trust regulation is used as an argument in the debate between the government and the multiple professional sports that base their economic activity on 'trust-like' organisational forms (NBA; NFL; National Hockey League, NHL).

Questions of a different nature are asked about the origins of the very large sums of money that circulate in professional spectator sports. Professional sports lack transparency and accountability when it comes to money matters (Lenskyj, 2000). This allows for a business model that would be unacceptable in other areas of economic activity. Moreover, corruption, illegal activities and other 'grey zone' economic practices are increasingly coming to the attention of public authorities. Estimates of €100 billion of illegal gambling, for example, are of obvious concern to public authority in the sphere of economic oversight and regulation, if not to the legal system. The fact that a number of football clubs are operating with 'criminal money', or 'dictatorial money' is also becoming more and more part of the public debate about sports (Foer, 2004).

Linked to the previous two points is the issue of taxation. Much debate exists about the tax regime for sports and athletes. What will be the tax base, the tax rate, the exemptions regime, and so on? The answers to these questions can signify large additional income or losses for public authorities. An extreme example is the 'tax free profit expatriation' regime that is negotiated by the FIFA time and time again. At lower levels, the payments to players with black money or without proper documentation, is another example of the practice of tax evasion in the football world. At the same time, the sports world is asking for access to public funds, or expects governments to 'invest' in sports. Building stadiums, public transport infrastructures, public television contracts for competition, investments in 'training centres' for the next crop of professional competitors, not to speak of some of the central tasks of the government which are solicited by the organisers of professional sports events such as security and traffic control.

A second main driving force is the globalisation of sports (Boniface, 2006). The production chain of the commodity 'professional sports' has become global, as has the reach of its consumer power. The athletes themselves, considered to be the 'raw material' of professional sports, are increasingly produced in global commodity chains. Think of global scouting and farming systems, where this raw material is gathered, groomed and eventually sold on the world market for football players. The fact that this type of production chain also produces much 'human waste' (players who will not function at the professional level), is hardly discussed within the football world, but has led to serious debates, and calls for public intervention. Competition, too, has become a global product (e.g., UEFA Champions League; NBA; Grand Slam tennis tournaments), and the important market for spin-off products, so-called merchandising, has global reach. This last aspect is definitely subject to private commercial and trade governance based on a monopoly system which is very much to the liking of those who invest their capital in the commodity of sports.

A third and underestimated reason for public regulation of (parts of) the sports world is the connection between sports as a social activity and multiple policy domains. These include health, education, youth, equal opportunities, employment, media, culture, and the like (Tokarski et al., 2006; Tokarski et al., 2009; Scheerder et al., 2007). It is obvious that in order to establish socially beneficial links between sports and these other concerns, much more than the voluntary self-governance of sports federations is required. This is certainly the case when one narrows the issue down to professional competitive sports. Although the discourse of FIFA, the International Association of Athletics Federations (IAAF) or the IOC has shifted towards these themes (e.g., the bid books for the major events), the reality remains sobering. Besides mostly unconvincing but well-packaged and glibly promoted lip-service, very little attention is paid to the abovementioned themes. Sepp Blatter is most obviously not interested in equal opportunities or health issues, as long as the commercial interests of FIFA are served. It would take forceful public interference to align the social reality of sports with other social objectives.

A fourth dynamic is related to a number of transgressions and scandals in the sports world that have prompted the debate for more public oversight and control over the world of sports. In the medical sphere we can refer to doping, especially visible in cycling, but also in smaller disciplines such as wrestling and weightlifting. In the sphere of interpersonal relations, the issue of racism comes to mind. Present (mainly in Europe) during football games at all levels, it is a problem that has proven hard to tackle. For some football clubs it is an essential part of their identity although the club leaders will deny so in public (Partizan Belgrado and AS Roma, for example) (Foer, 2004). For other clubs it is problematic from within the fan-base and is particularly directed against black (mostly African) players. Yet it has become a matter of public concern that football games often produce discourse and behaviour that go against fundamental state laws on racism and discrimination.[2] Violence during sports and by spectators, corruption scandals, tax evasion, money laundering . . . ; the list of transgressions is indeed very long. It is at the highest level of sports organisations that these practices seem to coalesce in their most visible and blatant form. The selection process of Olympic and of FIFA World Cup venues is the culmination point. Hardly any bidding round has been completed without corruption, bribery, the questioning of its legitimacy, and without the arrogant denial of the very top officials in sports.

Over the last decade, civil society as well as public authorities have asked legitimate questions about the setting of rules and norms, about compliance and sanctions, as well as about the distribution of costs and benefits within the sports organisations The large degree of autonomy, the global dimension and the scandals, together with the ever more visible and explicit linkages between sports and other policy domains, have laid the basis for coherent and structured attempts to exert some measure of public authority over sports.

GOVERNING SPORTS: A TOUGH CHALLENGE OR COMPETITION BETWEEN PROFESSIONAL SPORTS AND PUBLIC INTERESTS

When we refer back to the three interpretations of governance—governance as steering, governance as networked authority and good governance—we can uncover the fundamental objections of powerful actors in sports against more public control over norm setting and regulation. It is against the backdrop of this anti-regulatory sentiment that we need to understand the formation of current governance arrangements at the national, regional and global level.

It is obvious that governance as steering is a problematic notion for the large players in the sports world. In general, sports federations and other important actors in the sport world have been used to steering, and not to being steered. Examples of this are the organisation of large sports events, where FIFA, UEFA or IOC have clearly set the standards. It needs to be emphasized that they have, by and large, been very successful. This has reached a sort of symbolic *nec plus ultra* as regards the football World Cup. FIFA now even demands from organising countries that they change certain laws related to profit expatriation, monopoly protection, security, and so on. The fact that a number of countries are willing to go along with these demands demonstrates the power and influence of FIFA and is emblematic of its role as a hegemonic ruler or norm-setter.

The second characteristic, namely networked governance, also has its problems. Sports federations are eager to work in networks but only based on their own terms and conditions. Regardless of the term 'partners' so often used by IOC, FIFA or UEFA, commercial actors, or actors that consolidate the position of the sports federation or ensure the occurrence of the event, that are meant. They strengthen the position of private authority and governance as they do not fundamentally challenge the self-regulatory nature of sports. In addition, these networks tend to be of a closed nature as partnerships are based on a logic of 'exclusive partners'. This type of networking practice, however, is not the networking logic embedded in theories of governance, which refers to networks as horizontal forms of organisation, lacking strict hierarchy and with shifting composition (Spaargaren et al., 2006).

The third interpretation, namely the notion of good governance, remains the most contentious part of the governance debate. Transparency, accountability and legitimacy at times seem to be as rare as a snowball in the desert within the functioning of the largest sports federations. This precondition for the creation of functioning governance arrangements remains highly problematic therefore.

Although the preconditions for a greater mix of public and private authority in sports are not very favourable, several new forms of governance are being developed. In fact, several different 'routes' or strategies to exert more public authority over (mainly) professional sports (i.e., sports federations and large events) have already been sketchily used during the last two decades. One important route has been the legal one and more specifically, intervention by means of court cases. Three bodies with legal competence stand out: labour law, commercial law and competition law. The most well-known example is probably the Bosman ruling (1995), which laid the groundwork for policy interventions at the level of the EU, based on labour law. The fact that football and by extension other sports, did not get an exemption from rigorous labour laws, provided an important precedent.

> This ruling . . . set a process in motion that changed sports and the organizational structure of sports. While the institutions at European level were now able to influence sports more so than ever before, sport

clubs and associations realized that sport would no longer remain limited solely to the arena of autonomous self-organisation. (Tokarski et al., 2009: 50)

The second route has been the slow development of a European sports policy. Since the 1990s the European Union (EU) has developed an embryonic strategy for direct and indirect sports policy (Tokarski et al., 2009). By means of initiatives, addenda to treaties (Amsterdam and Nice) and finally a White Paper (2005), the European Commission and Parliament (which played a crucial role in stimulating the debate and preparing initiatives, e.g. ,the Bellet report), have started to shape this domain of policy. Article 165 of the Lisbon Treaty provides the European Union with a soft competence on sport (European Union, 2008). This means that the Commission will develop a specific EU sports programme, supported by a budget line. The competence also allows for better horizontal integration and coordination between sport and other EU policy areas and programmes, such as health and education. The treaty provisions further give the EU the opportunity to speak with one voice in international forums and vis-à-vis third countries. This is important as the reality of European sports competitions rarely, if ever, coincides with the membership of the EU. Just as important is that EU sports ministers will begin meeting in official Sports Council meetings. The Lisbon Treaty requires the Commission to contribute to the promotion of European sporting issues 'while taking account of the specific nature of sport, its structures based on voluntary activity and its social and educational function'. It asks the European dimension in sport to be developed 'by promoting fairness and openness in sporting competitions and cooperation between bodies responsible for sports, and by protecting the physical and moral integrity of sports people'. This last quote refers to the notions of good governance and networked responsibility. However, the former quote refers to the autonomy of sports. The 'specific nature of sports' concerns all aspects related to its functioning, economic conditions, labour regulations, etc. Governance as steering still remains a contentious issue. Yet, it is undeniably the case that the EU is taking serious steps in a coordinated governance approach to sport. As in many other policy areas, the EU is the first regional organisation to develop such an integrated and coordinated multilateral approach. The fact that other regional organisations or regulations hardly exist, weakens a more global approach.

The more global multilateral dimension of sports governance is certainly lacking in coherent ambitions and outcomes. The World Anti-Doping Agency (WADA) is probably the most encompassing attempt. Set up by the IOC in 1999 and thus hardly independent, WADA has moved away from Lausanne to Montreal and is now receiving about 50 percent of its financial means through contributions from countries and has gained, under the leadership of its previous director (Dick Pound), a certain degree of independence and legitimacy. Contributing to this is the co-management arrangement whereby countries and representatives of the sports world are part of the governing body (i.e., networked governance). Another part of the emerging global sports governance puzzle is the Court of Arbitration for Sport (CAS), mostly named by its French acronym TAS. C/TAS was founded by the IOC in 1984. Antonio Samaranch, the infamous president of the IOC, was hoping to develop an independent sports jurisdiction body, staying completely within the autonomous approach to sports regulation. It has several hundred arbitrators in several countries and deals with hundreds of cases every year. Just like WADA, C/TAS has gained more independence from the IOC (after a Swiss court ruling which stated that it was not independent enough from the IOC) and is now recognized as the 'Supreme Court' of sports.

The UNESCO International Convention against Doping in Sport is the first global international treaty against doping in sport and the legal cornerstone of the emerging global sports governance. It was unanimously adopted by 191 governments at the UNESCO General Conference in October 2005 and came into force in February 2007. The Convention is in principle legally binding and aims to

> align domestic doping policy with the World Anti-Doping Code, thus harmonizing the rules governing anti-doping in sport, including on how to organize and facilitate doping controls, through supporting national testing programs; encouraging the establishment of 'best practices' in the labelling, marketing, and distribution of products that might contain prohibited substances; withholding financial support from those who engage in or support doping; taking measures against manufacturing and trafficking; encouraging the establishment of codes of conduct for professions relating to sport and anti-doping; and funding education and research. (UNESCO Web site)

Regardless of the EU's emerging sports policy and the embryonic attempts at the multilateral level, it is fair to say that public regulation of sports in the international arena remains surprisingly weak for a sector that represents such an important social and financial reality and leans so heavily on public support and funding for its functioning (day-to-day as well as for large events).

REACTIONS FROM THE WORLD OF SPORTS

The world of sports has reacted in three ways to the increased demands for public governance.

First, it has set up stronger systems of self-governance on certain issues; or at least changed the discourse or made promises to do so. With the notion of stronger self-regulation it sends a double message, namely: 'we have understood your concerns, but do not intervene in our business, we can and will take care of this ourselves'. Examples of this involve nearly all the problematic aspects of professional sports. In the case of doping, professional sports federations have been trying to improve internal procedures and self-governance for about fifteen years already in a more or less serious fashion. In the case of racism, painfully present in football, international and national federations have designed policies, started programmes, instructed umpires, and have even changed certain rules in order to set norms and standards to counter racism in football. In terms of financial misconduct, FIFA and even more so UEFA, have been through a number of internal exercises to 'clean up' the business. Yet, until now these have not resulted in transparent, legitimate or convincingly effective governance arrangements.

Second, major sports organisations have sought to network with multilateral institutions to create legitimacy and networked authority. The IOC and UEFA, for example, have cooperated with several organisations within the UN on such issues as development (UNDP), culture and education (UNESCO) and the environment (UNEP). The IOC even has a Commission for International Relations. The Commission 'facilitates and promotes the relationship between the Olympic Movement, particularly the IOC and NOCs, and governments and public authorities.' (IOC Web site). However, what this commission does is nearly impossible to find out, as there is no information for it on the IOC's website nor in the IOC's library in Lausanne.

Thirdly, regardless of the shift in discourse, major sports federations are still lobbying heavily against further public or 'external' regulation for (professional) sports. The EU has been the focal point of lobbying against public regulation. With the new article 165 in the Lisbon Treaty the EU has gained the explicit competency to develop a European sports policy. The International Olympic Committee said it was "delighted to see the position of sport in the EU strengthened" by the Lisbon Treaty, but stressed that the EU should "support and not regulate sport". FIFA President Sepp Blatter hailed the "recognition of the specific nature of sport" in Article 165. This stands for protecting the universality of sports "in a world which is increasingly divided" and for "maintaining existing sports structure". Both statements thus refer unambiguously to the autonomous nature of sports governance. Public support——read: financial means, infrastructure and security—are welcome, but regulation should be avoided.

CRITICISM OF THE CURRENT GOVERNANCE ARRANGEMENTS FOR PROFESSIONAL SPORTS

The current public impact on top commercial sports through regulation and public policy is slowly gaining a footing. Yet several critiques can be formulated.

First, the focus is to a large extent on top-level sport and limited to, or driven by, a couple of sports, namely football and the Olympics. In addition, many regulations are reactive and event- or scandal-driven. Also, there is very little public impact on important issues of transparency, legitimacy and accountability. Recent scandals revolving around the bidding and selection process of the 2018 and 2022 FIFA World Cup demonstrated this in a painful manner. Although the organisation of a World Cup is very much a public event, involving massive investments, public works, a host of political decisions to be made, public security, and so forth, governments and public opinion accept the fact that the selection process is far from transparent, is highly illegitimate and lacks every form of accountability. That corruption and bribery are deeply embedded in the system is obvious, yet football federations, which often have very close and friendly relationships with selected politicians, seem to elect the same people to sports leadership without any problem and hardly any questions about the process or the outcomes are asked in public. In the meantime millions are lost in the bidding process, and billions will be spent on actually hosting the event. National parliaments are hardly involved, indeed those who ask critical questions about the opportunity cost of bidding for an event are regarded as disloyal or unpatriotic.

Second, there is an obvious lack of authority and hierarchy in the current dynamics of governance. The relations between the different bodies is unclear, caused by overlapping or parallel responsibilities, leading to multilevel conflicts and endless procedural battles that undermine the legitimacy of the whole construction and create governance insecurities. The Contador case illustrates this nicely as procedural and competence battles prevent a clear, univocal and timely decision on his status as a professional cyclist.

Third, in addition to these more direct questions about the nature of public governance of commercial sports, it is interesting to consider some less concrete issues. One example is the way in which the world of sports is implicitly creating norms about identity. Take, for example, the notion of 'Europe' and its boundaries. This debate is undoubtedly of political importance. One just has to analyse the debate about potential Turkish membership to understand this. Yet the UEFA has stretched the notion of Europe in several directions: Kazachstan, Azerbeidjan, Armenia, Georgia and Turkey are members although purely geographically they belong to the Asian continent. In fact Kazachstan borders China and reaches as far East as countries like Nepal and India. Even Israel, admittedly a special case, has ended up in the UEFA football association. The question needs to be asked what the public reaction would be if the UEFA were to decide—which it could independently—to add Morocco, the Palestinian Territories or Lebanon. It is unlikely that we would accept Anderlecht having to play against FC Beirut or Marakesh CF, let alone Fatah Ramallah. Yet sports governance is creating new mental and physical boundaries for Europe in many different ways.

The same can be said about the relationship between national identity, nationalism and sports. Northern Ireland has its own soccer team, yet the Basque region or Catalonia do not. In addition, different sports create different mental boundaries and identities. Rugby and football accept four teams from the UK, yet cycling (International Cycling Union, UCI) and track and field (IAAF) do not. Cycling, on the other hand, has no problem with the strong Basque identity of the Euskatel team. In any case, the boundaries of Europe seem to be very flexible (different for nearly every sport), stretch as far as the Alaskan border (someone from Vladivostok can become European champion in track and field, yet a Moroccan cannot), historically shift (the case of Israel) and in no way do they dovetail with more traditional geographical, historical, cultural or political approaches to the delineation of Europe (if such an endeavour makes sense at all in the first place).

This has serious consequences for the approaches towards a European sports policy or European sports governance. EU sports policy or other policies that apply to the world of sports (labour, commercial, etc.) by definition do not apply to non-member states. This includes a substantial number of members of UEFA such as the above-mentioned Asian countries. Yet, the same is true for Norway, Croatia and more importantly, Switzerland. This last country has become 'location of choice' for international (sports) organisations. Its legal system allows practices that would be unacceptable in EU-member states, it protects the leaders of international organisations and has a tax system that makes it very attractive to locate head quarters. The IOC and FIFA have managed to escape numerous potential court cases that might otherwise have led to further public scrutiny and regulation. This hampers the further development of truly effective, transparent, participatory and legitimate network arrangements for the world of sports. Yet it is our belief that the steps taken by the EU, WADA and TAS are slowly and irreversibly going in the right direction.

NOTES

1. It is rather obvious that the link between the state and sports is often very strong in authoritarian regimes which have framed sports as an important element of nationalism, propaganda and international identity. This has been historically the case (Nazi Germany), yet is also present today in countries like China and those of the Middle East (e.g., the 'import' of Ethiopian and Kenyan athletes to run middle and long distances). Yet, for this chapter this is not the lens through which we will consider sports governance. We will emphasize those practices that exist in democratic and international contexts.

2. On a personal note: during nearly every football game that I have attended, I have come to the conclusion that it would be easy to condemn a fairly large number of fans for breaking the Belgian law on racism. That is incidently also the reason that I have quit going to football games, as the experience became repugnant.

REFERENCES

Arts, B. J. M., Leroy, P. & van Tatenhove, J. P. M. (2006), 'Political Modernisation and Policy Arrangements: A Framework for Understanding Environmental Policy Change', *Public Organization Review*, 6(2), 93–106.

Barney, R. K., Wenn, S. R. & Martyn, S. G. (2002), *Selling the Five Rings: The International Olympic Committee and the Rise of Olympic Commercialism*, Salt Lake City: The University of Utah Press.

Boniface, P. (2006), *Football et Mondialisation*, Paris: Armand Colin.

Bruyninckx, H. (2009), 'Spelen met macht. Het IOC en de macht van een niet-statelijke actor', in J. Scheerder & B. Meulders (eds), *Wedijver in een internationale arena. Sport, bestuur en macht*, Gent: Academia Press, pp. 103–135.

Bruyninckx, H. & Scheerder, J. (2009), 'Sport, macht en internationale politiek. Een politicologisch kader', in J. Scheerder & B. Meulders (eds), *Wedijver in een internationale arena. Sport, bestuur en macht*, Gent: Academia Press, pp. 1–19.

European Union (2008), 'Treaty of Lisbon Amending the Treaty on European Union and the Treaty Establishing the European Community', *Official Journal of the European Union* (C 115), Article 165.

Foer, F. (2004), *How Soccer Explains the World: An Unlikely Theory of Globalization*, New York: HarperCollins.

Geeraert, A., Scheerder, J. & Bruyninckx, H. (2012), 'The Governance Network of European Football: Introducing New Governance Approaches to Steer Football at the EU Level', *International Journal of Sport Policy*, 4(2).

Güldenpfennig, S. (2003), 'Politikwissenschaft und Sport. Sportpolitik', in H. Haag (ed.), *Theoriefelder der Sportwissenschaft*, Schorndorf: Hofmann.

Lenskyj, H. (2000), *Inside the Olympic Industry: Power, Politics and Activism*, Albany, NY: State University of New York Press.

Pound, D. (2004), *Inside the Olympics. A Behind-the-Scenes Look at the Politics, the Scandals, and the Glory of the Games*, Etobicoke, Ontario: John Wiley & Sons.

Scheerder, J., van Tuyckom, C. & Vermeersch, A. (eds) (2007), *Europa in Beweging*, Gent: Academia Press.

Senn, A. (1999), *Power Politics and the Olympic Games*, Champaign, Illinois: Human Kinetics Publishing.

Simson, V. & Jennings, A. (1992), *Dishonored Games: Corruption, Money, and Greed at the Olympics*, Toronto: Shapolsky Publishing.

Spaargaren, G., Mol, A. P. J. & Bruyninckx, H. (2006), 'Introduction: Governing Environmental Flows in Global Modernity', in G. Spaargaren, A. P. J. Mol & F. H. Buttel (eds.), *Governing Environmental Flows*, Cambridge, MA: MIT Press, pp. 1–36.

Tokarski, W., Petry, K., & Jesse, B. (eds) (2006), *Sportpolitik: theorie- und praxisfelder von Governance im Sport*, Köln: Sportverlag Strauss.

Tokarski, W., Petry, K., Groll, M., & Mittag, J. (2009), *Perfect Match? Sport in the European Union*, Aachen: Meyer & Meyer Verlag.

UNESCO, www.unesco.org.

Young, O., Schroeder, H. & King, L.A. (2008), *Institutions and Environmental Change Principal Findings, Applications, and Research Frontiers*, Massachusetts: MIT Press.

9   The Magicians of Sport
How the Greatest Corruption Scandal in the World of Sport Vanished Before We Knew It Existed

Jens Sejer Andersen

Usually, I am a great admirer of magicians. People who can make elephants appear out of nowhere or escape from underwater cages handcuffed and wrapped in chains really deserve respect.

There are, however, some magicians that we should beware of and quite a few of them perform their tricks in sport. I am not referring to artists like Lionel Messi or Justine Henin who can make a ball do unimaginable things. No, the magicians I would like to talk about are exercising their craft more discreetly.

They do not seek our admiration for their skills. On the contrary, they shun the public eye so much that they have become experts in one aspect of magic; they know how to make us look in one direction while they do their work in the other direction, and more than that, when we look back we do not even notice that something mysterious has happened.

Thanks to these skills in magic, a number of corruption scandals in the highest ranks of sports leadership continue to vanish even before we realise that they actually exist.

Where were your eyes directed for instance in late June of 2010? I suppose that they, like mine, were glued to a flatscreen TV to follow the last matches in the group stage of the International Federation of Football Association (FIFA) world cup in South Africa.

Abracadabra! While we were staring at one of the greatest shows on earth, the biggest corruption scandal ever documented in sport vanished into thin air.

Did you notice?

If not, do not feel ashamed. It was not meant for you to see.

While events in South Africa held the world spellbound, a dry and formal sheet of paper was produced more than 8,000 kilometres away by the public prosecutor in Zug, the Swiss canton in which FIFA resides.

On 24 June 2010, the prosecutor ended eight years of legal proceedings with a statement that put an end to the so-called ISL affair.

Simultaneously, FIFA noted in a very brief media release that 'FIFA is pleased that the prosecutor of Zug has finalised his investigations'.

FIFA had reasons to be satisfied indeed. For although the Swiss prosecutor that day confirmed that FIFA officials had received millions of Swiss francs from ISL and kept them in their pockets and that FIFA should hence pay a compensation of 5.5 million Swiss francs—around 4 million euros— things could have turned out much worse for football's governing body.

THE COLLAPSE OF A MARKETING GIANT

ISL was no street vendor of services to FIFA. ISL stands for International Sport and Leisure and was, from the early 1980s to its collapse in 2001, by far the biggest sport marketing company in the world. It was founded by Horst Dassle whose family owned Adidas.

ISL bought TV and marketing rights from the international sports feder- ations and the International Olympic Committee and re-sold them to media companies and private sponsors. Thanks to its close personal relations to FIFA and other big federations it became a driving force in the explosive commercialisation of elite sport.

However, even a booming company in a booming sector can make mis- takes and in 2001 ISL collapsed because it had seriously overestimated the value of its products.

When the Swiss administrators took over bankrupt ISL and started looking at the books they soon discovered some strange payments. The liquidator of the company, Thomas Baur, found first of all that at least 3.5 million Swiss francs (at the time 2.2 million euros) had been paid out in personal commissions and they started writing to leading sports officials in order to get the money back.

In 2004, Mr Bauer did indeed get most of that money back. Not in many small portions but in one big cheque for 2,5 million Swiss francs. It would of course be interesting to know where this sum came from and on behalf of which sports leaders it was paid back, but despite hard work from a splendid Swiss lawyer, Peter Nobel, the Federal Court, the highest court in Switzerland, ruled that no names should be mentioned.

Peter Nobel is not only an excellent player in the court room—a magi- cian in his field you could say—he was also the man who issued the big cheque. Further, coincidentally perhaps, he has for many years been the personal lawyer of Joseph S. Blatter, President of FIFA.

This however, was only the beginning. Other parts of the Swiss justice system had an interest in ISL and one investigative judge, Thomas Hild- brand, was particularly active, launching an investigation into how six ISL directors managed their affairs and another one into the relation between FIFA and ISL.

140 MILLION SWISS FRANCS IN KICKBACKS

In 2008, the court in the Swiss city of Zug concluded the first of these two cases, the proceedings against six former ISL directors, charged with embezzling large portions of money belonging to FIFA. The case itself ended with a number of acquittals and lenient sentences since the defendants were able to convince the judges that in reality FIFA had accepted the way ISL handled FIFA's money.

But in the indictment a stunning revelation was brought forward and confirmed by the defendants in the court room; over a period of twelve years, from 1989 to its bankruptcy in 2001, ISL handed out no less than 140 million Swiss francs—then 88 million euros—in personal commissions to sports leaders in order to get lucrative TV and marketing contracts.

The payments were channelled to the private pockets or bank accounts of high-ranking sports leaders through an advanced system of secret funds in Liechtenstein and the British Virgin Islands. Some of the kickbacks were handed over personally by the top executive of ISL, Jean-Marie Weber, who travelled around the world with a suitcase filled with cash.

BRIBES AS SALARIES FOR SPORTS LEADERS

According to the defendant ISL directors, these payments were a normal and integral part of the daily business of sports and a precondition for ISL to sign contracts with their customers.

'I was told the company would not have existed if it had not made such payments', said former chief executive of ISL Christoph Malms, and he was backed by the former director of finances, Hans-Jürgen Schmid.

'It was like paying salaries. Otherwise they would have stopped working immediately', he said about the sports officials.

How come the six directors admitted these secret personal commissions so freely? The answer is simple. In Switzerland this kind of kickback or bribe was not a criminal act until new anti-corruption legislation was passed in 2006. And although the directors were quite loose-tongued, they did not risk their future careers by dropping names in court.

All we know is that, when ISL flourished, some of its most important customers besides FIFA, were ATP in tennis (Association of Tennis Professionals), IAAF in athletics (International Association of Athletics Federations), FINA in swimming (International Federation for swimming), FIBA in basketball (International Basketball Federation) and, for some years also, the IOC (International Olympic Committee).

You would perhaps expect these organisations to react to the revelations in Zug by tracing corrupt sports leaders in their own ranks or at least distancing themselves publicly from such malicious practices. From the international sports community, however, there has only been one reaction to what is beyond doubt the biggest known corruption scandal in sport: unanimous and complete silence. After the verdicts in Zug in 2008, one hope still remained that perhaps the third and last criminal investigation could help us answer the simple question: who took the bribes?

How much did they get each? After all, 87 million euros is a lot of money and not that many individuals were in charge of TV and marketing contracts. Do these persons still hold important positions in sport?

Unfortunately, the end of the ISL-affair did not answer any of these questions.

The settlement does confirm what FIFA has long denied: that FIFA officials had taken millions of Swiss francs from ISL in return for contracts, and it did oblige FIFA to pay back some of the money stolen from sport.

But even if we assume that all cheques have been paid by FIFA—2.5 million Swiss francs to the liquidators, 5.5 million Swiss francs in the recent decision plus the costs of the legal procedure—we are still far from the impressive 138 million Swiss francs that went into corruption. The financial balance is clearly in favour of those who cheated.

Before I go deeper into analysing the mechanisms that allow such a huge scandal to pass almost unnoticed by the world public, one more important question arises from the ISL case: is this the end of the magic performance?

Did corruption in sports organisations die with ISL in 2001, and is the buying and selling of TV and marketing rights now a clean business?

NO ANSWERS GIVEN AT THE OLYMPIC CONGRESS

I raised this question during a session about 'Good governance and ethics' at the Olympic Congress in Copenhagen last year where over 1,200 high-ranking sports officials gathered to discuss the challenges to sport. The answer from the moderator, Youssoupha Ndiaye from the IOC Ethics Commission, was easy to understand:

'The panel does not answer questions'.

To be fair, the audience was quite amused by that response. Well, perhaps not all—probably not the man sitting a few rows from me, Jean-Marie Weber, the man who once travelled the world with a suitcase full of money.

I do not know which tasks the elegant Mister Weber had at the Olympic Congress but it cost the IOC President Rogge some sweat explaining Weber's presence. It was apparently not the IOC itself that had invited him, but still, to get an accredited entry through the strict security measures of that meeting one had to have very good connections in the so-called Olympic family of sport.

Only several weeks after the congress, Mr Rogge declared that Mr Weber would not get Olympic accreditation in the future.

Although Jean-Marie Weber was in his time by far the most influential sorcerer in sport, he was not (and is not) the only one and there are several cases that prove that corruption in sport did not vanish with the bankruptcy of ISL.

THE ROYALTIES OF VOLLEYBALL

Take, for instance, the great leader of world volleyball from 1984 until 2008, Ruben Acosta from Mexico, or Dr. Acosta as he prefers to be called though no papers support this doctoral title.

As a President of the Féderation Internationale du Volleyball (FIVB), Ruben Acosta—very actively assisted by his flamboyant wife Malú—introduced a kind of management style that is comparable to absolute monarchy.

Ruben Acosta made the FIVB a resounding commercial success. He changed the counting system of volleyball, he decreed tiny shorts for female players and last but not least, he embraced and developed beach volley with its flavour of sun, sex and soft drinks. All these initiatives were aimed at making the ailing sport more appetising on the TV screens. And again, while you and I were staring at the scarcely dressed suntanned men and women playing in the sand, the magician went to work. Without asking anyone, he introduced a rule through which every person who signed a TV or marketing contract on behalf of FIVB was entitled to a personal commission of 10 percent of the contract sum. He also introduced another rule, being that the president should sign all contracts. According to their critics, these procedures may have secured at least US$25 million for the Acosta family. Sooner or later, this practice had to be ratified by the General Assembly. When some volleyball leaders began to pose questions, a code of conduct was duly introduced according to which anyone who criticises volleyball or its institutions could be excluded by the president. Following this, several respected international volleyball leaders have had to retire involuntarily in the last decade. They are not even allowed to enter the local volleyball club, so, in fact, they are deprived of a basic civic right, the right to take part in associations.

A CRITICAL AUDITOR'S NOTE REMOVED

Even magicians sometimes fail, however. When the FIVB accounts for 2001 showed that Ruben Acosta had, that year alone, received 8.4 million Swiss francs and over 5 million euros in personal commissions, Acosta decided to hide the number by grouping it with other amounts. The auditors, however, took the rare step of making a critical note on the accounts because the personal commission was not transparent. This worried Acosta; how would the General Assembly handle such a complex message? Acosta decided to delete the critical note of the auditors before the FIVB accounts were published. This action is illegal in most countries, even in Switzerland. In 2006 the local court in Lausanne therefore decided that Acosta and his nearest aides at the FIVB offices had really done something wrong. However, as the judge felt that no harm had been done and there had been no criminal intent, Acosta was acquitted. His only obligation was to pay legal costs to the amount of 4,300 Swiss francs. Again, he received a good financial result for the cheater. Acosta's magic tricks did not go unnoticed at the IOC. The IOC's Ethics Commission already produced a devastating report about Acosta's mismanagement in 2004. However, because Acosta reacted by leaving his IOC seat in anger and protest, the IOC decided to keep the report secret and Acosta received four more years as FIVB President, harvesting the money that belonged to volleyball.

THE HANDBALL PHARAOH

Acosta's successor from 2008, long-standing Vice-President Jizhong Wei from China, has fortunately decided to replace his loyalty to Acosta with loyalty to his sport. Wei has stopped all payments to Acosta, upsetting many of Acosta's friends and he has taken many other positive steps; however, he has still not succeeded in rehabilitating those volleyball leaders that were excluded from volleyball because of a sense of ethics. This sense is not predominant in another sport where the top reaches for rather more than the ball.

The Egyptian businessman Hassan Moustafa has had a firm control of the International Handball Federation (IHF) for the past ten years and has his own way of understanding good governance. It is well-documented that he has tried to influence the outcome of Olympic qualifiers, that he has travelled for more than 300,000 euros without presenting receipts, and that he has demanded insight into the doping testing plans for national teams. At the General Assembly of the IFH in Cairo in 2009, it was also evident that the European opponents were not allowed to speak. A rival for the presidency, the Luxembourger Jean Kaiser, simply had his microphone cut off. These facts did not impress the assembly, which re-elected Hassan Moustafa by an overwhelming majority, 115 against 25 votes. A similar majority ousted the long-standing secretary-general Peter Mühlematter, who had dared to tell the public what Moustafa was doing with handball's money. In 2010 a new story has been confirmed. From 2007 to 2009, Hassan Moustafa was employed as an advisor by the German marketing company Sportfive. Moustafa's salary was 602,000 euros. Curiously, during that same period, Sportfive acquired the TV rights for the games of the International Handball Federation. Even more curiously, when Sportfive's director, Robert Müller von Vultejus, left his position and went to rival company UFA, a very new player in sports marketing, it was this company which won the next bid for the IHF TV rights. Thought-provoking?

THE BERMUDA TRIANGLE: SPORT, SPONSORS, MEDIA

Would it have hindered the re-election of Moustafa if his constituency had heard about these magic events? One supposes not. Moustafa is simply a typical representative of the power structures developed within international sport since the early 1980s, thanks to visionary businessmen like the late Horst Dassler. Thirty years ago a triangle was created which one might call the 'Bermuda Triangle' of sport—a triangle where transparency, accountability and true democratic standards always mysteriously disappear. Explained in broad terms, the triangle has three sides that support each other: sports organisations, multinational companies and TV companies. Adidas and other consumer goods producers give sponsorships to sports organisations to ensure that they are run by people with the right mindset; some of the first to benefit from this was the late IOC President Juan Antonio Samaranch and the former FIFA President Joao Havelange. In return, these outstanding sports leaders ensured that their sponsors attained exposure and access to emerging markets everywhere in the world. By signing marketing contracts with national federations the sponsors could get an even stronger foothold in local markets. The globalisation of TV was of course a driving force in this development. TV companies saw the potential of elite sport to build up audiences and were willing to invest huge sums in acquiring broadcasting rights. These rights were paid either with taxpayers' money or, in the case of private TV companies, with money from advertising by consumer goods producers. TV and corporate companies have one thing in common; they are in a highly competitive market. They need sport in this competition and they are ready to raise the stakes to get sport on their side. This has been to the great advantage of sports organisations, who, for their part, are in a market with very little competition. Within each sport they are de facto monopolies. Internationally and nationally there is only one federation in every sport. As a result, sport has been able to gather ever-increasing revenues from sponsors as well as from media companies.

A BREEDING GROUND FOR CORRUPTION

Much of this money has been used by sports presidents to globalise sport and to strengthen their own position. The main procedure has been to establish new federations in poor countries with no infrastructure for athletics, handball, volleyball, or any other sport and to provide these new federations with generous grants and other kinds of privileges. They have been so eager to recruit new members that FIFA and some other sports federations have more member countries than the United Nations.

The upside of this development is that the leaders of sport can claim that they are breaking the colonial scheme of sport, fulfilling the goal of making their specific sport accessible to the whole world, also to less privileged people and countries. By involving new groups and giving each new member state a vote, they can with some right say that they are making sport more global and more democratic. However, there is also a remarkable downside. The 'one-country-one-vote' system is also yielding a lot of power to countries with no particular stake in a given sport, and—if you take into account that the generous amounts are distributed without strict control over their use—power is also given to sports leaders who may think more about their own fortune than about the fate of their sport. When we talk about sport in a development context, this is a factor that has to be taken seriously. Can we say without blushing that the fortunes that the international federations have distributed to developing countries for the past twenty-five years have had an important impact on sports participation of the native population? Are the international federations efficient and reliable partners in the expansion of grassroots sporting activity? At the second Magglingen conference for sport and development in Switzerland in 2005, I had the opportunity to briefly encourage small grassroots sports projects to prepare for a situation where corruption in one project might destroy the reputation of sport in development more broadly. Immediately a middle-aged man grabbed the microphone and declared he was 'livid'. There is no corruption at all in sport for development, he stated, and I owed everybody an apology! I was quite surprised by this reaction. I became even more surprised when I found out that the furious man was the Zimbabwean Tommy Ganda Sithole, prominent IOC director of international cooperation and development. It is not only surprising, but deeply worrying that a man in such a position rejects the idea that sport is vulnerable to corruption everywhere, even in developing countries. The fact is that sports organisations are all too often breeding grounds for corruption and there is no real interest in stopping this state of affairs from the inside. On the contrary, the powerbase of the leadership of sport is built on this system of patronage, of quid pro quo.

THE FAMILY CULTURE

Those few sports leaders who dare speak up against this kind of governance are met with ridicule, exclusion or marginalisation. Such behaviour not only threatens the power structures, not being loyal to your leaders is also incompatible with the cultural concept that sports leaders like to promote, namely sport as a family. Over and over again, Sepp Blatter and his ilk refer to their sport as a family, the football family, the family of volleyball and above all, the all-embracing Olympic family. The 'family'-word may produce good feelings in the corridors of power but is not as innocent and heart-warming as it may seem. The ideal of family unity is also invoked as a defence against open internal debates. In a family we are loyal to each other. We do not have any real conflicts of interest. We do not hang our dirty laundry out to dry and, at the end of the day, Daddy knows what is best for us.

If sport were to be regarded as a community rather than a family, conditions for the debate would change radically. They might even become truly democratic. The notion of family is based on the idea that we all share the same interests. Democracy is based on an understanding that we have different interests and that it offers us a way of resolving our conflicts. To do so, it is a prerequisite that the conflicts are visible and can be discussed publicly.

If the affairs of sport really were a matter for sport only, we could leave the family members to mind their own business. However, during the last thirty years, sport has developed into an unparalleled economic, political and cultural power and it is therefore of fundamental importance to democratic societies that sport takes its internal democracy serious as being exactly that—and hence stops seeing itself as a family. If not, the world of sport runs the risk of blending into other industrious groups that handle big fortunes, live outside the law, operate freely across borders and are based on family values. We have a name for this type of organisation, a word borrowed from Italian.

THE MEDIA AS PART OF THE FAN CROWD

I have now discussed some of the most important internal factors that make sport unable to clean up its style of governance by itself. Let me—again in broad terms—look at those external forces that one would expect to exercise some control. First of all, let's look at the world I come from as a journalist, the media. I am embarrassed to say that one should not expect too much. Very few, if any, major sport scandals have been revealed by investigative journalists in the first instance. Sports journalism emerged as a twin of sport in the late nineteenth century. From the outset, sports journalists have seen themselves as fans, only too glad to assist sport with bringing out its message of character building, national pride and peace in the world. The fact that sport was always an item that could attract readers and advertisers has probably greased the media's willingness to cooperate. In recent times, this commercial partnership has grown enormously with TV being one of the sides in the aforementioned Bermuda Triangle of sport. So, although sport exercises considerable influence in society, journalists are still focused on the battle field rather than on the games in the corridors.

For example, when I was searching through the international newspaper database, Lexis-Nexis, which covers most of the Western Hemisphere, I found only 44 articles mentioning ISL and FIFA after the decision to settle the case. The articles reached only 12 out of the 208 member nations of FIFA. We often regard the media as the fourth pillar of power in democracies. Sport is a notable exception.

PROTECTING THE AUTONOMY OF SPORT

With such silence from within the world of sports as well as from the media, it is hard to blame our elected politicians if they do not react. Why should they?

Sport is regarded as widely popular and politicians would not like to provoke their voters by opposing sport. Also, sport might single out critical politicians and stop inviting them to and prevent them from getting media exposure at national team games and medal ceremonies. Moreover, in many countries sport is seen as a part of independent civil society, a no-go zone for politicians and protecting sport's autonomy is top of the agenda for all sports organisations. Whenever the IOC mentions the need for good governance, they also mention the autonomy of sport. There is a clear underlying warning to politicians that if they do not listen, sport will react. Every now and then FIFA issues a bulletin against a member nation's government for interfering in football's internal issues. Sometimes FIFA might be within its right to do so, but we have seen many cases in which FIFA has intervened against governments that have tried to stop corrupt football leaders—for instance in Poland, in Greece, in Kenya or right now in Nigeria. It would seem that, independently of the reasons, when FIFA threatens a country with being suspended from international football, most governments pull back.

Last but not least, sports organisations prevent political and police intervention by placing their headquarters in countries that have very favourable working conditions. Home country number one is, of course, Switzerland where the organisations enjoy special tax privileges plus the same legal status as any local bowling or household association. This means that the kind of corruption that distorts business competition, as in the ISL case, may well be illegal now, yet it is still not illegal to hand over personal commissions in relation to internal events, like elections or choosing hosts for sporting events.

What can we do therefore other than to demand transparency, democracy and fair play from such important and potent players in a global, billion-dollar entertainment industry, which is intimately linked to the largest consumer good producers, protected by media conglomerates and blessed with enormous political, financial and cultural influence?

A SOLUTION DERIVED FROM AN EMERGING THREAT

The solution may be helped forward from an unexpected side, from people who care even less about sport's integrity and are even more powerful and unscrupulous. In the past years, the combination of match-fixing and illegal gambling on the Internet has become a growing industry and a growing threat to sport, especially to sport as a business. Match-fixing is indeed a significant threat. Experts assess that annual revenues in the world gambling market can reach US$350 billion, of which US$100 billion is derived from the illegal market, dominated by organised crime in Asia. If the public in general loses confidence in how sporting results are arrived at—in equality of competition with uncertainty of the outcome—it would not just affect the state gambling companies that finance sports organisations in most of Europe and many other countries around the world, it would also seriously affect the lucrative Bermuda Triangle and the core business interests of sport, the media and sponsors.

This threat is by nature global, ranging across sports as well as geographical boundaries. An increasing number of sports officials understand that a global, comprehensive threat must be confronted with a global comprehensive answer.

A GLOBAL COALITION FOR GOOD GOVERNANCE

Play the Game suggested in 2006, at a seminar organised by the European Council and UEFA, that we ought to let ourselves be inspired by the World Anti Doping Agency which has proved that a legally binding cooperation between governments, supranational institutions and sport can create considerable progress. It is time now to create a new world institution: a 'Global Coalition for Good Governance in Sport'. This new anti-corruption body should be run jointly by the International Olympic Committee and the international sports federations, by the United Nations, by governmental organisations like the EU and the European Council, and—as a supplement to the structure we know from the World Anti-Doping Agency—should also invite representatives from the media, the scientific community, the fan trusts and the sports business world to the board.

The 'Global Coalition for Good Governance in Sport' should

- Define minimum standards for transparency, accountability and democratic procedures;
- Have administrative capacity to ensure that the minimum standards are respected;
- Build up a global co-operation between the betting industry and governments to counter illegal gambling and match-fixing;
- Actively welcome sports leaders and administrators, media professionals, sports researchers and other stakeholders to report irregularities;
- Have a legal mandate and the professional expertise to investigate cases of mismanagement and corruption, including the right to search sports offices, archives, and the like without prior notice;
- Be empowered with the right to issue bans against individuals or groups who violate the global standards and suspend those who are under investigation;
- Be provided with a legal status that enables it to report supposed violations to national or international legal authorities for further trial;
- Communicate its findings to the public through annual reports, conferences, and so on.

Though the focus of late is mostly on match-fixing, it would be a great failure to only focus narrowly on this aspect of corruption which is managed by organised crime. In any case sports organisations and their leaders must accept that they should be held accountable for their practices.

RAYS OF HOPE

Quite recently, the Secretary General of WADA, David Howman, suggested exactly such a WADA-style anti-corruption body to the sports ministers from the Commonwealth countries and the European Union. Indeed, sports ministers from the European Council agreed to act against match-fixing. Although I may have painted quite a dark picture of sports politics, there is some hope in these recent developments. More than that, there is hope in the fact that sport really can be used to more noble ends than filling the pockets and bolstering the prestige of a privileged few magicians in sport. Let us not turn our eyes away from these magicians, let us instead take a much closer look at them and see if their tricks will survive our attention. Let me end by quoting an author who has highlighted magic more than anybody else, the creator of Harry Potter, J. K. Rowling. She once said that we do not need magic to change the world because we carry all the power we need inside ourselves already; we have the power to imagine better.

EPILOGUE: A LANDSLIDE ON THE WAY?

The text above was presented on Saturday 16 October 2010, a date which seemed to mark the end of a stable decade in sports politics.

The following day the British newspaper the *Sunday Times* published articles and video footage proving that two FIFA Executive Committee members, Amos Adamu from Nigeria and Reynald Temarii from Tahiti, were ready to sell their votes in the bidding process for the World Cups 2018 and 2022. Other officials confirmed that vote selling is common practice. The allegations set off a series of reactions and debates inside and outside FIFA. The Swiss Minister of Sport, Ueli Maurer, asked for a review of the legislation that covers more than forty international sports federations based in Switzerland. FIFA decided to suspend the two committee members charged with fraud. In late November 2010, the British reporter Andrew Jennings concluded ten years of investigations into FIFA politics by publishing documents naming some of the, still functioning, FIFA officials that have taken money in the ISL affair. The documents were shown on BBC Panorama, one of the world's oldest and most respected investigative TV programmes, fueling the debate about sports governance further.

When FIFA chose Russia and Qatar on 2 December 2010 as hosts for the disputed World Cups, nations not particularly renowned for transparency and fair business practice, public worries about past and future irregularities rose to new heights. The Swiss MP and former ISL employee, Roland Rino Büchel, filed an anti-corruption initiative in parliament, a step backed by a cross-party group of sixty politicians. As his first move in 2011, FIFA President Sepp Blatter announced he was going to set up a new compliance body with high-ranking international personalities from all parts of society. No details were revealed. The IOC has so far remained silent, but in late January it announced that it would gather key stakeholders for a symposium dealing with match-fixing and illegal betting. At the EU Sport Forum in Budapest in February 2011, the President of the International Weightlifting Federation and Honorary IOC Member, the Hungarian Tamás Aján, made a stunning statement: he declared that corruption was omnipresent within the international federations, in elections and in doping testing and he urged the EU to intervene. He called for public awareness and he warned that a new generation of sports leaders was emerging from countries 'where money seems to grow on trees'.

On 1 March 2011, the IOC Symposium on match-fixing and illegal betting gathered forty carefully selected delegates and forty observers from sport, the gambling industry, Interpol, a handful of governments, transnational institutions and other stakeholders. After a day in which it kept strict control over the agenda the IOC issued a joint declaration to the effect that the IOC would soon form a working group which would define which measures to take. Deliberately, there was no mention of corruption inside the structure of sport, and only time will tell if the working group is ready and permitted, to bring that issue up. After all, a momentum has now gained speed which the magicians of sport may not be able to control. It looks like a slow, but forceful landslide and it will take some years to see how much real change it will bring.

10 A Governance Perspective on Sport Mega-Events

The 2010 Football World Cup
in South Africa as a Lubricant in
Domestic and International Affairs?

*Bert Meulders, Bart Vanreusel, Hans
Bruyninckx, Marion Keim and André Travill*

INCREASING COMPETITION FOR GROWING MEGA-EVENTS IN SPORTS

Global competition between countries and cities to host the world's most important mega-events or so-called 'hallmark events', such as the Olympic Games and the FIFA World Cup, has seriously intensified in the last few decades (Tomlinson, Bass & Pillay, 2009). The game of football has become strongly globalised as a result of continued and predictable increases in the largest economies worldwide, real rises in disposable income in those economies, the growing commercial significance of football, the consolidation of international television coverage by dominant, trans-national broadcasting firms and the increased corporatisation of football through private capital (Cornelissen, 2010). With more than 200 recognised football associations, the international administrative body of football or FIFA (Fédération Internationale de Football Association) has more nations as members than the United Nations itself. The increasing significance and size of the World Cup tournament is one of the most explicit components of this trend. The number of national teams participating in the finals of the event increased in the last few decades, from sixteen to twenty-four participating countries in 1982, to thirty-two countries in 1998. According to FIFA figures, the World Cup in France (1998) generated 135 million Swiss Francs (1 Swiss Francs = 0.68 Euros, 25 January 2010) in broadcasting revenues (Forster & Pope, 2004). More recently, television broadcasting rights with a total value of 1,66 billion Swiss Francs were sold for the 2006 World Cup in Germany (Davies, 2009), accounting for more than half of FIFA's total revenue. Huge cumulative television audiences totalling some 26 billion viewers for the 2006 World Cup (Tomlinson et al., 2009) go pretty far in explaining why so-called event sponsors are willing to invest heavily in association with the tournament. The six corporations signing exclusive contracts with FIFA as first tier firms for the 2010 World

Cup in South Africa, paying R700 million each (1 South African Rand = 0.09 Euros, 25 January 2010), are McDonald's, MTN, Budweiser, Castrol, Continental and Satyam Computer Services. As it is arguably the world's largest sporting and media event, taking place only once every four years, the hosting rights of the FIFA World Cup provide a scarce and prestigious product, prompting intense competition between nations to win the support of FIFA and its constituencies in the bidding process (Forster & Pope, 2004; Cornelissen & Swart, 2006; Black, 2007).

A QUEST FOR PROFIT AND PRESTIGE?

Preuss (2000) identified nine broad objectives associated with the hosting of mega-events like the Olympics: putting the country 'on the map', showcasing the region, promoting the political system, creating new trading partners, attracting investment, boosting tourism, creating jobs and business opportunities, urban renewal including housing and infrastructure and building a legacy of sports infrastructure. Other scholars make a distinction between direct financial gains associated with the duration of the event through expenditure by tourists, teams, media and organising agents; longer-term gains through infrastructure constructed for the event and the benefits these will generate as a result of future visitors; technological and human capital spill-overs from these investments; and non-financial benefits, for instance through political impacts, enhanced prestige effects and a potential feel-good component (du Plessis & Maennig, 2009). According to the economics of public expenditure, governments can justify investments of public funding based on solid arguments that the productive return on the investment will exceed all other investments or that a specific re-allocation of resources will generate higher revenues in the future (Noll & Zimbalist, 1997). Despite the firm grip of FIFA and its corporate and media partners on the main revenue streams of the World Cup (Sugden & Tomlinson, 1998; Cornelissen, 2007; 2010; du Plessis & Maennig, 2009; Davies, 2009), governmental parties appear to be remarkably willing to carry large portions of the costs of infrastructure development that are necessary to organise such a mega-event. Bearing in mind the growing reservations of many economists as to the direct economic benefits of mega-events for the host cities or host nations (Baade & Matheson, 2004; Horne & Manzenreiter, 2004; Bohlmann & Van Heerden, 2008; Pillay & Bass, 2009), the role of governments in funding commercial spectacles seems even more remarkable. It suggests that mega-events have the potential to bring about indirect, intangible outcomes which are hard to measure or at least that decision makers do not exclusively apply evidence-based rationales in their efforts to acquire the hosting rights for mega-events. Van der Westhuizen (2007) stresses the importance and under-studied character of political symbolism in the pursuit of mega-projects. Or to put it in the words of Flyvberg: 'It is not necessarily the best mega-projects that get built, but those projects for which proponents best succeed in conjuring a fantasy world of underestimated costs, overestimated revenues, undervalued environmental impacts and overvalued developmental effects' (Siemiatycki, 2006: 72).

DEVELOPING NATIONS JOIN THE RACE

An increased political awareness of developing nations in general and African states in particular, was marked among other things by their entrance, in the latter half of the twentieth century, into the global football arena, largely through lobbying efforts to increase the number of berths for African national teams to compete in the finals of the World Cup and more recently through bids for the hosting rights of the World Cup (Sugden & Tomlinson, 1998; Darby, 2005, 2008; Bolsmann & Brewster, 2009; van der Merwe, 2009). The wave of de-colonisation that gradually took off after World War II stimulated many newly independent African nation states to manifest and legitimise themselves by applying for membership of international organisations such as the United Nations and FIFA. Whereas FIFA contained no more than four African affiliates (South Africa, Egypt, Ethiopia and Sudan) in the early 1960s, more than thirty nations had joined the 'global football fraternity' by the mid-1960s (Darby, 2008). At the same time, the Confédération Africaine de Football (CAF), established in 1957, provided a platform for the pan-African movement to articulate the interest of the (African) Third World in global football (Sugden & Tomlinson, 1998). CAF played a prominent role in the suspensions of the Football Association of South Africa (FASA) in 1961 and 1964 and its later exclusion in 1976 from FIFA, due to its segregationist policies which excluded black players (Darby, 2008; van der Merwe, 2009). It needs to be noted, however, that the support for the 'African cause' of the Brazilian João Havelange was fed at least as much by his personal interest in becoming FIFA president in 1974 than by the ambition to be a champion of the oppressed nations (Sugden & Tomlinson, 1998; Jennings, 2006). Notwithstanding the real and significant reconfiguration of the power balance in the structures of international football taking place today, the globalisation of football in the last 30 years has been strongly driven by commercial interest and the desire of FIFA to increase its profits, an objective for which the Third World offered an interesting and untapped market (Sugden & Tomlinson, 1998; van der Merwe, 2009; Cornelissen, 2010). The decision of FIFA in 2001 to introduce a continental rotation system for the World Cup Finals, which opened the door for South Africa to jump on the 'global stage of football', also has to be interpreted with that commercial motive in mind. The policy of continental rotation has been revoked since 2007, after the 2014 World Cup was awarded to Brazil.

SOUTH AFRICA ON THE GLOBAL STAGE

At FIFA's Executive Committee meeting in Zurich on 15 May 2004, ten years after its first democratic elections, South Africa won the right to stage the first World Cup on the African continent, despite all four votes from CAF representatives going to Morocco (Bolsmann & Brewster, 2009). As such, after hosting the 1995 Rugby World Cup, the 2003 Cricket World Cup, the 1996 African Cup of Nations and failed bids for the 2004 Olympics (by Cape Town) and the 2006 Football World Cup, South Africa has managed to secure a new milestone in its recent history of attracting major sporting events. Similar to the way in which newly independent African states sought legitimisation through membership of international sporting bodies after de-colonisation, the new political elite that was installed in South Africa after the breakdown of the apartheid system actively sought ways to confirm and consolidate its status as a new democracy (Black & van der Westhuizen, 2004; van der Merwe, 2006; van der Merwe & van der Westhuizen, 2006). Highly aware of the symbolic power of sport due to the role it played in the abolition of apartheid and drawing upon the iconic status of Nelson Mandela, the successes in hosting events like the 1995 Rugby World Cup (in which the Springboks were victorious) and the 2003 Cricket World Cup were a stimulus for the South African (sporting) leaders to go for better and bigger. As a developing nation, attracting the global media through mega-events offers specific opportunities for South Africa to 'punch above its weight' in world affairs, relative to its actual size and strategic importance (van der Merwe, 2007). Cornelissen and Swart (2006) describe three foreign policy goals for developing countries implemented through sports mega-events: delivering particular messages to the international community, engaging in international activities that go beyond objective measures of its international capacity and compensating for a lack of sources of power and influence in the international sphere.

In addition to international political legitimisation and foreign policy goals, as was highlighted in the bidding process and the official communication in the preparatory phases running up to the event, the promoters of the South African 2010 World Cup had an ambitious domestic agenda. The power of sport to construct bridges in a divided society and to build a unified rainbow nation had been continuously hailed by political and sporting leaders since Nelson Mandela embraced the white South African Springbok captain Francois Pienaar after he led his rugby team to win the Webb Ellis Cup (Rugby World Cup) on 24 June 1995, an image that sent a message of forgiveness and reconciliation to the entire population and the rest of the world[1]. The significance of football as 'the people's game', as opposed to rugby and cricket which has historically been dominated by white South Africans, usefully added to the rhetoric of nation-building through sport. To further justify the large government investments in infrastructure that are required to organise an event of this magnitude, the South African drivers of the bid for the 2010 World Cup emphasized the capacity of the event to create jobs, stimulate economic growth, bring about improved service delivery and upgrade public (transport) infrastructure (Pillay & Bass, 2008; 2009). The tone of the discourse by the South African leaders on the development potential of the 2010 event is quite nicely illustrated by the former premier of the Gauteng Province, Mbhazima Shilowa, who argued in The Star (27 June 2007) that 'the South African vision remains that of halving poverty and unemployment by 2014, and the 2010 World Cup provides an opportunity to fast-track development towards attainment of this vision'.

THE 2010 WORLD CUP: THE EGG OF COLUMBUS OR A TROJAN HORSE?

With a cumulative television audience of 2.629 billion viewers for the 2006 World Cup in Germany and the anticipation of an even bigger number of football fans watching the 2010 tournament in South Africa, it is hard to imagine a larger opportunity for a country to capture the attention of the world media. For a country (and a continent) that struggles to shake off the stereotypical features associated with African nations as places of depression, crime, corruption and underdevelopment, the successful hosting of the world's most important single sporting event could prove a major break in challenging ideas of Afro-pessimism (Donaldson & Ferreira, 2007). Similarly, the perceived global image of Germany improved significantly as a result of the 2006 World Cup, as measured through the Anholt Nation Brands Index (Kersting, 2007; Allmers & Maennig, 2008). For South Africa, this prospect is particularly attractive as tourism has recently been identified as a 'priority economic sector' by the national Department of Trade and Industry and the Accelerated and Shared Growth Initiative for South Africa (Cornelissen, 2009). With a share more than 3 percent of the South African GDP and employing more than 400,000 people, tourism is one of the sectors that has seen the most meaningful advance in South Africa since 1994 (Swart & Bob, 2007; Cornelissen, 2009). The influx of 230,000 to 475,000 foreign tourists and more importantly, the medium- to long-term effect on tourism of a potentially improved international profile could provide a major boost to the South African tourism industry (du Plessis & Maennig, 2009). Consultancy company Grant Thornton (2004) predicted a net economic gain of R21.3 billion, good for an increase of 1.5 percent in GDP, as well as 159,000 new jobs (3.5 percent of the unemployed South Africans) and R7.2 billion in additional tax income for the South African government.

This firm belief in a significant and positive impact of the 2010 World Cup on the South African economy, is not, however, shared by most economists. The political rationale that underlies most impact projections for mega-events has led to a skewed 'science of overestimation' (Baade &

Matheson, 2004; Matheson & Baade, 2004; Crompton, 2006). Main critiques have been directed at the deliberate misapplication of multipliers (that suggest a further spending by initial spending on mega-events but ignore the benefits of alternative spending) and the deceptive inclusion of domestic (displacement) spending as direct benefits in the equation (Bohlmann & Van Heerden, 2008; du Plessis & Maennig, 2009; Pillay & Bass, 2009; Swinnen & Vandemoortele, 2009). Caution has also been called for in order to avoid overstating the impact of the event on tourism, claims for which should not be accepted at face value, bearing in mind that media tend to perpetuate negative stereotypes and images rather than challenging them (Atkinson, 2009; Pillay & Bass, 2009). A study by Baade and Matheson (2004) that has estimated income growth for the host cities of the 1994 World Cup in the United States, found that in fact nine out of thirteen host cities suffered from declines in growth. Very few ex post studies find significant positive effects from sport events (du Plessis & Maennig, 2009; Swinnen & Vandemoortele, 2009; Tomlinson et al., 2009). Indeed, over a thirty-year period, Szymanski (2002) found that economic growth was significantly lower in host countries in World Cup years. The excessive cost overruns in South Africa for stadiums[2] and other infrastructure projects, for which the different tiers of government are almost exclusive accountable—whereas more than 60 percent of the investments in 2006 World Cup stadiums in Germany were made by private partners—are not helping to make the picture look any brighter, especially since opportunity costs for investment tend to be higher in developing nations (Davies, 2009; du Plessis & Maennig, 2009; Pillay & Bass, 2009). As a consequence, the risk of the poor and marginalised groups in South Africa being affected negatively by the 2010 World Cup is acute, as investment projects in the public interest might be delayed, resources will be concentrated in urban centres that aspire to become 'world class' and low-paying temporary job creation is unlikely to compensate for permanent rises in food and transportation prices (Pillay & Bass, 2009; Tomlinson, 2009; Desai & Vahed, 2010; Ngonyama, 2010).

GOVERNING THE 2010 LEGACY IN SOUTH AFRICA: GEARING UP FOR THE FUTURE OR CULTIVATING INEQUALITY?

In a country where about half of the population (of 49.3 million) lives in Third World conditions, 34 percent live below the poverty line, and between 28 percent to 40 percent are unemployed (World Bank, 2008), a government's economic policies and spending should strive to find a balance between creating a supportive environment for economic sectors with obvious competitive advantages and cultivating an enabling environment for all people without exception (Pillay, 2004). As a host for the 2010 World Cup football, this implies that the South African government needs to promote and act upon the vision that the potential benefits associated with the event are not the exclusive rights of any one South African stakeholder but national public goods and therefore it should attempt to balance investments with the socio-economic needs of the population as a whole (Cornelissen & Swart, 2006; Meulders, 2009; Pillay & Bass, 2009). Even though it is a prominent party and main funder in the institutional arrangement for the 2010 World Cup, government stakeholders do not hold the monopoly of the governance process of the 2010 World Cup and as such have to embark in negotiation processes with other stakeholders to defend public interest. A few rich entrepreneurs who own elite-level clubs in South Africa and who hold key positions in the Premier Soccer League Board and/or SAFA's (South African Football Federation) Executive Committee, were instrumental in conceiving and steering South Africa's bid to host the 2010 World Cup[3] (Cornelissen, 2010; Darby & Solberg, 2010). As commercial owner of the event, FIFA and a small group of commercial and media partners have a firm grip on the parameters for broadcasting, marketing, ticketing, imaging and to some extent, infrastructure development. A small South African elite is benefiting from large tenders for infrastructure development, including old, white construction companies and a new black elite (Alegi, 2007). Host cities are competing with each other to attract funding from higher ranks in government, some, like Johannesburg, embracing a neo-liberal, market-oriented approach in an attempt to position themselves in a global hierarchy of competitive metropolitan areas. Frustration about limited employment opportunities has resulted in outbursts of xenophobic violence against immigrants from neighbouring African countries who have taken up jobs in the construction industry (Desai & Vahed, 2010). One could even question whether any meaningful openings were left for national and regional authorities to cash in on potential opportunities to fast-track development as was envisioned in national development policies. As Cornelissen (2010) argues, it is the interplay between international and domestic processes of sport, commerce and politics that will determine the legacy of the 2010 World Cup for South Africa.

The aim is to shed some light on these governance processes by teasing out the nature of the relations between all relevant stakeholders and assessing the political will and governance capacity to engage in a participatory, transparent and pro-poor event strategy. To do this in a meaningful and useful manner, the South African 2010 World Cup is considered within its broader sporting and political-economic context at local, regional, national and international levels. Answers are provided to questions on the dubious character of unequally distributed legacies that can be expected to result from the nineteenth FIFA World Cup. This requires the combination of a critical sense in exposing legacy politics which merely reflect the need of politicians to be seen to be spreading the benefits of the 2010 World Cup on the one hand and an appreciation of a genuine commitment to a pro-poor development agenda and of the unified leadership, sense of urgency and focus needed to deliver on the massive requirements for hosting a mega-event on the other hand.

A GOVERNANCE APPROACH TO THE STUDY OF
THE FOOTBALL WORLD CUP IN SOUTH AFRICA

> One of the key factors that would determine the nature and extent of the imprints left from the [2010 World Cup] event [in South Africa] is the way in which a broad amalgam of corporate, commercial, sport and political actors, all of whom have a stake in the event, interact, collaborate and rival to set planning and profit parameters. [. . .] [It is] the interplay between international and domestic processes of sport commerce and politics and current courses of planning that could determine the event's aftermath. (Cornelissen, 2010: 132)

A lot of the criticism surrounding the 2010 FIFA World Cup revolves around the skepticism and suspicion of critics about the ability of the South African event organisers to generate 'a reasonable return on investment' for South African society at large that would justify the allocation of public resources to this end. Over and above the intricate and highly political debate on what constitutes such a reasonable return on investment, the quote from Cornelissen above suggests that the space in which the South African event organisers operate is competitive and densely populated. As outlined before, South African governmental stakeholders do not have 'carte blanche' to plan and construct the event to fit their goals and objectives. A number of domestic and international non-governmental players with diverse interests also assert a level of ownership over the event and its planning processes. This is partly due to the nature of the (commercial) sport sector that has traditionally claimed a unique status as a separate sphere in society exempt from normal regulation by governmental authorities (Bruyninckx & Scheerder, 2009). On the other hand, the extensive mixing of public and private interests that shape the planning and implementation strategies of the 19th FIFA World Cup can be seen as symptomatic of a broader shift in the manner in which governments operate. Indeed, entering the twenty-first century, nation states have lost their monopoly over policy processes only to be replaced by new 'power constellations' that include a variety of players such as corporate actors, financial institutions, scientific representatives, civic associations and international organisations (Arts, Leroy & van Tatenhove, 2006; Spaargaren, Mol & Bruyninckx, 2006). Due to the changing political environment—characterised by the joint effects of globalisation, liberalisation and privatization—which has pervaded most societal domains, the capacity of national governments to solely manage issue areas and give adequate responses to structural needs has disappointed (Mol & Spaargaren, 2006). The resulting functional shift in political dynamics between governmental agents, market actors and representatives from civil society, marked by diminishing contrasts in distinctive features and tasks, has introduced a new approach to the political sciences in their study of the mechanisms underlying policy processes. The replacement of 'government' by the concept of 'governance' is indicative of this new line of thought.

The governance approach is particularly suitable for our analysis of the 2010 World Cup for several reasons. First, it recognises the importance of cross-sectoral links in policy processes for any given society and this provides a window of opportunity to study the manner in which inter-actions between governmental stakeholders and football administrators shape the World Cup event and set limits to the political space to formulate a developmental agenda for it. Second, the governance approach was devised to fit the contextual circumstances of powerful supra-national forces that have re-framed many policy issues. Such an analytical scope is obviously required to understand the foundations of the FIFA World Cup, which is by definition an international affair as the event is commercially owned by the governing body for world football, FIFA. Finally, governance theory includes useful concepts and components that can be used to systematically deconstruct the 2010 World Cup as a unique part of a South African development strategy. In other words, this approach provides a scientific instrumentarium with which to understand the constitutive factors of the capacity of governance to engage in a participatory, transparent, pro-poor event strategy. The analytical components of the 'governance arrangements' approach relevant to this study will be described in further detail.

MULTIDIMENSIONAL, ACTOR-BASED GOVERNANCE ARRANGEMENTS

The processes of transformation in the political sphere of society, brought about as a response to structural changes in the economic, social and cultural domains, are sometimes referred to as 'political modernisation'. It can be viewed as a later stage of 'early modernisation', which is situated in the period after the Second World War when national states of Western societies were perceived as forces for steering progress in society (van Tatenhove, 1999; Arts & van Tatenhove, 2004; Arts et al., 2006). Current political modernisation, on the contrary, is characterised by the appearance of coalescing, hybrid networks between the institutions of state, market and civil society in the political sphere. Yet, the process of political modernisation should not be interpreted as a simple, diachronic and evolutionary process. Rather, it takes place as an uneven, complex, synchronic and largely unplanned phenomenon, entrenched in domestic societal forces as well as a global political economy (Nelissen, 2002; Arts & van Tatenhove, 2004; Stevis & Bruyninckx, 2006). Indeed, despite globalising forces crossing national boundaries, local socio-political circumstances constitute the soil in which multiple networks can take root.

The devolving of policy-shaping powers from national governments to both supra-national levels and local levels is described as the vertical dimension of governance networks (see Figure 10.1), hence the terminology of multilevel governance arrangements. Arts et al. (2006) define policy arrangements as the temporary stabilisation of content and organisation in specific policy areas. For our analysis of the 2010 Football World Cup, however, we use the concept of governance instead of policy, as the 2010 FIFA World Cup cannot in itself be regarded as a policy domain, considering its clear-cut and relatively short-term time frame.

The entrance of non-governmental actors in policy processes that occurs within national boundaries can also be observed at the international level. The process of political globalisation is accompanied by a process of economic globalisation (Jänicke, 2006). Multinational corporations systematically scout the globe to find the most attractive economic conditions and markets to produce and sell goods or services. In his multidimensional governance arrangement model, Jänicke (2006) labels the growing interdependence of governmental agents, market actors and representatives from civil society as the horizontal or multi-stakeholder dimension of governance, as is shown in Figure 10.1.

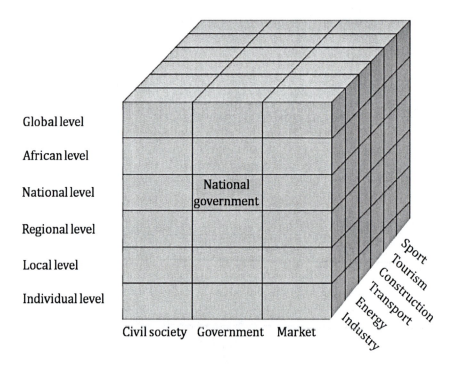

Figure 10.1   Multidimensional actor-based governance arrangement model (based on Jänicke, 2006).

The complexity of governance processes is enlarged even more as actors from different sectors interfere in specific issue areas (in Figure 10.1 represented as the in-depth or multi-sectoral dimension of governance). In the case of the 2010 World Cup, for instance, the governance space is penetrated by a myriad of interests and actors that comprise a complex system of directly and indirectly involved parties. The seventeen government guarantees to FIFA on deliverables associated with the 2010 FIFA World Cup are illustrative of the multi-sectoral nature of the event, with involvement of the national departments for sport, home affairs, finance, communications, public works, safety and security, minerals and energy, environment and tourism, health and transport.

The fragmentation of authority in governance processes is not entirely new, but the extent to which it takes place is, mirroring the fading distinctions between the roles and responsibilities of different types of stakeholders (Mol & Spaargaren, 2006; Bruyninckx & Scheerder, 2009). Governments adopt commercial rationalities and step into public-private partnerships, market actors take on tasks 'traditionally' reserved for states and some NGOs begin to act as multinational corporations and operate in official systems. The shift from government to governance through hybrid arrangements thus represents a more fundamental change than a mere scaling-up of national processes as a result of globalisation (Mol & Spaargaren, 2006).

Despite the more diffuse and competitive governance environment, nation states are by no means becoming superfluous institutions. In a network society, with no strict hierarchy between national and international political levels, states have become strategic actors instead of sovereign subjects directing all policy processes (Mol & Spaargaren, 2006). Yet, in several policy areas, as Jänicke (2006) has demonstrated for environmental affairs, there is no functional equivalent for the nation state in terms of financial resources, expertise, coercive power or pressure for legitimisation.

In the case of the 2010 FIFA World Cup, for instance, sufficient support was found to put environmental and ecological issues on the agenda, resulting in a Green Goal 2010 Programme, in which issues such as waste management, renewable energy usage, carbon emission and ecologically sustainable tourism were addressed.

CONCLUSION

To conclude, it could be said that a governance approach can be used as a benchmark for analyses of mega-events in sport such as the 2010 FIFA World Cup. Given the extensive investment of public means, all South African citizens can be considered as stakeholders in the event, providing an argument for collective ownership of any fruits accrued through the hosting of the Football World Cup. In fact, looking at the 2010 Football World Cup from a governance perspective, the complete event strategy and all preparatory processes ought to rest on a broad societal consensus. A general consensus, however, should not be confused with full consensus—as in solid democracies which can stand the test of opposition—but depends on a participatory, consultative process with all relevant stakeholders. The credibility and acceptability of any given governance scheme has a three-fold foundation: the provision of a mandate by the constituency, transparency in the formulation of targets and strategies, and internal and external accountability (Bruyninckx & Scheerder, 2009). Determining factors for governance capacity, such as a short democratic history for South Africa and a consequently limited institutional memory of government, a heterogeneous and polarised civil society, as well as a FIFA-dominated governance arrangement, is fitting for appraisal by means of a governance framework. The contextual social, political and economic conditions that set the stage for mega-events in sport such as the 2010 FIFA World Cup need to be spelled out in further detail in order to understand and manage their future place in local and global societies.

NOTES

1. This powerful image and highly symbolic moment became the central theme for a 2009 Hollywood film, *Invictus*, directed by Clint Eastwood and starring Morgan Freeman as President Nelson Mandela and Matt Damon as Francois Pienaar.
2. Ten stadiums in nine host cities have been selected for the 2010 FIFA World Cup tournament, of which five have been newly constructed and five have been moderately or greatly upgraded: Cape Town: Green Point Stadium; Durban: Moses Mabhida Stadium; Nelspruit: Mbombela Stadium; Polokwane: Peter Mokaba Stadium; Port Elizabeth: Nelson Mandela Bay Stadium; Bloemfontein: Mangaung Stadium; Johannesburg: Soccer City Stadium and Ellis Park Stadium; Pretoria: Loftus Versveld Stadium; and Rustenburg: Royal Bafokeng Stadium.
3. FIFA President Sepp Blatter refers to 'the three musketeers' at the core of the South African bid team: Molefi Oliphant (SAFA President), Irvin Khoza (SAFA Vice-President, PSL Chair, Orlando Pirates owner and chair of the 2010 LOC), and Danny Jordaan (CEO of the 2010 LOC). (City Press, 20 September 2008)

REFERENCES

Alegi, P. (2007), 'The Political Economy of Mega-stadiums and the Underdevelopment of Grassroots Football in South Africa', *Politikon*, 34(4): 315–331.

Allmers, S. & Maennig, W. (2008), 'South Africa 2010: Economic Scope and Limits', *Hamburg Contemporary Economic Discussions*, 21, online version available at http://www.hced.uni-hamburg.de/WorkingPapers/021.pdf (accessed 20 April 2009).

Arts, B. & van Tatenhove, J. (2004), 'Policy and Power: A Conceptual Framework Between the 'Old' and 'New' Policy Idioms', *Policy Sciences*, 37: 339–356.

Arts, B., Leroy, P. & van Tatenhove, J. (2006), 'Political Modernisation and Policy Arrangements: A Framework for Understanding Environmental Policy Change', *Public Organization Review*, 6: 93–106.

Atkinson, D. (2009), 'The 2010 World Cup and the Rural Hinterland: Maximising Advantage from Mega-events', in U. Pillay, R. Tomlinson & O. Bass (eds), *Development and Dreams. The Urban Legacy of the 2010 Football World Cup*, Cape Town: HSRC Press.

Baade, R. A. & Matheson, V. A. (2004), 'The Quest for the Cup: Assessing the Economic Impact of the World Cup', *Regional Studies*, 38(4): 343–354.

Black, D. (2007), 'The Symbolic Politics of Sport Mega-events: 2010 in Comparative Perspective', *Politikon*, 34(3): 261–276.

Black, D. & van der Westhuizen, J. (2004), 'The Allure of Global Games for 'Semiperipheral' Polities and Spaces: A Research Agenda', *Third World Quarterly*, 25(7): 1195–1214.

Bohlmann, H. R. & Van Heerden, J. H. (2008), 'Predicting the Economic Impact of the 2010 FIFA World Cup on South Africa', *International Journal of Sport Management and Marketing*, 3(4): 383–396.

Bolsmann, C. & Brewster, K. (2009), 'Mexico 1968 and South Africa 2010: Development, Leadership and Legacies', *Sport in Society*, 12(10): 1284–1298.

Bruyninckx, H. & Scheerder, J. (2009), 'Sport, macht en internationale politiek: een politicologisch kader', in J. Scheerder & B. Meulders (eds), *Wedijver in een internationale arena: Sport, bestuur en macht*, Gent: Academia Press.

Cornelissen, S. (2007), 'Crafting Legacies: The Changing Political Economy of Global Sport and the 2010 FIFA World Cup™', *Politikon*, 34(3): 241–259.

Cornelissen, S. (2009), 'Sport, Mega-events and Urban Tourism: Exploring the Patterns, Constraints and Prospects of the 2010 World Cup', in U. Pillay, R. Tomlinson & O. Bass (eds), *Development and Dreams. The Urban Legacy of the 2010 Football World Cup*; Cape Town: HSRC Press.

Cornelissen, S. (2010), 'Football's Tsars: Proprietorship, Corporatism and Politics in the 2010 FIFA World Cup', *Soccer & Society*, 11(1–2): 131–143.

Cornelissen, S. & Swart, K. (2006), 'The 2010 Football World Cup as a Political Construct: The Challenge of Making Good on an African Promise', *Sociological Review*, 54(s2), 108–123.

Crompton, J. (2006), 'Economic Impact Studies: Instruments for Political Shenanigans', *Journal of Travel Research*, 45(1): 67–82.

Darby, P. (2005), 'Africa and the 'World' Cup: FIFA Politics, Eurocentrism and Resistance', *International Journal of the History of Sport*, 22(5): 883–905.

Darby, P. (2008), 'Stanley Rous's "Own Goal": Football Politics, South Africa and the Contest for the FIFA Presidency in 1974', *Soccer & Society*, 9(2): 259–272.

Darby, P. & Solberg, E. (2010), 'Differing Trajectories: Football Development and Patterns of Player Migration in South Africa and Ghana', *Soccer & Society*, 11(1): 118–130.

Davies, G. (2009), 'Managing the Alchemy of the 2010 Football World Cup', in U. Pillay, R. Tomlinson & O. Bass (eds), *Development and Dreams. The Urban Legacy of the 2010 Football World Cup*, Cape Town: HSRC Press.

Desai, A. & Vahed, G. (2010), 'World Cup 2010: Africa's Turn or the Turn on Africa?', *Soccer & Society*, 11(1): 154–167.

Donaldson, R. & Ferreira, S. (2007), 'Crime, Perceptions and Touristic Decision Making: Some Empirical Evidence and Prospects for the 2010 World Cup', *Politikon*, 34(3): 353–371.

du Plessis, S. & Maennig, W. (2009), 'South Africa 2010: Initial Dreams and Sobering Economic Perspectives', in U. Pillay, R. Tomlinson & O. Bass (eds), *Development and Dreams. The Urban Legacy of the 2010 Football World Cup*, Cape Town: HSRC Press.

Forster, J. & Pope, N. (2004), *The Political Economy of Global Sporting Organisations*, New York: Routledge.

Horne, J. & Manzenreiter, W. (2004), 'Accounting for Mega-Events: Forecasts and Actual Impacts of the 2002 Football World Cup Finals on Host Countries Japan/Korea', *International Review for the Sociology of Sport*, 39(2): 187–203.

Jänicke, M. (2006), 'The Environmental State and Environmental Flows: The Need to Reinvent the Nation State', in G. Spaargaren, A. P. J. Mol & H. Bruyninckx (eds), *Governing Environmental Flows. Global Challenges to Social Theory*, Cambridge, MA: MIT Press.

Jennings, A. (2006), *Foul! The Secret World of FIFA: Bribes, Vote Rigging and Ticket Scandals*, London: Harper Sport.

Kersting, N. (2007), 'Sport and National Identity: A Comparison of the 2006 and 2010 FIFA World Cups™', *Politikon*, 34(3): 277–293.

Matheson, V. A. & Baade R. A. (2004), 'Mega-Sporting Events in Developing Nations: Playing the Way to Prosperity?', *The South African Journal of Economics*, 72(5): 1085–1096.

Meulders, B. (2009), 'Wedijveren voor ontwikkeling. Het wereldkampioenschap voetbal als ontwikkelingsmotor voor Zuid-Afrika?', in J. Scheerder & B. Meulders (eds), *Wedijver in een internationale arena: Sport, bestuur en macht*, Gent: Academia Press.

Mol, A. P. J. & Spaargaren, G. (2006), 'Towards a Sociology of Environmental Flows: A New Agenda for Twenty-First Century Environmental Sociology', in G. Spaargaren, A. P. J. Mol & H. Bruyninckx (eds), *Governing Environmental Flows. Global Challenges to Social Theory*, Cambridge, MA: MIT Press.

Nelissen, N. (2002), 'The Administrative Capacity of New Types of Governance', *Public Organization Review*, 2: 5–22.

Ngonyama, P. (2010), 'The 2010 FIFA World Cup: Critical Voices from Below', *Soccer & Society*, 11(1): 168–180.

Noll, R. & Zimbalist, A. (1997), *Sports, Jobs and Taxes*, Washington DC: Brookings Institution.

Pillay, U. (2004), 'Are Globally Competitive 'City Regions' Developing in South Africa? Formulaic Aspirations or New Imaginations?', *Urban Forum*, 15(4): 340–364.

Pillay, U. & Bass, O. (2008), 'Mega-Events as a Response to Poverty Reduction: The 2010 FIFA World Cup and Its Urban Development Implications', *Urban Forum*, 19(3): 329–346.

Pillay, U. & Bass, O. (2009), 'Mega-Events as a Response to Poverty Reduction: The 2010 World Cup and Urban Development', in U. Pillay, R. Tomlinson & O. Bass (eds), *Development and Dreams. The Urban Legacy of the 2010 Football World Cup*, Cape Town: HSRC Press.

Preuss, H. (2000), *Economics of the Olympic Games. Hosting the Games 1972–2000*, Sydney: Walla Walla Press.

Siemiatycki, M. (2006), 'Message in a Metro: Building Urban Rail Infrastructure and Image in Delhi, India', *International Journal of Urban and Regional Research*, 30(2): 277–292.

Spaargaren, G., Mol, A. P. J. & Bruyninckx, H. (2006), 'Introduction: Governing Environmental Flows in Global Modernity', in G. Spaargaren, A. P. J. Mol & H. Bruyninckx (eds), *Governing Environmental Flows. Global Challenges to Social Theory*, Cambridge, MA: MIT Press.

Stevis, D. & Bruyninckx, H. (2006), 'Looking Through the State at Environmental Flows and Governance', in G. Spaargaren, A. P. J. Mol & H. Bruyninckx (eds), *Governing Environmental Flows. Global Challenges to Social Theory*, Cambridge, MA: MIT Press.

Sugden, J. & Tomlinson, A. (1998), 'Power and Resistance in the Governance of World Football: Theorizing FIFA's Transnational Impact', *Journal of Sport & Social Issues*, 22(3): 299–316.

Swart, K. & Bob, U. (2007), 'The Eluding Link: Toward Developing a National Sport Tourism Strategy in South Africa Beyond 2010', *Politikon*, 34(3): 373–391.

Swinnen, J. F. M. & Vandemoortele, T. (2009), 'Sport en ontwikkeling: Een economische visie op de impact van de Wereldbeker 2010 in Zuid-Afrika', in J. Scheerder & B. Meulders (eds), *Wedijver in een internationale arena: Sport, bestuur en macht*, Gent: Academia Press.

Szymanski, S. (2002), 'The Economic Impact of the World Cup', *World Economics*, 3(1): 169–177.

Thornton, G. (2004), '2010 Soccer World Cup Facts You Should Know', online version accessed 4 September 2006 at: http://www.gauteng.net/research/pdf/soccer1.pdf.

Tomlinson, R. (2009), 'Anticipating 2011', in U. Pillay, R. Tomlinson & O. Bass (eds), *Development and Dreams. The Urban Legacy of the 2010 Football World Cup*, Cape Town: HSRC Press.

Tomlinson, R., Bass, O. & Pillay, U. (2009), 'Introduction', in U. Pillay, R. Tomlinson & O. Bass (eds), *Development and Dreams. The Urban Legacy of the 2010 Football World Cup*, Cape Town: HSRC Press.

van der Merwe, J. (2006), 'Comparing South Africa's Hosting of the Rugby and Cricket World Cups: Lessons for the 2010 Football World Cup and Beyond', paper presented at WISER, CUBES, HSRC and Goethe Institute Symposium on 2010 and the life of the city, Witwatersrand, September 2006.

van der Merwe, J. (2007), 'In Conversation with Justin van der Merwe: Safaris, Soccer and the Silver Screen', *HSRC Review*, 5(2), online version available at http://www.hsrc.ac.za/HSRC_Review_Article-56.phtml (accessed 20 September 2007).

#van der Merwe, J. (2009), 'The Road to Africa: South Africa's Hosting of the "African" World Cup', in U. Pillay, R. Tomlinson & O. Bass (eds), *Development and Dreams. The Urban Legacy of the 2010 Football World Cup*, Cape Town: HSRC Press.

van der Merwe, J. & van der Westhuizen, J. (2006), 'The Branding Game: The Role of Sport in South African Foreign Policy', *Global Insight*, 67: 1–3.

van der Westhuizen, J. (2007), 'Glitz, Glamour and the Gautrain: Mega-projects as Political Symbols', *Politikon*, 34(3): 333–351.

van Tatenhove, J. (1999), 'Political Modernisation and the Institutionalisation of Environmental Policy', in M. Wissenburg, G. Orhan & U. Collier (eds), *European Discourses on Environmental Policy*, Aldershot: Ashgate.

World Bank (2008), South Africa: Data and Statistics, online version accessed 125 April 2009 at: http://web.worldbank.org/wbsite/external/datastatistics.

11 Popular Deception by IOC and FIFA

Stefan Késenne

Every time a city or a nation offers to host the Olympic games or the World Cup, without fail a study appears of the economic impact on the host nation, region or city, which invariably and predictably tells of the marvelous economic benefits of such a mega-sporting event. These studies are usually commissioned by one or other lobby group which needs to find the results that will be approved by IOC (International Olympic Committee) or FIFA (International Federation of Football Association). If they do not, the study will disappear forever in a dark drawer or even the wastepaper basket. These studies are usually swarming with calculation errors: double counting, blanking out of effects of substitution, displacement and crowding-out, over-estimation of impacts through the use of unrealistic multipliers and dubious long-term effects. Even if the economic impact studies were to be correct they would still be meaningless because they do not provide the relevant information for the policy makers who need to decide on whether to support and subsidize a sporting event or not.

ECONOMIC IMPACTS, COSTS AND BENEFITS

What an economic impact study actually does is calculate the extra income flows, such as added value and income and the extra job opportunities and taxation revenues that a mega-sporting event creates. This suits the IOC and FIFA very well for these financial flows tell us nothing about the costs and revenues of the event for the natives of the host country and in particular nothing about who carries these costs (the taxpayer) and who pockets the revenue (the IOC and FIFA).

This useful information can only be gained through a serious cost-benefit analysis of the organization of a sporting event. A cost-benefit analysis differs fundamentally from an economic impact study because it separates out the income flows generated, which are bundled together in the former, into costs and benefits (see Késenne, 2005). Not all revenue flows are profits; for example, the income of workers building new stadiums ought to be counted as costs to the sporting organisation, but in most impact studies they are reckoned as benefits.

A vastly simplified example can illustrate the differences between a cost-benefit analysis, a correctly conducted economic impact study and a wrongly calculated one.

Let us assume that in order to organize a football game a new field needs to be laid out and that the only outlay will be the labour cost of 100,000 euro paid by the local council of the organizing region. To this end eighty workers are hired of which forty were jobless without unemployment benefits. Further assume that the general taxation rate, both income and value added, is 40 percent.

The spectators who come to watch are solely local inhabitants of the region and together spend 20,000 euro on tickets which are sold by the international sports federation, who also receive the television rights and sponsoring money up to the value of 50,000 euros. The incorrect impact study will present the results as in Table 11.1.

The correctly conducted impact study will take into account the crowding-out effects: if only forty of the eighty hired hands were unemployed, only forty new jobs are created and so only 50,000 euros of extra added value and income. The other forty are taken off another job, and this counts as a displacement effect. Moreover, there is also a potential loss of 20,000 euros to the region because local supporters spent it on tickets and assuming a constant savings rate, not on purchases with local suppliers. The ticket income of 20,000 euros goes straight to the international sporting federation. The net income generation in the host region is therefore only 30,000 euros and only twenty-four extra job opportunities. This more realistic impact study is given in Table 11.2.

If the sporting event were to reverse the tendency to save so that more cash were freed up for consumption, this could in turn have a negative long-term impact because, via a rise in interest rates, more productive investments would be discouraged. These correct figures look rather less attractive than the faulty calculations.

Table 11.1   Incorrect Economic Impact Study for Host Region

Income generation	120,000 euros
Job creation	96 jobs
Taxation revenue	48,000 euros

Table 11.2   The More Realistic Economic Impact Study for the Host Region

Income generation	30,000 euros
Job creation	24 jobs
Taxation revenue	12,000 euros

A cost-benefit analysis would show that the total opportunity cost of organizing this sporting event and therefore not the actual financial cost, was 90,000 euros. For forty workers were previously employed elsewhere and have been removed from other productive employment in the region or foreign workers would have had to be imported (like many Eastern European construction workers in the West). This represents an opportunity cost or leak of 50,000 euros. On top of this there is an opportunity cost of 20,000 euros for local suppliers because supporters have spent their money on tickets. Because this income is pocketed directly by the International Sport Federation it represents an additional leak of 20,000 euros.

The benefits of the event are the 20,000 euros in ticket sales, added to the consumer surplus which we can estimate at 10,000 euros. A consumer surplus arises when a supporter is prepared to pay over the odds for his ticket. Under certain circumstances it can be shown that the consumer surplus amounts to half of the sum spent on tickets. Together, the benefits are then 30,000 euros. The net profit for the organiser of the sport event is therefore negative:

Profit minus costs = 30,000—90,000 =−60,000 euros.

Economically, this is a bad deal for the host country. It becomes even more interesting when we try to find out who bears the costs and who walks away with the profits. Some of the winners are the newly employed forty workers who were jobless before and now have a net income after tax of 30,000 euros. Also in the winning camp are the local supporters with their consumer surplus of 10,000 euros. The losers are the local businesses who will see their income reduced by 12,000 euros. The biggest loser is the state (i.e., the taxpayer) of the host country who has forked out 100,000 euro to build the field and only recovered 12,000 in taxes. The taxpayer therefore loses no less than 88,000 euros. (See Table 11.3.)

When added up, this tallies exactly with the negative net profit of−60,000 euros (100,000 for the losers and 40,000 for the winners). What a contrast with the attractive results of the economic impact studies!

In this simplified example it is also clear that the big winners in these sporting events are the international sporting federations, namely FIFA and IOC. Their ticket sales (20,000), television rights and sponsorship deals (50,000) all together yield them 70,000. They could have mitigated the

Table 11.3   The Winners and Losers

Winners:	
40 workers (net income)	30,000 euros
Local supporters (consumer surplus)	10,000 euros
Losers:	
Local business (net income)	12,000 euros
State or taxpayer	88,000 euros

60,000 euro loss of the host nation with it but prefer to use the money to live in luxury for four years.

THE REAL FIGURES

The fictitious example above does not of course prove anything as it serves only to illustrate the difference between an economic impact study and a cost-benefit analysis. That is why we will present here a selection of quotations from renowned sport economists who have carried out serious and objective research on this topic.

'If the main argument for hosting a mega-event, like the Olympics, is its long-term economic impact, it is a waste of money' (Spilling, 1999).

'A new sports facility has an extremely small, perhaps even negative, effect on overall economic activity and employment' (Noll & Zimbalist, 1997).

'A proper measurement of the Super Bowl's economic impact would show that the event has had no impact' (Porter, 1999).

'Based on macroeconomic indicators, large sports events and sports stadiums have rarely identified significant net economic benefits, not in the short run, not in the long run' (Maennig & Hagn, 2008). This is the final result of studies of the Football World Cup in Germany in 1974 and in 2006.

'Even the most generous measure of net benefit of the Winter Olympics in Vancouver 2010—event benefits minus event costs—is negative (-$101m)' (McHugh, 2006).

From many serious studies carried out by the most respected sport economists in the world it is very clear that organizing large-scale sporting events does not bring significant positive economic benefits. On the contrary, the big losers are always the tax payers of the organizing country or town. The inhabitants of, for example, Montréal (Olympic Games of 1976) have had to pay a special tax until 2006 (that is, for thirty years) to finance the huge losses of the games. The IOC and FIFA are also to blame for this. By orchestrating a bidding round between competing candidate cities or countries and awarding the candidate promising the most modern, advanced, prestigious and expensive sporting infrastructure, they are also responsible for the huge increases in costs (40 billion euros for the Games in Beijing 2008). Both organisations often defend themselves with the argument that this wonderful infrastructure will benefit the local community for many years to come. First of all this argument does not hold in a cost-benefit analysis. If the sporting and other accommodation units would not have been built without the Games or World Cup, it implies that these investments had no political priority and that the financial means would have been allocated to other priorities, such as social housing in impoverished townships in South Africa. Moreover Olympic installations are often broken down after the Games because they cannot be exploited profitably or upkeep proves to be too expensive. In Portugal some of the football stadiums built for Euro 2004 will be demolished. In Cape Town there were already plans, even before WC 2010 had begun and the stadium was finished, to break down their ultra-modern and highly expensive Green-Point stadium. That would also be an extra cost. This ought to be a lesson for small countries like Belgium and the Netherlands when hoping to attract the World Cup of 2018. This would need, in Belgium alone, five new stadiums of 40,000 seats each minimum (FIFA regulation). One can guess who would pay the lion's share of these costs. What would happen to them after the World Cup? There are no teams in Belgium that could attract 40,000 spectators on average. The big stadiums would therefore not be commercially interesting to Belgian clubs. The question then is why so many countries vie for the opportunity to host events like the Olympic Games and the World Cup? The answer can only be that political prestige is at stake or that politicians allow themselves to be misled by the senseless economic impact studies that they are bombarded with (see Baade & Matheson, 2002).

CONCLUSION

Does all this mean it would be better not to organise the Olympic Games or World Cup at all? Certainly not. Both events are particularly fascinating and often well-organized and of the highest level allowing brilliant athletes to compete and give enjoyment to many people (including this author) in stadiums or on television. My only contention is that we should stop persuading the people that the organisation of such events brings more economic and financial benefits than costs to a country.

REFERENCES

Baade, R. & Matheson, V. (2002), 'Bidding for the Olympics, Fools' Gold?', in C. Barros, M. Ibrahimo & S. Szymanski, (eds), *Transatlantic Sport: The Comparative Economics of North American and European Sports*, Cheltenham: Edward Elgar.

Késenne, S. (2005), 'Do We Need an Economic Impact Study or a Cost-Benefit Analysis of a Sports event?', *European Sport Management Quarterly*, 5(2): 133–142.

Maennig, W. & Hagn, F. (2008), 'Employment Effects of the Football World Cup 1974 in Germany', *Labour Economics*, 15(5): 1062–1075.

McHugh, D. (2006), 'A Cost-Benefit Analysis of an Olympic Games', accessed 9 March 2012 at at SSRN: http://ssrn.com/abstract=974724.

Noll, R. & Zimbalist, A. (1997), *Sports, Jobs and Taxes, the Economic Impact of Sports Teams and Stadiums*, Washington, DC: Brookings Institution Press.

Porter, P. (1999), 'Mega-sports Events as Municipal Investments: A Critique of Impact Analysis', in J. Fizel, E. Gustafson & L. Hadley (eds), *Sports Economics: Current Research*, Westport: Greenwood Publishing Group.

Spilling, O. (1999), 'Long-term Impacts of Mega-events: The Case of Lillehammer 1994', in C. Jeanrenaud (ed.), *The Economic Impact of Sports Events*, Neuchâtel: Editions CIES, Université de Neuchâtel.

12 Football Academies and Player Migration in Developing Countries

Jeroen Schokkaert, Johan F. M. Swinnen and Thijs Vandemoortele

Ever since the establishment of the World Cup in the early 1930s, migration of football players between different countries has been an important element of professional football competitions (Taylor, 2006). Football migration has been predominantly arranged through intermediary agents and scouts who actively recruit foreign players on the transfer market (Cornelissen & Solberg, 2007). This type of migration increased with the 1995 Bosman ruling, which removed restrictions on the number of foreign players that European clubs could recruit from other European countries. The ruling was later extended to include other countries (and sports) by the Malaja, Kolpak and Simutenkov cases and the 2000 Cotonou agreement.[1]

However, similar to general concerns that international migration drains developing countries of their human capital (i.e., the so-called brain drain[2]), the globalisation of the market for football players has been accused of causing a 'muscle drain' in developing countries by depriving them of their most talented players for the benefit of rich countries' leagues (see e.g. Gerrard, 2002; Magee & Sugden, 2002; Andreff, 2004; 2009; Poli, 2006a; 2006b; 2008; Darby, 2007a; 2007b; Darby, Akindes & Kirwin, 2007).[3] In an attempt to mitigate these alleged negative effects of football migration from developing countries to developed countries, FIFA (Fédération Internationale de Football Association) introduced a new set of transfer regulations in 2001 (Darby, 2007b). The key clauses of these new regulations on migration of players from developing countries consist of a training compensation, a solidarity mechanism, and better protection of minors (Gerrard, 2002; Andreff, 2004).[4]

Despite the introduction of these stricter transfer regulations, football migration from developing countries—especially Africa—has continued to increase over the past decade. The growing migration of African football players has been facilitated by the emergence of a particular organisational structure to train and transfer African players, namely football academies. These academies can be broadly defined as 'facilities or coaching programs designed to produce football talent' (Darby et al., 2007: 148) and serve as an institutional instrument to transfer talented African football players to European leagues, in addition to the traditional transfer system through intermediary agents and scouts (see, e.g., Cornelissen & Solberg, 2007; Darby, 2007b; Darby et al., 2007; Darby & Solberg, 2010).

Football clubs can use two different methods to source football players from a certain country, namely the establishment of a football academy or the recruitment of players on the transfer market. This chapter discusses the economic rationale behind these two recruitment strategies and investigates its relationship with a country's economic development. Our prediction is that a change in economic development involves a trade-off between the different costs of both recruitment strategies. We provide empirical evidence and compare two countries with different levels of economic development, namely Senegal and South Africa.

The rest of this chapter is organised as follows. The second section discusses the economic rationale behind the recruitment strategies of football clubs. The next two sections present the characteristics of football academies and the transfer market in Senegal and South Africa. The last section concludes.

THE ECONOMIC RATIONALE BEHIND RECRUITMENT STRATEGIES OF FOOTBALL CLUBS

The organisation of a football club and its recruitment strategies show some interesting similarities with that of a commercial firm (Ericson, 2000). Firstly, both employees and football players participate as members of a team and invest continuously in their human capital during their career via formal training programs and informal on-the-job training. Secondly, both employees and football players have a market value as a potential team member of another firm. Firms and football clubs can obtain high-quality workers either by training their own workers or by using the market to attract workers trained by other firms. In football, setting up a football academy to train young players is an extreme version of such in-house training. The other extreme is to purchase ready-trained players on the transfer market. In economics, one refers to the latter organisational form as 'spot market' transactions, while the former is a typical example of vertical integration (VI) in which a downstream agent owns the upstream company.[5]

Transfers of players from developing countries to leagues in developed countries have been organised predominantly through a network of agents and scouts recruiting players on the transfer market (Cornelissen & Solberg, 2007). Although this spot market strategy is still widely used, factors such as stricter transfer regulations have triggered the growth of football academies as an additional means to source talented football players from less-developed countries.

In the remainder of this section, we explain the economic motivations behind the recruitment strategies of football clubs. We introduce a conceptual framework that allows comparison, from a club's point of view of the costs and benefits of either setting up a football academy or recruiting players on the transfer market. Using our conceptual framework, we investigate how economic development of a country may influence the recruitment strategy of a club to either establish a football academy in that country or to recruit football players from that country on the transfer market.[6]

A Conceptual Framework

In a competitive football players' labour market, a club needs to employ a certain number of high-quality players to generate revenues by providing and winning football games. We assume that a club has only two ways of recruiting high quality players: a club has to decide whether to employ players who are trained in a football academy (VI strategy) or who are recruited on the transfer market (spot market strategy).[7] Clubs will compare the costs and benefits of both strategies.

We first discuss the costs and benefits of the VI strategy. In general, a club's revenue, strictly speaking, increases with the quality of its football players (Feess & Stähler, 2009). When a club establishes its own football academy to recruit and train players, it suffers the risk that the young trainee will not evolve into a professional football player.[8] Hence, a club's expected revenue depends on the probability of training a young trainee endowed with the necessary skills to become a high-quality player after training.[9] The costs of the VI strategy are actually investment costs and bureaucratic costs. The investment costs are both set-up costs and operating costs. Set-up costs are the fixed costs of either acquiring a stake in an existing academy or setting up the necessary football (and educational) facilities. The operating costs involve variable training costs such as, amongst others, wage costs of the academy's employees, purchasing football (and educational) equipment, costs of providing accommodation, etc.[10] These investment costs increase with the quality of the football players (Fella, 2005). The other costs of the VI strategy are bureaucratic costs. These costs relate to decreased incentives of owners and other bureaucratic distortions that might occur under internal organisation (Williamson, 1985).

The spot market strategy involves costs and benefits of a different nature. When a club purchases a player on the transfer market, the player is transferred to a club of high quality, observable from previous performance in football competitions (Kahn, 2000). The revenue that a club generates through the employment of high-quality football players from the transfer market is on average higher than the expected revenue of a club that establishes a football academy because of the uncertainty regarding the final quality of football academy graduates. The costs on the transfer market are transaction costs and the transfer price. Transaction costs can be broken down into four costs, namely search costs, contracting costs, monitoring costs and enforcement costs (Williamson, 1985; North, 1990).[11] In the football labour market, search costs consist of both the wage costs of talent scouts and agents who search for highly talented players, and the costs of coordinating this recruitment process. The latter three costs can be generalised into the bargaining costs with respect to a player's contract. The transfer price is the other cost of spot market transactions in the football player's labour market.[12]

The different costs and benefits of the two recruitment strategies imply a trade-off that determines which strategy is optimal for a club. A club will establish a football academy instead of sourcing a player on the spot market if, and only if, the sum of transaction costs and the transfer price of transfer market recruitment exceed foregone revenues, investment costs and the bureaucratic costs of football academy recruitment.

So far, our conceptual framework points at the recruitment strategies of football clubs as 'pure strategies' (i.e., as either sourcing players through the establishment of a football academy or through recruitment on the transfer market). However, in reality, the recruitment policy of nearly all football clubs is oriented towards a 'mixed strategy' of both training players in a football academy and recruiting players on the transfer market.[13] The reason for adopting a mixed strategy is that the transfer market has some additional benefits with respect to the establishment of a football academy which are not taken up in the costs and revenues already discussed. For example, most football academies source their players from a rather geographically restricted area, whereas the spot market allows tapping into the global talent pool. Another crucial advantage of the transfer market is its recruitment flexibility in case of an unexpected need for replacement or in case of a need for players that have already gained substantial experience in professional football competitions.

The Effect of Economic Development

Football clubs may look for players in their own country or in other countries. The optimal recruitment strategy may differ depending on the characteristics of the country where it wants to recruit players from (the country of 'origin' or source country). This issue is particularly important when analysing the flow of African players to European clubs. Through a comparison of how the different costs are affected, we can analyse how a source country's economic development may influence the recruitment strategy of football clubs to import football players from that country.

With respect to the VI strategy of the establishment of a football academy, two opposing forces are at work. First, investment costs are positively related to the source country's economic development, amongst others due to increasing labour and input costs (Krugman & Obstfeld, 2006). Second, bureaucratic costs decrease in a source country's economic development through the higher quality of institutions. An increase in economic development improves the quality of a country's institutions (North, 1990), and higher quality of institutions decreases the organisational distortions in establishing a firm (Meyer, 2001).

Also, with respect to the spot market strategy of transfer market recruitment of football players, a trade-off exists between two effects. First, similar to bureaucratic costs under the VI strategy, a negative relationship exists between the source country's economic development and transactions costs on the spot market (North, 1990). An increase in a country's economic development increases the quality of its institutions and hence reduces transaction costs. Second, an increase in the source country's economic development has a positive impact on the transfer price. Wealthier countries are likely to spend more time and resources on leisure activities, including sports such as football (Houston & Wilson, 2002). The resulting increase in demand for football creates an upward pressure on the transfer price of players on the transfer market.[14]

In summary, our analysis suggests that a change in a source country's economic development has multiple effects. First, when a country's economic development increases, the establishment of a football academy becomes more attractive because of decreasing bureaucratic costs, but less so due to increasing investment costs. Secondly, when a country's economic development increases, recruitment on the transfer market becomes more expensive due to a higher transfer price but less expensive because of lower transaction costs. Consequently, the effect of economic development on the recruitment strategy of football clubs is ambiguous from a conceptual perspective, and the effect may go in either direction.

Empirical Evidence

In the rest of this chapter, we present empirical evidence on this issue by studying football academies and the transfer market in two African countries: Senegal and South Africa. Per capita income in South Africa is more than seven times higher than per capita income in Senegal (IMF, 2010). Hence, by comparing football academies and the transfer market of these two countries with different levels of economic development, the results may shed light on our hypotheses on the effect of a change in economic development on the costs of recruiting players either through the establishment of a football academy or through recruitment on the transfer market.

FOOTBALL ACADEMIES

In this section, we describe several football academies based on our own field research in Senegal and South Africa. Information on the characteristics of football academies was gathered during extensive interviews with directors, coaches and other officials of several football academies in Senegal and South Africa. The Senegalese data were gathered during

Table 12.1 Main Characteristics of Selected Football Academies, Senegal and South Africa

Name	Country	Year of Foundation	Type	Academic Education	Boarding School	Registration Fee (Euro)	Admission Test	Number of Students
CASE	Senegal	1991	Formal	Full	Limited	1,740 to 1,920	Limited	175
Alizé Elite Foot	Senegal	2000	Formal	Limited	Limited	Around 900	Limited	Around 65
Kenza Mariste	Senegal	2005	Formal	None	Limited	0	Limited	160
SAFA-Transnet	South Africa	1994	Formal	Full	Yes	0	Yes	100
Diambars	South Africa	2010	Formal	Full	Yes	0	Yes	20
CUSSE	South Africa	2009	Formal	Limited	Yes	0	Yes	32
Ajax	South Africa	1999	Formal	None	No	0	Yes	Around 120
Cape Town	South Africa	2005	Informal	None	No	0	No	20-40
Durrheim	South Africa	2001	Informal	Full	No	0	No	150

Notes: (i) Information with regard to Senegal based on fieldwork in 2007, information with regard to South Africa based on fieldwork in 2010. (ii) Diambars Senegal and Génération Foot were not visited, so these football academies are not included in the table.

semi-structured, qualitative interviews from July to August 2007 in the region of Dakar. Additional information was gathered during an interview with the director of administration of the Fédération Sénégalaise de Football (FSF). The South African data were gathered during semi-structured, qualitative interviews in September 2010 in the regions of Cape Town and Johannesburg. Table 12.1 lists a summary of the main characteristics of these football academies.

Football academies in developing countries have been established both in the formal and in the informal economy (Darby, 2010).[15] In general, most of the academies belonging to the formal sector adopt a professional approach to football training and offer additional services to their trainees. Frequently, on top of professional football training, these football academies provide official academic education and supply the requisite football equipment, medical support and physiotherapy. This contrasts with the academies belonging to the informal sector, which are established on an ad hoc basis, have poorly qualified staff and facilities and do not offer additional services such as academic education.

Football Academies in Senegal

In this section, several Senegalese football academies from the region of Dakar are discussed. Field work revealed that academies belonging to the informal sector grew rapidly in Senegal in the wake of the national team's outstanding performance at the 2002 World Cup.[16] According to the FSF, there are nearly 300 such football academies in the region of Dakar alone. Unfortunately, we were unable to structurally survey these informal football academies. In the following we provide information on the formal academies.

Collège Africain Sports-Études

One of the most important professional football academies in Dakar is the Collège Africain Sports-Études (CASE), a football training centre that additionally provides basketball and tennis training. The centre was established in 1992 as the Centre Aldo Gentina by El Hadji Malick Sy, the current president of CASE and former Senegalese Minister of Tourism and former President of the FSF.

Initially, the academy consisted of a partnership between the Senegalese club ASC Jeanne d'Arc and the French club AS Monaco. In exchange for a substantial financial contribution, AS Monaco had the right to select the best players that graduated from the centre. In the first decade, the centre only provided football training. Since 2004, the centre added official academic (secondary) education and other sports training. To emphasize this fundamental change in priorities, the centre altered its name to CASE. According to the president, the reason for this turnaround and focus on academic education was that every child, whether it becomes a professional football player or not, needs a decent basic education. First, he argues, not all graduates are able to enter into a professional football career. For these trainees, regular academic education is of the utmost importance in successfully entering the regular labour market. Secondly, those pupils who do become professional football players also need an academic education that allows them to understand and negotiate their future football contracts and to understand the tactical explanations of coaches. Additionally, even professional football players may need to enter the regular labour market at the end of their football career.

Around the time of its priority switch, CASE lost its funding from AS Monaco after some management restructuring at the French club.[17] Due to the subsequent lack of funds, the centre entered into some sponsorship deals with foreign and domestic corporations in order to secure (financial) stability and the smooth functioning of the centre. Additionally, the academy introduced substantial registration fees.[18] Each year around thirty pupils who lack financial means are selected on the basis of their football talent and offered a scholarship that exempts them from the registration fee. Other players are not subject to selection criteria for admission.

Besides revenues from sponsors and registration fees, the transfers of some of their players also generate revenues.[19] These transfers to, or testing of players with foreign clubs, proceed according to national and international FIFA transfer regulations. In 2007, there were 175 students enrolled (12 to 20 years old). The trainees mainly originate from Dakar and its surroundings but some also come from other regions in Senegal or even from other African countries.

Alizé Elite Foot

Another football academy in Dakar is Alizé Elite Foot, established in 2000 by retired Senegalese internationals such as Pape Idrissa Thiam, a former professional football player in France. Additional funds are provided by an anonymous private U.S. partner.

From the outset, this football academy has been providing some academic education—for the same reasons as CASE. However, while CASE delivers graduates with an officially recognised secondary degree, Alizé Elite Foot does not provide the complete package of secondary academic education. Instead, they organise specific courses to develop what they consider to be important assets for a future professional football career, such as courses in information technology, English and French. Additionally, only the resident pupils (around fifteen) have an academic commitment while the non-residents (around fifty) do not.[20]

The resident pupils pay a registration fee but those in financial distress are exempt.[21] Students are mainly from the Dakar region and are between 11 and 19 years old. Formerly, the centre organised week-long football trials to test future pupils. Although the youngest cohorts are still subject to these tests, they are no longer conditional for entry to the academy. Transfers of players to, and tests with, European clubs are managed by the president of the centre, who resides in France and concentrates his efforts on establishing networks with European clubs.

Kenza Mariste

Kenza Mariste was established in 2005 by an African businessman Djibril Traoré.[22] The academy does not provide any academic education but compels its pupils to show their monthly school reports. Children who perform below par at (regular) school are banned from the football academy until their academic performance is again at an acceptable level.

Until the age of fifteen, trainees are not subject to any qualifying trials to enrol in the academy; older trainees are tested on their football talent before admission.[23] No registration fee is charged, and the centre has no strategic partnerships or other funds.[24] The academy has no limit on capacity and all trainees are non-residents. In 2007, 160 trainees between the ages of 5 and 18 were enrolled, mainly from the Dakar region but also from other parts of Senegal and other African countries.

The academy has a small boarding school to temporarily accommodate those trainees who are accepted for performing tests with a foreign club. Transfers of players to foreign clubs are arranged through official agents.

The Diambars Institute

The Diambars Institute, a professional football academy, operates both in Senegal and South Africa. Located south of Dakar at Saly, Diambars Senegal was established in 2003 by Saer Seck, the Vice-President of the FSF, Patrick Vieira and Bernard Lama, two retired French internationals, and Jimmy Adjovi-Boco, a retired Beninese international. The first official partners of the Diambars Institute (at that time only in Senegal) were the French Nord-Pas-de-Calais region and the Senegalese government. The former financed the feasibility studies of the Diambars project; the latter donated the site on which Diambars Senegal was built (Mbapndah, 2010). Graduates from Diambars Senegal are currently playing for clubs in the first divisions of France and Norway.

Génération Foot

Established in 2000 by a former football player Mady Touré, Génération Foot is currently in partnership with the French club FC Metz. FC Metz provides the academy with the necessary football equipment and the trainees with educational guidance. In return, the French club is granted first choice of the best graduates. With the support of 'godfathers' such as the Togolese ex-international Emmanuel Adebayor and the Senegalese international Babacar Gueye, Génération Foot has been remarkably successful in transferring its graduates to European professional leagues.[25]

Football Academies in South Africa

In this section, we describe a set of South African football academies from the region of Johannesburg and Cape Town. Table 12.1 summarises their main characteristics.

SAFA-Transnet Football School of Excellence

Located in Johannesburg, the SAFA-Transnet Football School of Excellence is the 'flagship of soccer development' in South Africa (McKinley, 2010: 91). The football academy was established in 1994 by the South African Football Association (SAFA) and Transnet, South Africa's national transport company. Within this partnership, SAFA provides the technical know-how, skills training and equipment support, and Transnet provides the working budget.

Admission to the academy—except for the school uniform—is free. The academy provides both academic education and football training. Pupils follow the official South African educational program. All players are resident pupils, most of the time also during weekends because of the remoteness of the trainees' home towns. To recruit trainees, the academy's coaches attend trials organised by several football clubs in different South African provinces. SAFA-Transnet applies a rotational system such that each year around twenty players graduate and are replaced by new freshmen.

The SAFA-Transnet Football School of Excellence has delivered several football players who are now playing in European leagues or in the South African Premier Soccer League.[26] On top of that, several academy players have successfully obtained a university degree after graduating from the football academy.

The Diambars Institute

Another South African football academy in Johannesburg, the Diambars Institute, is an expansion of the successful Senegalese project (see above). Diambars South Africa was formally established in 2010 with a first intake of twenty players.[27] The Diambars Institute is supported by a large group of committed partners, both in Senegal and South Africa. Aside from the involvement of ex-internationals such as Patrick Vieira and Bernard Lama, the Diambars Institute also attracts sponsorships from large (sports) companies such as Adidas.

Due to a delay in acquiring authorisation to set up its own educational and sports infrastructure, the football academy temporarily collaborates with a public school in Boksburg, a city near Johannesburg. All players are resident pupils and are currently accommodated at the public school in Boksburg which is also endowed with football training facilities. Academy trainees follow regular classes with the other (non-Diambars) students. In contrast to the SAFA-Transnet Football School of Excellence where the pass rate equals almost 100 percent, the director of Diambars South Africa stressed that pupils who continuously perform below par at school will be dismissed from the Diambars Institute.[28]

Trainees are only recruited after a rigorous selection procedure and are required to meet criteria of academic proficiency, football talent and a particular demographic and geographic representation. No registration fees are charged. The institute's financial sustainability is ensured by revenues from renting out the academy's facilities for activities such as football camps and corporate programs by FIFA's training compensation and by fundraising operations. The project in South Africa is still in its infancy, but if results live up to those of Diambars Senegal, the outlook is positive.

Cape United Soccer School of Excellence

Another recently established football academy is Cape United Soccer School of Excellence (CUSSE) in Cape Town. It was founded in 2009 by the English businessman Mike Steptoe and the former South African football player, coach and manager Colin Gie. CUSSE was able to acquire its facilities through funds raised with private investors and (former) professional football players such as the English ex-international Ian Wright. CUSSE owns a residential school, where players between the ages of fifteen and eighteen can stay.

In contrast to the above two South African football academies, CUSSE only offers an unofficial and specific academic curriculum with English and mathematics as core subjects, largely similar to Alizé Elite Foot in Senegal. The main priority of CUSSE is developing the footballing skills of the players.

Currently, thirty-two trainees are registered with the academy, mainly from the Western and Eastern Cape provinces. There are also some players from some other African countries. Selection of the trainees is based on open trials, organised during academic holidays. No registration fee is charged. Concentrating their efforts on establishing transfer networks with European clubs, CUSSE expects considerable revenues from transfer fees of some of their graduates in the near future.

Ajax Cape Town

In 1999, the Dutch club Ajax acquired a 51 percent controlling stake in the merger of two Cape Town clubs, Seven Stars and Cape Town Spurs. Ajax subsequently renamed the merger club to Ajax Cape Town and simultaneously created its well-known football academy near Cape Town. The Ajax Cape Town team participates in the PSL.

The Ajax Cape Town football academy does not provide any academic tuition. All trainees are non-residents and the football academy transports its pupils from their regular school to the football academy. However, two days per week, the academy organises tutoring for its trainees. In addition, the football academy monitors the academic grades of its trainees through contact with the pupils' parents and regular teachers.

Currently the football academy organises open trials to recruit trainees. However, to improve its recruitment efficiency, the management will switch to a new recruitment strategy by establishing its own scouting network in the Cape Town province. The pupils are enrolled in the academy from the age of 10 until the age of 18, after which they either join the senior Ajax Cape Town team or leave the club. According to club officials, around 70 percent of the senior Ajax Cape Town team has been trained in its academy. Additionally, the academy's ambition is to transfer one or two graduates per year to Ajax. Unfortunately, no complete data are available on the frequency with which academy graduates are transferred to other teams in the PSL or overseas. Since the football academy is part of the professional Ajax Cape Town club, daily academy activities are financed through the club's general revenues, mainly consisting of broadcasting revenues and commercial revenues.[29]

The final South African football academy is an example of a more informal football academy. In South Africa, numerous such academies were established around the time of its hosting of the 2010 World Cup. The one discussed here already existed before this.

Durrheim Soccer Academy

The Durrheim Soccer Academy was founded in 2006 in Charlesville near Cape Town. Football trainings are organised twice a week and take place on a football field without goals, provided for free by the local community. The academy owner finances the other necessary football equipment. Every child between the ages of 8 and 15 is allowed to join the academy at no cost. Although trainees only play friendly games on a monthly basis, the purpose of the academy is to set up a network by integrating their graduates into academies of local professional clubs. Up to now no single trainee has succeeded in signing a contract with a professional club, neither in South Africa nor in Europe.

THE TRANSFER MARKET

In this section, we compare the transfer markets of South Africa and Senegal with each other.

Table 12.2   Migration Patterns of Graduated Academy Players, Senegal and South Africa

Academy	Country	Player	Current Team	League	Division
Génération Foot	Senegal	Babacar Gueye	Alemannia Aachen	Germany	2
Génération Foot	Senegal	Cheikh Gueye	FC Metz	France	2
Génération Foot	Senegal	Momar N'Diaye	FSV Frankfurt	Germany	2
Génération Foot	Senegal	Papiss Cissé	SC Freiburg	Germany	1
Génération Foot	Senegal	Oumar Pouye	FC Metz	France	2
Génération Foot	Senegal	Rahmane Barry	AS Beauvais	France	3
Génération Foot	Senegal	Mamadou Baldé	Langon Castets FC	France	5
Génération Foot	Senegal	Moustapha Sall	AS Saint-Étienne	France	1
Génération Foot	Senegal	Baye Fall	Locomotiv Moscow	Russia	1
Diambars	Senegal	Diafra Sakho	FC Metz	France	2
Diambars	Senegal	Omar Wade	Lille OSC	France	1
Diambars	Senegal	Papa Souré	Lille OSC	France	1
Diambars	Senegal	Idrissa Gueye	Lille OSC	France	1
Diambars	Senegal	Papa N'Diaye	ASC Xam Xam	Senegal	1
Diambars	Senegal	Serigne Mbodj	Tromsø IL	Norway	1

Continued

Table 12.2 Continued

Academy	Country	Player	Current Team	League	Division
Safa-Transnet	Senegal	Saliou Ciss	Tromsø IL	Norway	1
Safa-Transnet	South Africa	Bryce Moon	Golden Arrows	South Africa	1
Safa-Transnet	South Africa	Daine Klate	Orlando Pirates	South Africa	1
Safa-Transnet	South Africa	Mabuti Khenyeza	Mamelodi Sundowns	South Africa	1
Safa-Transnet	South Africa	Masilo Modubi	KVC Westerlo	Belgium	1
Safa-Transnet	South Africa	Jeffrey Ntuka	SuperSport United	South Africa	1
Safa-Transnet	South Africa	Bernard Parker	FC Twente	The Netherlands	1
Safa-Transnet	South Africa	Jackson Mabokgwane	Mamelodi Sundowns	South Africa	1
Ajax Cape Town	South Africa	Couldrin Coetzee	Platinum Stars FC	South Africa	1
Ajax Cape Town	South Africa	Clifford Ngobeni	Orlando Pirates	South Africa	1
Ajax Cape Town	South Africa	Franklin Cale	Mamelodi Sundowns FC	South Africa	1
Ajax Cape Town	South Africa	Nathan Paulse	Bloemfontein Celtic	South Africa	1
Ajax Cape Town	South Africa	Stanton Lewis	Ajax Cape Town	South Africa	1
Ajax Cape Town	South Africa	Daylon Claasen	Lierse SK	Belgium	

In South Africa, football became more professional and commercial with the inception of the Premier Soccer League in 1996 (Cornelissen & Solberg, 2007; Darby & Solberg, 2010). Corporate sponsorship and broadcasting revenue has transformed many local clubs into professional football clubs that employ players who are relatively well paid, have access to good training and facilities and enjoy a certain degree of labour protection. Therefore, the PSL has been able to retain skilled South African football players and attract football players from foreign African countries (Cornelissen & Solberg, 2007; Darby & Solberg, 2010).[30] In contrast, in Senegal, organisational weaknesses and the fragility of the professional sporting economy have dominated the domestic football league, which is unattractive for skilled Senegalese football players (Lafranchi & Taylor, 2001). As a consequence, Senegalese football players aspire to foreign football careers and migrate to Europe whenever the opportunity presents itself.

These observations suggest that the majority of South African players are employed by domestic clubs, whereas the majority of Senegalese players are employed by European clubs. Table 12.2 provides evidence for these migration patterns. It lists the current football clubs of academy players who graduated during the last decade from the two most successful football academies in both countries, namely Génération Foot and The Diambars Institute in Senegal and SAFA-Transnet Football School of Excellence and Ajax Cape Town in South Africa. Table 12.2 shows that successful Senegalese graduates have almost exclusively been transferred to European clubs, whereas the majority of graduates from South African football academies are employed by domestic South African clubs.[31]

These findings are also consistent with the migration flows of Senegalese and South African football players towards clubs from the 'Big Five' European football leagues England, Spain, Germany, Italy and France. From the 2005/06 season until the 2008/09 season, 'Big Five' clubs employed on average twenty-eight Senegalese players and only seven South African players (CIES, 2011).

CONCLUSION

In this chapter comparison has been made between—from a club's point of view—the costs and benefits of recruiting football players either by setting up a football academy or by recruiting on the transfer market. Furthermore, the effect of a change in a country's economic development on the costs of these two recruitment strategies has been investigated. We provided empirical evidence and compared two countries with different levels of economic development, namely Senegal and South Africa. The analysis of several football academies and the transfer market in Senegal and South Africa highlighted some interesting observations.

First, foreign club involvement in football academies in developing countries seems to be rather modest. In our sample, only one VI strategy exists in which a foreign club owns a football academy in a developing country. This is the South African club Ajax Cape Town, in which the Dutch club Ajax has a controlling stake. The establishment of a football academy requires a substantial upfront set-up cost, which seems to deter football clubs from developed countries to vertically integrate with football academies/clubs from developing countries. This is confirmed by our observation that, rather than acquiring controlling stakes in football clubs, by establishing official partnerships, European clubs set up a new academy—or upgrade an existing one—in exchange for a free transfer of its best graduates. Examples are the Senegalese football academy Génération Foot, which has an official partnership with the French club FC Metz and Feyenoord Fetteh, a Ghanaian football academy set up by the Dutch club Feyenoord.

Second, field research revealed that football academies in developing countries are often established by (former) football players and/or (foreign) companies. In the spirit of our conceptual framework, these representatives are often able to raise sufficient means to finance the set-up costs of the football academy. Moreover, operational costs are partially financed by revenues from transfer fees of some of their graduates. In our sample, notable examples of such football academies are Alizé Elite Foot, the Diambars Institute and CUSSE.[32]

A third finding relates to the analysis of the transfer market in Senegal and South Africa. We observe that most successful Senegalese football players have been transferred to European clubs and that the majority of South African football players are employed by domestic South African clubs. Within our conceptual framework, the higher concentration of high-quality players in the more developed country South Africa is likely to lower search costs on the transfer market. Since these search costs are part of the transaction costs, transaction costs of transfer market recruitment will be lower in the more developed source country. Moreover, the trend towards commercialisation of football in South Africa resulted in increasing attraction to the game from wealthy individuals inside and outside football (Kunene, 2006). This increase in demand for football creates an upward pressure on the transfer price. This analysis seems to confirm our prediction that the effect of an increase in a source country's economic development has both a positive and a negative effect on the costs of recruitment of football players on the transfer market. While transaction costs decrease, the transfer price increases.

Although football academies play an important role in the migration of African football players, many aspects remain open for future research. Empirically, we are extending our research to locate and characterise additional African football academies and those in other continents and to further analyse differences between football academies, both within and between (African) countries. Additionally, there is at present no theoretical framework to formalise this type of institutional migration. Future research will develop formal theoretical analyses to gain future insights in the economic incentives and organisation of (African) football academies.

NOTES

1. The Malaja, Kolpak and Simutenkov cases extended the Bosman jurisprudence to different sports and to citizens of Central Eastern European countries and 'of former Soviet Republics of the Commonwealth of Independent States (CIS) (Andreff, 2006). The 2000 Cotonou agreement, signed by the European Union and seventy-seven African, Caribbean and Pacific countries, allows athlete transfers from the latter area under the qualification of assimilated Europeans (Chaix, 2004). For more information, see Berlinschi, Schokkaert and Swinnen (2010).

2. However, recent empirical work shows that the 'brain drain' is generally limited (see, e.g., Adams, 2003) and that the net impact may even turn into a 'brain gain' when dynamic investment effects are taken into account (see, e.g., Boucher, Stark & Taylor, 2009).

3. See Swinnen and Vandemoortele (2009) for a critical review.

4. More specifically, a compensation for training costs incurred between the ages of 12 and 21 has to be paid to the club which provided the training when the player signed his first professional contract and on each subsequent transfer to another team, up to the age of 23. Additionally, the solidarity mechanism guarantees that five percent of all transfer payments for players over the age of 23 is redistributed to those clubs involved in the training of the player from the age of 12 to 23. Finally, international transfers of minors are prohibited unless the player's family migrates for non-football-related reasons.

5. Important theoretical contributions in the area of vertical integration include Williamson (1975; 1985), Klein, Crawford and Alchian (1978), Grossman and Hart (1986), and Hart and Moore (1990). We make abstraction of existing hybrid forms of recruiting football players such as cooperation agreements between clubs from higher ranked leagues and lower ranked 'feeder clubs' to lend out players to the feeder team, allowing them to gain experience.

6. The transfer market is a global trading place for football players. However, we focus on the transfer market of players within one country to allow a ceteris paribus analysis with respect to the strategy of the establishment of a football academy.

7. Terviö (2006) provides a model that determines the fraction of football clubs that decides to recruit inexperienced players with unknown talent or experienced players with known talent. Focusing on European professional football, he omits training because, as he argues, training costs are negligible compared to the high level of transfer fees that are observed within and across these wealthy football leagues.

8. In general, the chances of becoming a professional football player after training are low. Moreover, attrition rates are higher than in other industries (Monk, 2000).

9. We refrain from including registration fees as extra revenues, which often accompany the establishment of a football academy.

10. Operating costs also include the search costs of selecting young trainees to enrol in the academy. If no such selection process exists, uncertainty regarding the graduates' final quality increases.

11. Liebermann (1991) argues that the presence of transaction costs in the spot market is one of the main determinants of vertical integration. For example, vertical integration is more common in countries and sectors where it is more difficult to conclude long-term contracts between upstream and downstream firms (see, e.g., Williamson, 1975; 1985).

12. Since the 1995 Bosman ruling, a transfer price is no longer applicable to players who are transferred after expiration of their contract with their club.

Since in that case the club foregoes substantial revenues, the policy of professional clubs is to sell their players when they are still under contract (Ericson, 2000; Feess, Gerfin & Muehlheusser, 2010). In general, transfer prices have been defended as a necessary incentive for clubs to invest in training of young players (see, e.g., Simmons, 1997; Antonioni & Cubbin, 2000; Feess & Muehlheusser, 2003; Terviö, 2006).

13. This corresponds with equilibrium behaviour in the general labour market where firms obtain high-quality workers by training their own workers and by purchasing workers that are trained by other firms (Guasch & Sobel, 1983).

14. Several other factors such as the contract's length and a player's experience may affect the transfer price. See Frick (2007) for a review of the literature on the determinants of transfer prices.

15. In the labour market, a distinction is made between employment in the regulated formal economy and employment in the unregulated informal economy (De Soto, 1989). The presence of the informal economy is a very important characteristic of developing countries (Loayza, 1996). Also in this respect the football labour market is not different from the usual labour market.

16. For an analysis of how the World Cup affects the development of football academies, see Schokkaert, Swinnen and Vandemoortele (2012).

17. Unfortunately, it is unclear whether CASE's shift in priorities influenced AS Monaco's decision to withdraw, or vice versa.

18. Based on the information provided by CASE and our own calculations, the 2007 registration fee varied from 1,140,000 to 1,260,000 CFA francs per year (between 1,740 and 1,920 euros). The International Monetary Fund (IMF) estimates that the Senegalese per capita income was slightly lower than 700 euros per year in 2007 (IMF 2007).

19. CASE has been a major source of talent for clubs overseas and for the Senegalese national team: five graduates were part of the Senegalese national team which reached the quarter finals in the 2002 World Cup (Alegi 2010).

20. School attendance outside the academy is not monitored, so no information is available about the academic involvement of the non-resident pupils.

21. The yearly fee was 600,000 CFA francs (around 900 euros) in 2007.

22. El-Hadji Diouf, a Senegalese player currently participating in the English Premier League, is the godfather of Kenza Mariste.

23. The centre makes this distinction because it believes that older pupils cannot be formed as easily as younger ones and therefore should have a considerable football aptitude before being admitted.

24. However, a voluntary contribution is demanded from parents with sufficient financial means.

25. Babacar Gueye himself was one of the first graduates from Génération Foot.

26. The Premier Soccer League (PSL) is the trading name of the National Soccer League (NSL), which is currently composed of sixteen clubs in the first tier of South African football (ABSA Premiership) and one league of sixteen clubs in the second tier of South African football (National First Division).

27. The same rotational system as in the SAFA-Transnet Football School of Excellence applies.

28. According to the director of Diambars South Africa, only two or three out of twenty football academy players will eventually become professional football players.

29. Match day revenues are limited as football is, since the 1950s, mainly the sport of the poorer, black population in South Africa (Cornelissen & Solberg, 2007).

30. Most (foreign) African players in the PSL tend to consider South Africa as a transit point in the football migration market, serving as a stepping stone for later migration to Europe where quality of training and competition are on average higher (Cornelissen & Solberg, 2007).
31. Note that France is the most important migration destination for Senegalese graduates. Colonial links and the subsequent establishment of transfer networks are important in understanding migratory flows of football players (see e.g. Poli, 2006b; 2008: 2010; Darby, 2007a; 2007b; Darby et al., 2007).
32. Numerous such academies also exist in other African countries. Examples are the Pepsi Football Academy in Nigeria, founded by Kashimawo Laloko, a former coach and a former technical director of the Nigeria Football Association (NFA), the Right to Dream Academy in Ghana, founded by Tom Vernon, a former scout of the English Premier League club Manchester United and the Centre Salif Keita in Mali, founded by the Malian ex-international Salif Keita.

REFERENCES

Adams, R. H. J. (2003), 'International Migration, Remittances, and the Brain Drain. A Study of 24 Labor-Exporting Countries', *Policy Research Working Paper No. 3069*, Washington, DC: The World Bank.

Alegi, P. (2010), *African Soccerscapes: How a Continent Changed the World's Game*, Athens, Ohio: Ohio University Press.

Andreff, W. (2004), 'The Taxation of Player Moves from Developing Countries', in R. Fort & J. Fizel (eds.), *International Sports Economic Comparisons*, Westport and London: Praeger, pp. 87–103.

Andreff, W. (2006), 'Pistes de réflexion économique', in D. Oswald (ed.), *La nationalité dans le sport. Enjeux et problèmes*, Neuchâtel: CIES, pp. 171–191.

Antonioni, P. & Cubbin, J. (2000), 'The Bosman Ruling and the Emergence of a Single Market in Soccer Talent', *European Journal of Law and Economics*, 9(2): 157–173.

Berlinschi, R., Schokkaert, J. & Swinnen, J. F. M. (2010), 'When Drains and Gains Coincide: Migration and International Football Performance', *Discussion Paper No. 265*, LICOS Centre for Institutions and Economic Performance, Leuven.

Boucher, S., Stark, O. & Taylor, J. E. (2009), 'A Gain with a Drain? Evidence from Rural Mexico on the New Economics of the Brain Drain', in J. Kornai, L. Mátyás & G. Roland (eds), *Corruption, Development and Institutional Design*, Basingstoke: Palgrave Macmillan, pp. 100–119.

Chaix, P. (2004), *Le rugby professionnel en France. Enjeux économiques et sociaux*, Paris: L'Harmattan.

CIES (2011), *Mapping Players*, accessed 1 March 2011 at: www.eurofootplayers. org.

Cornelissen, S. & Solberg, E. (2007), 'Sport Mobility and Circuits of Power: The Dynamics of Football Migration in Africa and the 2010 World Cup', *Politikon*, 34(3): 295–314.

Darby, P. (2007a), 'African Football Labour Migration to Portugal: Colonial and Neo-Colonial Resource', *Soccer & Society*, 8(4): 495–509.

Darby, P. (2007b), 'Out of Africa: The Exodus of African Football Talent to Europe', *WorkingUSA: The Journal of Labour and Society*, 10(4): 443–456.

Darby, P. (2010), 'Go Outside: The History, Economics and Geography of Ghanian Football Labour Migration', *African Historical Review*, 42(1): 19–41.

#Darby, P. & Solberg, E. (2010), 'Differing Trajectories: Football Development and Patterns of Player Migration in South Africa and Ghana', *Soccer & Society*, 11(1–2): 118–130.

Darby, P., Akindes, G. & Kirwin, M. (2007), 'Football Academies and the Migration of African Football Labor to Europe', *Journal of Sport & Social Issues*, 31(2): 143–161.

De Soto, H. (1989), *The Other Path: The Invisible Revolution in the Third World*, New York: Harper and Row.

Ericson, T. (2000), 'The Bosman Case: Effects of the Abolition of the Transfer Fee', *Journal of Sports Economics*, 1(3): 203–218.

Feess, E., Gerfin, M. & Muehlheusser, G. (2010), 'Contracts as Rent-Seeking Devices: Evidence from German Soccer', *Discussion Paper No. 15*, Department of Economics, Bern.

Feess, E. & Muehlheusser, G. (2003), 'Transfer Fee Regulations in European Football', *European Economic Review*, 47(4): 645–668.

Feess, E. & Stähler, F. (2009), 'Revenue Sharing in Professional Sports Leagues', *Scottish Journal of Political Economy*, 56(2): 255–265.

Fella, G. (2005), 'Termination Restrictions and Investment in General Training', *European Economic Review*, 49(6): 1479–1499.

Frick, B. (2007), 'The Football Player's Labor Market: Empirical Evidence from the Major European Leagues', *Scottish Journal of Political Economy*, 54(3): 422–446.

Gerrard, B. (2002), 'The Muscle Drain, Coubertobin-Type Taxes and the International Transfer System in Association Football', *European Sport Management Quarterly*, 2(1), 47–56.

Grossman, S. & Hart, O. (1986), 'The Costs and Benefits of Ownership: A Theory of Vertical and Lateral Integration', *Journal of Political Economy*, 94(4): 691–719.

Guasch, J. M. & Sobel, J. (1983), 'Breeding and Raiding: A Theory of Strategic Production of Skills', *European Economic Review*, 22(1): 97–115.

Hart, O. & Moore, J. (1990), 'Property Rights and the Nature of the Firm', *Journal of Political Economy*, 98(6): 1119–1158.

Houston, R.G. & Wilson, D.P. (2002), 'Income, Leisure and Proficiency: An Economic Study of Football Performance', *Applied Economic Letters*, 9(14): 939–943.

IMF (2007), *World Economic Outlook Database*, Accessed 1 February 2011 at: www.imf.org.

IMF (2010), *World Economic Outlook Database*, accessed 1 February 2011 at: www.imf.org.

Kahn, L.M. (2000), 'The Sports Business as a Labor Market Laboratory', *The Journal of Economic Perspectives*, 14(3): 75–94.

Klein, B., Crawford, R.G. & Alchian, A.A. (1978), 'Vertical Integration, Appropriable Rents, and the Competitive Contracting Process', *Journal of Law and Economics*, 21(2): 297–326.

Krugman, P. R. & Obstfeld, M. (2006), *International Economics: Theory & Policy*, Boston: Pearson International Edition.

Kunene, M. (2006), 'Winning the Cup But Losing the Plot? The Troubled State of South African Soccer', in S. Buhlungu, J. Daniel, R. Southall & J. Lutchman (eds), *State of the Nation South Africa 2005–2006*, Cape Town: HSRC Press, pp. 369–391.

Lanfranchi, P. & Taylor, M. (2001), *Moving with the Ball: The Migration of Professional Footballers*, Oxford: Berg.

Lieberman, M. B. (1991), 'Determinants of Vertical Integration: An Empirical Test', *The Journal of Industrial Economics*, 39(5): 451–466.

Loayza, N. V. (1996), 'The Economics of the Informal Sector: A Simple Model and Some Empirical Evidence from Latin America', *Carnegie-Rochester Conference Series on Public Policy*, 45(1): 129–162.

Magee, J. & Sugden, J. (2002), '"The World at Their Feet": Professional Football and International Labor Migration', *Journal of Sport & Social Issues*, 26(4): 421–437.

Mbapndah, A. (2010), *Making a Difference in Africa: The Amazing Story of The Diambars Football Institute, Senegal* accessed 11 January 2011 at: www.panafricanvisions.com.

McKinley, D. T. (2010). '"Transformation" from Above: The Upside-Down State of Contemporary South African Soccer', in A. Desai (ed.), *The Race to Transform: Sport in Post-apartheid South Africa*, Cape Town: HSRC Press, pp. 80–104.

Meyer, K. E. (2001), 'Institutions, Transaction Costs and Entry Mode Choice in Eastern Europe', *Journal of International Business Studies*, 32(2): 357–367.

Monk, D. (2000), 'Modern Apprenticeships in Football: Success or Failure?', *Industrial and Commercial Training*, 32(2): 52–60.

North, D. C. (1990), *Institutions, Institutional Change and Economic Performance*, Cambridge: Cambridge University Press.

Poli, R. (2006a), 'Africans' Status in the European Football Players' Labour Market', *Soccer & Society*, 7(2): 278–291.

Poli, R. (2006b), 'Migrations and Trade of African Football Players: Historic, Geographical and Cultural Aspects', *Afrika Spectrum*, 41(3): 393–414.

Poli, R. (2008), 'Explaining the "Muscle Drain" of African Football Players: World-System Theory and Beyond', *Working paper No. 01*, Basler Afrika Bibliographien, Basel.

Poli, R. (2010), 'Understanding Globalization Through Football: The New International Division of Labour, Migratory Channels and Transnational Trade Circuits', *International Review for the Sociology of Sport*, 45(4): 491–506.

Schokkaert, J., Swinnen, J. F. M. & Vandemoortele, T. (2012), 'Mega-Events and Sports Institutional Development: The Impact of the World Cup on Football Academies in Africa', in A. Zimbalist & W. Maennig (eds.), *Handbook of Economics of Mega Sporting Events*, Cheltenham and Northampton: Edward Elgar, forthcoming.

Simmons, R. (1997), 'Implications of the Bosman Ruling for Football Transfer Markets', *Economic Affairs*, 17(3): 13–18.

Swinnen, J. F. M. & Vandemoortele, T. (2009), 'Sport en ontwikkeling: een economische visie op de impact van de Wereldbeker 2010 in Zuid-Afrika', in J. Scheerder & B. Meulders (eds), *Wedijver in een internationale arena. Sport, bestuur & macht*, Ghent: Academia Press, pp. 185–205.

Taylor, M. (2006), 'Global Players? Football, Migration and Globalization, c. 1930–2000', *Historical Social Research*, 31(1): 7–30.

Terviö, M. (2006), 'Transfer Fee Regulations and Player Development', *Journal of the European Economic Association*, 4(5): 957–987.

Williamson, O. (1975), *Markets and Hierarchies: Analysis and Antitrust Implications*, New York: The Free Press.

Williamson, O. (1985), *The Economic Institutions of Capitalism*, New York: The Free Press.

13 Rules of Law in the Business of Sport

Frank Hendrickx

SPORT, ETHICS AND THE LAW

In an ethical context, the moral judgment of human behaviour or human activity stands central. The final assessment of whether something is right or wrong is made at the level of morality. Moral approval or rejection may, nevertheless, influence human behaviour.

In a legal context, there is also a central concern to find the mechanisms that can influence human behaviour. Even though law is concerned with ordering society, or sub-strata in society, as well as with prohibiting or stimulating certain kinds of behaviour, the main problem is the enforcement of what the law lays down. At the level of enforcement, reference is often made to governmental instruments and state-based outcomes, such as judicial systems applying criminal sanctions, allowing tort mechanisms and contractual liabilities or administrative procedures producing administrative sanctions.

Ethics in sport is a broad concept. There are nevertheless various points to be made about regulating morally acceptable or unacceptable behaviour, such as (Canadian Centre for Ethics in Sport, 1997):

- The impact of behaviour on the potential damages at the physical, mental, emotional or financial level;
- The impact of principles of fairness; This is often not much more than a generally accepted feeling about right and wrong but is nevertheless important in the game of sport and often called 'fair play';
- The impact of and the respect for other human beings; this implies respect for the interests, wishes and desires of others.

What remains important here is the fact that policy interventions in the area of sports ethics require choices about which values are considered in need of protection. Equally important is the choice of method of operation. From the point of view of legal policy intervention, what has to be assessed is whether hard legal intervention, centralised or de-centralised intervention, sanctions or incentive schemes, direct regulation or self-regulation, is the right approach. Furthermore, ethical issues may pose a problem. When looking at the large variety of ethical themes and streams of thought that exist, it is not evident that opening up a wide range of issues to legal intervention based on public policy is the right way. In a given society, legal intervention in the ethical field has to go hand-in-hand with the respect for individual liberty and freedom of decision-making, whether at the individual, ethical level or at the group level. In other words, management of ethics at policy level requires a balance between legal intervention in ethical issues on the one hand and a certain distance from the individual's autonomous behavioural or decision-making level on the other hand.

This may be called the legal dilemma, which implies a question with a double bind:

- How do we promote, on the one hand, ethically sound behaviour, while maintaining respect for freedom and autonomy of individuals and organisations;
- How, on the other hand, do we guarantee in our intervention that the norms are binding and lived up to?

This is the scope of the present contribution. It basically requires an investigation into the role of the law in management of ethics at the policy level of sport. This contribution, therefore, focuses on the legal dilemmas that arise in this field and which are concerned with the characteristics of sports law, the respect for autonomy and the prospects for self-regulation. Within the spectrum of legal responses, it will be shown that added value is to be found in bottom-up instead of top-down regulation, such as in forms of soft law, self-regulation or the open method of coordination, which fits in interdisciplinary approaches and responsive regulatory frameworks.

SPORTS LAW: AUTONOMY VERSUS INTERVENTION

The tension between public, governmental intervention in sports issues and the autonomy of sports organisations themselves can be found in the very nature of sports law. The specific characteristics of sports law have given rise to a doctrine of the specificity of sport, developed in an EU legal context, which shields sports bodies from public regulatory initiatives.

The Characteristics of Sports Law

The law of sport has two faces. It is both public and private. Sports law deals with both autonomous as well as state-created rules regarding the variety of economic, social, commercial, cultural and political aspects of sports activities.

Sports law emanates primarily from the sports movement which is, in essence, a private initiative. This sports movement has established rather powerful organisations that possess strong powers to determine and regulate the activity of sport. This regulation mainly takes the form of self-regulation, e.g. by national and international associations or sports bodies (such as the International Olympic Committee [IOC], the World Anti-Doping Agency [WADA], the International Football Association [FIFA], among others).

These private regulations or by-laws, including organisational and disciplinary rules as well as rules of play, are sometimes labelled as so-called *lex sportiva* (Nafziger, 2006) and arguably constitute a genuine legal order. At the same time, the trend towards more professionalism in sport and the growing economic, social and cultural relevance of sport, have prompted an increasing reliance on legal rules adopted by the government, which are further diversified according to a particular type or sector of sport. Not only its own *lex sportiva*, but also the specific type of interplay between private and public rule-making, characterises sports law as a subject.

In developing the autonomous nature and characteristics of sports law, specific attention needs to be paid to the unique relationships and interests that govern the sports world, involving as it does, athletes, players, clubs, sports bodies, governments and the public at large. Furthermore, it would appear that regulating these relationships and interests and resolving eventual conflicts is determined by the various underlying values that are protected in sport, i.e. values of a social, cultural, economic, political nature. Along the lines of the arguments of M. J. Mitten (1997), it is assumed that there is a strong reciprocal relationship between sports and societal values.

This marks a special feature of the purpose of sports law. It aims at protecting sporting values. Sport is a human activity resting on fundamental social, educational and cultural values. It contributes to integration, involvement in social life, tolerance, the acceptance of differences and playing by the rules. It can also be seen as a vehicle for personal fulfilment, physical and social wellbeing and cultural identity. However, at the same time, the interdependence between sport and societal values needs to be addressed and can be defined as a public policy concern.

Public Policy Concerns and Sporting Interests in EU Law

The tension between sporting autonomy and (public) regulatory intervention is clearly present in the discourse of European sports law. In this context, the debate on the specificity of sport has enabled arguments in favour of immunities for sports bodies with respect to public regulatory intervention.

With regard to the politics of sports regulation in the European Union it can be argued that the body of sports law that exists on this level, either originating from Council, Commission, Parliament or Court, aspires— either implicitly or explicitly—to integrate social, cultural and economic policies (Parrish, 2003).

Typical of the European sports law debate, is the 'European model of sports' and, as referred to above, the doctrine of the so-called 'specificity of sport'. It would appear likely that sports law in the EU does not only turn out to be strongly related to the Union's limited competences but is also dependent on the models of regulation, such as a market model, a welfare model, a socio-cultural model or a political model (Parrish, 2003). The question also has to be raised as to what extent European integration models influence the integration of social, cultural and economic values through EU law (Hepple, 1995).

It should be remembered that the European Court of Justice has held that, in regard to the objectives of the Community, sport is subject to Community law only in so far as it constitutes an economic activity within the meaning of the treaties.[1] This doctrine of Walrave and Koch, confirmed in later case law, has allowed the Court to exclude certain matters from the scope or operation of the Treaty. As the Court's proposition would seem to be that sport does not, in principle, fall under Community law, unless it concerns an economic activity, it could be referred to as supporting the doctrine of the specificity of sport. This implies that matters pertaining purely to sport cannot be regulated under European Union law.

This was confirmed in the European Court's case of Dona versus Mantero where it was accepted that there are 'reasons which are not of an economic nature, which relate to the particular nature and context of such matches and are thus of sporting interest only' (European Court of Justice, ECJ, *Dona v. Mantero*).[2]

Also in the famous Bosman case, the European Court held that 'it is certainly undeniable that the sports associations have the right and the duty to draw up rules for the practice and organization of the sport, and that that activity falls within the association's autonomy which is protected as a fundamental right' (§216, AG, Bosman).[3]

It has, however, become clear that the Court's concept of what constitutes an economic activity has been quite a broad one. The Court repeated its Walrave and Koch principle, in the case of Meca-Medina.[4] This case concerned two professional athletes, Mr Meca-Medina and Mr Majcen, who competed in long-distance swimming. During the World Cup in that sport they tested positive for Nandrolone (an anabolic substance). The International Swimming Federation (FINA) suspended them under the Olympic Movement's Anti-Doping Code for four years, a term subsequently reduced to two years by the Court of Arbitration for Sport. The two athletes filed a complaint with the European Commission, alleging that the International Olympic Committee's rules on doping control were not compatible with the Community rules on competition and freedom to provide services. The Commission rejected the complaint by decision on 1 August 2002. The two athletes brought an action before the Court of First Instance to have the decision set aside. The Court of First Instance dismissed the action by judgment on 30 September 2004, holding that the rules on doping control did not fall within the scope of Community law on competition and freedom to provide services. However, taking the view that the Court of First Instance had erred in law, Mr Meca-Medina and Mr Majcen brought an appeal against that judgment before the Court of Justice.

The Meca-Medina case is interesting in various ways. Here, the Court did not just repeat its position of Walrave and Koch. The Court also held that, 'it is apparent that the mere fact that a rule is purely sporting in nature does not have the effect of removing from the scope of the Treaty the person engaging in the activity governed by that rule or the body which has laid it down.' This leaves a lot of room for interpretation about the Court's view on sporting matters. However, it could be seen as a viewpoint that allows European legal intervention in areas that are of a purely sporting nature (Siekmann, 2008).

SOLVING THE LEGAL DILEMMA IN POLICY PERSPECTIVE: AUTONOMY VERSUS INTERVENTION

Let us refer back to the legal dilemma. From an interventionist point of view in relation to legal policy, what needs evaluating is whether it is hard legal intervention, centralised or de-centralised intervention, sanctions or incentive schemes, direct regulation or self-regulation, that is best applied. This implies a question with a double bind:

- How do we promote, on the one hand, ethically sound behaviour, while maintaining respect for the freedom and autonomy of individuals and organization?
- How do we, on the other hand, guarantee in our intervention that the norms are binding and lived up to?

What can be seen is that the area of sports ethics, as vast as it is, cannot easily be translated into a classical legal method of regulation. A slightly more modern view on regulatory intervention is therefore required.

This hypothesis can be tested on the basis of practical as well as theoretical legal or regulatory concerns.

In both the design and the practice of public policy it is necessary to determine the right (legal) method of operation in ethical issues in sports. It implies that some questions or steps have to be dealt with, such as:

- Who are the actors involved (who are the norms addressed to)?

- What are the problems faced or issues to be addressed (from a policy perspective)?
- How far is public policy intervention desired?

The Actors

Because in sports ethics the judgment of individual or collective human behaviour is at stake, the question is which kind of actor would be subject to any form of policy intervention.

It seems that this may concern a wide variety of subjects such as athletes, sport clubs, sport federations, coaches, medical practitioners, training staff, officials, sponsors, family members, supporters, agents, managers, the media.

Defining the Problem

It is up to the policy level to define what problem or issue needs to be dealt with. This requires a policy choice. It would also seem that, in the area of sports ethics, a public policy regulator may think of the following themes: fair play, health and doping, bribery, racism, violence, diligent management, due process, social responsibility, protection of children and young people and privacy.

How Far Is Public Policy Intervention Desired?

In order to define policy intervention, it can be said that two main considerations play an important role:

How can we keep the respect for individual and organisational freedom?

Do we want to either promote or to prohibit certain (ethical) actions?

Within this consideration, the following principles have to be taken into account.

Individual and Organisational Freedom

Individual freedom is connected with the role of the law. The degree of public policy intervention in a given society and, therefore, the extent to which individual freedom is respected, is a result of ideological consensus and public decision-making processes. In legal terms, public authorities are limited by the fundamental rights of individuals. Therefore, the guarantee of freedom of expression, freedom of opinion, or the right to privacy and personal autonomy will be able to limit the degree of regulatory interference in a legal context.

Freedom of association plays an important role in the organisational freedom of sports bodies. Freedom of association is recognised as a fundamental right and enshrined in many national and supranational constitutional documents. It is to be accepted that the organisational freedom of sports bodies is based on the freedom of association. This also implies that governmental interference should follow the principles laid down in article 11§2 of the European Convention of Human Rights (1950). It states:

> No restrictions shall be placed on the exercise of these rights other than such as are prescribed by law and are necessary in a democratic society in the interests of national security or public safety, for the prevention of disorder or crime, for the protection of health or morals or for the protection of the rights and freedoms of others. This article shall not prevent the imposition of lawful restrictions on the exercise of these rights by members of the armed forces, of the police or of the administration of the State.

It is therefore also necessary from a legal point of view to carefully weigh up governmental action in the field of sports with the respect for sporting autonomy.

To Promote or to Prohibit (Ethical) Behaviour

It seems obvious that public policy intervention is determined by the very nature of sports ethics. It would not appear evident, for example, to oblige citizens to behave in an ethical manner if ethics were not defined further. In a democratic, governmental setting, it is likely that there is a (severe) lack of consensus on what constitutes sound ethical behaviour.

International intervention in the sorts of issues and problems that are discussed under sports ethics also lead to the conclusion that a softer approach might be more desirable.

On an international level, one can invoke the Code of Sports Ethics, adopted by both UNESCO and the Council of Europe on 24 September 1992 and which has been modified by the Council of Europe on 16 May 2001.

This Code is not legally enforceable although it carries high political authority. It concerns a code of conduct, which indicates that it would be problematic to make strict and thus less programmatic, rules in the form of binding obligations.

Their subject matter refers in fact to general ethical obligations, expressing desires or programmes rather than strict legal obligations.

The basic principle of the Code of Sports Ethics is that ethical considerations leading to fair play are integral and not optional elements, of all sports activity, sports policy and management and apply to all levels of ability and commitment, including recreational as well as competitive sport. The Code aims to provide a 'sound ethical framework to combat the pressures in modern day society which appear to be undermining the traditional foundations of sport—foundations built on fair play and sportsmanship, and on the voluntary movement.'

The primary concern and focus of the Code concerns children and young people. Obviously, the Code is also aimed at the institutions and adults who have a direct or indirect influence on young people's involvement and participation in sport.

One of the challenging aspects of the Code is the provision of a definition of 'fair play'. It is described in the Code as follows:

> Fair play is defined as much more than playing with the rules. It incorporates the concepts of friendship, respect for others and always playing within the right spirit. Fair play is defined as a way of thinking, not just a way of behaving. It incorporates issues concerned with the elimination of cheating, gamesmanship, doping, violence (both physical and verbal), the sexual harassment and abuse of children, young people and women, exploitation, unequal opportunities, excessive commercialisation and corruption.

Fair play is a positive concept. Sport is a social and cultural activity which, practised fairly, enriches society and the friendship between nations. Sport is also recognised as an individual activity which, played fairly, offers the opportunity for self-knowledge, self-expression and fulfilment; personal achievement, skill acquisition and demonstration of ability; social interaction, enjoyment, good health and well-being. Sport promotes involvement and responsibility in society with its wide range of clubs and leaders working voluntarily. In addition, responsible involvement in some activities can help to promote sensitivity to the environment.

The Code is clearly addressed, amongst others, to public policy makers. With regard to public policy intervention in the various areas of the Code, it lists the tasks of governments as follows:

- To encourage the adoption of high ethical standards in all aspects of society within which sport operates;
- To stimulate and support those organisations and individuals who have demonstrated sound ethical principles in their work with sport;
- To encourage the education profession to include the promotion of sport and fair play as a central part of the physical education curriculum;
- To support initiatives aimed at promoting fair play in sport, particularly amongst the young, and encouraging institutions to place fair play as a central priority in their work;
- To encourage research both nationally and internationally which improves our understanding of the complex issues surrounding young people's involvement in sport and which identifies the extent of poor behaviour and the opportunities for promoting fair play.

The Code of sports ethics shows that the appropriate method of regulation is not always a hard law that is directly legally enforceable and provides for strict legal obligations. It shows that, at least from the nature of things as well as from a realistic, political point of view, soft law may be a proper way of handling issues of sports ethics.

This finding could imply that it is recommended to limit strong and direct governmental interference in those areas of sports ethics that concern the most severe forms of malpractice or improper human behaviour, such as sexual intimidation or harassment, child abuse or violence. Such extreme forms of unethical or undesirable behaviour is capable of being addressed in terms of prohibition, prosecution and sanction (for example through criminal law or administrative law procedures). A hard legal approach and hard regulatory intervention seem appropriate here. This would amount to a policy prohibiting certain categories of behaviour.

For less extreme and therefore broader ethical themes, such as, for example, inclusion, friendly environment, fair play, and so on, a less interventionist approach is more feasible. This may constitute an argument for fewer top-down approaches in return for bottom-up approaches in the area of sports ethics. In other words, classic top-down regulatory models may be less appropriate at this level. This would fit a policy promoting certain behaviour.

THEORETICAL DIMENSIONS: THE VALUE OF SOFT LAW, SELF-REGULATION AND RESPONSIVE REGULATION

Given the value of alternative modes of regulation in sports ethical issues, the value of interventions through soft law, self-regulation or disciplinary law needs to be looked at.

Soft Law

Soft law documents are often defined as 'non-binding instruments'. Soft law can be conceived of as the beginning of a gradual process in which further steps are needed. In a more indirect way, soft law instruments have an influence on parties that is not so different from that of top-down regulation. Soft law is intended to have a direct influence on the practice or behaviour of parties. To the extent that it is successful in doing so, it may lead to the creation of customary behaviour. As some experts explain, soft law may 'catalyse the creation of customary behaviour by expressing in normative terms certain principles whose general acceptance is already in the air, and thereby making it easier and more likely for parties to conform their conduct to them' (Szasz, 1992).

An analysis of legal writing on soft law reveals three core elements of this phenomenon:

1. 'rules of conduct' or 'commitments' are involved, which

2. are not devoid of all legal effect despite the fact that they have been laid down in instruments that have no legally binding force as such, and which

3. aim at or may lead to some practical effect or influence on behaviour. (Morand, 1970; Borchardt et al., 1989; Thürer, 1990; Snyder, 1994)

On this basis, the following definition of soft law can be given: rules of conduct that are laid down in instruments which have not been attributed legally binding force as such, but may nevertheless have certain (direct) legal effects and that are aimed at and may produce practical effects. As such, the concept of soft law can be considered as providing an umbrella concept for those instruments laying down rules of conduct whose legal status is unclear or uncertain (Senden, 2005).

Why might soft law instruments represent an attractive alternative to top- down law making? There are several reasons for this. First, soft law presents the advantage of allowing parties or addressees to gradually become familiar with the proposed standards before they are confronted with the adoption of enforceable rules at the national or international level. This gradual process leaves more room for discussion and achieving consensus on issues that are particularly complex or sensitive or liable to change.

Second, it may be easier to reach agreement when the format is soft law because parties are usually more reluctant to bind themselves to legislation that may restrict their sovereignty or even lead to sanctions in case of any violation of provisions (Guzman, 2005).

Third, the relatively short time that is needed to develop 'soft law instruments' is of great value in a domain characterised by rapid developments. It would not take several years of negotiation.

It would seem that all these advantages of soft law are applicable in the context of sports ethics.

Self-regulation

Self-regulation means that a person or an organisation creates and/or enforces norms with a certain degree of autonomy. It is important to see why the public authorities would prefer self-regulation over public regulation.

One reason to revert to self-regulation may be that there already is a wide span of governmental regulatory intervention. This often leads to problems of implementation and enforcement. The power of the legislature is also often overestimated. On the one hand, there is the demand to react more efficiently and effectively to the problems of an increasingly complex world, but, on the other hand, the growth in the number of rules and legislation has its own limits.

It is, therefore, obvious that public policy makers, like governments, have to reflect on their own tasks, purposes, responsibilities and the means to be used in policy making. Self-regulation may offer a solution one that can often work in cooperation with governmental policy or in joint regulatory settings (Eijlander, 1993).

It may also be that public policy makers are of the opinion that, from the perspective of public policy, certain problems in society need to be addressed but that the classical mechanisms of governmental interference are less feasible.

There are various types of self-regulatory frameworks, which are dependent on the freedom of the self-regulating group or organisation:

- Free self-regulation: The relevant interest groups or stakeholders have complete freedom in determining the envisaged regulation, as long as there is no violation of mandatory legal provisions.
- Replacement self-regulation: Interest groups or stakeholders are free to determine the envisaged regulation, but if there is no desired outcome, the government may intervene. The public policy maker only has a replacement function.
- Framework self-regulation: The self-regulation takes place within the margins of discretion or the goals and purposes that have been set by the government. The government then keeps control over the ultimate result. Public and self-regulation are complementary.
- Contract self-regulation: This is self-regulation in which the relevant stakeholders or the concerned organisations conclude an agreement with the public policy maker, where the norms for regulation are determined ad hoc.

These considerations would appear relevant in the context of ethical issues in sport such as apply to youth sport for example.

Disciplinary Law

Disciplinary law is a form of legal enforcement norm-conformity in human behaviour. The societal support for norm-conforming behaviour is as important as the manner in which the enforcement of this behaviour is organised. If a legal rule is not borne by those who implement it, its practical effect may be zero.

Disciplinary law takes place within this framework. It has a place in an ever- developing societal context in which norms are being created to deal with increasingly complex situations or human relationships. In this context, a balance has to be found between the responsibilities of public government and those of private individuals or organisations.

Disciplinary law is a field of law in full development. In this sense, it is not yet evident to clearly define the proper characteristics of disciplinary law, or to distinguish it from other legal disciplines. Nevertheless, some elements can be mentioned to indicate the specific place that disciplinary law receives in our legal systems:

in disciplinary law:

- Norms are founded on specific interests of specific groups in society;
- Sanctions have a moral or functional character;
- Violations of norms follow own procedures or sanction mechanisms;
- Disciplinary procedures require discretionary power as well as a degree of informality and flexibility, while limited by the principles of due process and fair trial;
- Norms and procedures are either based on agreement by the parties (e.g., contract or membership) or on governmental support (e.g., legislation).

The question here is what role governments have in the area of disciplinary law. The issue of 'delegation of public authority' can be mentioned here. Governments might not be able to divert their public policy responsibilities to private organisations so easily. This would mean that private groups in society should not, in principle, be looking after the general interest. Nevertheless, a shared responsibility might be possible and even feasible in certain areas.

The role of the government—and thus the public policy maker—versus private organisations in the arena of norm setting and norm enforcement marks the tension between public regulation and self-regulation.

BINDING THEORY WITH THE PRACTICE OF POLICY: RESPONSIVE REGULATION AND THE OPEN METHOD OF COORDINATION

At the more abstract level of legal theory, alternative approaches to classical top-down regulatory intervention can be argued for on the basis of insights offered by responsive regulation.

Responsive Regulation

Responsive regulation is a concept developed by Ayres and Braithwaite. It is set to transcend the regulation versus deregulation debate (Ayres & Braithwaite, 1995) and can be applied to regulatory approaches in the context of developing economies with limited regulatory capacity (Braithwaite, 2006). But it may also serve a much wider regulation debate such as the regulation of sports and sport ethics.

One characteristic of responsive regulation is its responsiveness to the logic of different regulatory strategies and tools.

> Different regulatory strategies can have different logics. They embody, or at the least place emphasis on, different understandings of the nature or behaviour or of an institutional environment, and in turn have different preconditions for effectiveness. (Bladwin & Black, 2008)

For example, Howe and Landau have argued that forms of 'light touch' regulation may be envisaged within a responsive regulatory context:

> We consider that, to be effective and accountable, regulation must take account of the complexity of relationships within its 'regulatory space', acknowledging the interaction between different actors, social and economic forces and between public and private modes of regulation. (Howe & Landau, 2007)

Responsive regulation, therefore, is applied best in an interdisciplinary context, where, in responding to societal problems, insights from various disciplines such as law, sociology, psychology, economy, ethics, etc. are required. It may therefore also fit into a regulatory approach for issues in sports ethics.

Responsive regulation can also be seen as calling on the various processes that influence human behaviour. Behaviour, or human conduct, can be influenced by various drivers, as the following overview shows:

- human behaviour <=> moral pressure;
- human behaviour <=> social pressure;
- human behaviour <=> legal pressure.

Towards Policy Action: The Open Method of Coordination

Taking into account the findings above, it is obviously important to use a method of regulation that optimises public policy intervention in the field of sports ethics in general and youth sport ethics in particular.

It would appear that the open method of coordination (OMC) has added value in a perspective that demands a plurality of initiatives in the regulation of sports ethics. It may serve as a bridge between public policy concern and private autonomy.

This set of methods and techniques is widely used in the context of European Union policy, such as, in particular, the European employment strategy. The Lisbon Council Meeting of 2000 is often seen as the birth of the OMC. In this context, the OMC can be defined as an instance of transnational target-setting between (national) governments and other actors, with the ultimate aim of starting a learning process between (national) governments and other actors about how to respond with (national) policies to universal political and social challenges.

The four elements of the OMC can be identified as follows:

- Fixing guidelines, combined with specific timetables for achieving goals set in the short, medium and long term;
- Establishing, where appropriate, quantitative and qualitative indicators and benchmarks by means of the best available models or examples in the world and tailored to the needs of states or sectors;

- Translating the fixed guidelines into national, regional or sectoral policies by setting specific targets and adopting measures, taking into account national, regional or sectoral differences;
- Periodic monitoring, evaluation and peer reviewing organised as a mutual learning process. Through this peer review, a mutual learning process takes place between governments and other actors.

In the literature concerning the OMC, various explanations have been given for the choice of this 'new mode of governance' (Kenner, 1999; de la Porte & Pochet, 2004). An important line of reasoning focuses on the capacity of the OMC for accommodating diversity (Scharpf, 2001; WRR, 2003) and flexibility. It is stated that by using the OMC at the level of the European Union, member states are able to respond to the specific problems they are facing with solutions that are compatible with their specific policy legacies and that can be implemented within their existing institutional frameworks. It supports a bottom-up approach. It does not involve hard legal intervention, but insists on softer ways of enforcement, such as peer pressure.

This model could be applied in the area of sports ethics. Governments and sports organisations may decide to work towards developing a coordinated strategy for sports ethics. The public policy maker would draw up guidelines each year which the sports organisations would then take into account when setting their sports ethics policies. Each sports organisation addressed would provide the public policy maker with an annual (or multi-annual) report on the principal measures taken to implement its sports ethics policy in the light of the guidelines set by the public policy maker. In the context of this reporting, meetings and debates may take place with the public policy maker and all relevant stakeholders, so that peer reviews and an exchange of viewpoints can take place. This process could serve the purpose of providing information, learning, sharing best practices, transferability of best practices and peer pressure. This approach has the advantage of being focused on public policy concerns and a public procedure for the setting of guidelines, while promoting a bottom-up approach, flexibility for sports organisations as well as individual choice in thorny ethical contexts for a wide variety of ethical themes.

Applications in the EU: The Sport Article

The adoption at a European level of the Treaty establishing a Constitution for Europe in 2004 and the subsequent double 'no' in national referenda, in 2005, brought a new period of reflection on the issue of European integration. This resulted in a draft Reform Treaty, agreed at an Intergovernmental Conference in October 2007. The Treaty amends the EU Treaty and EC Treaty and was signed in Lisbon on 13 December 2007.

The inclusion of a sport article contributes to the idea that Europe is set to become more than a construct that is solely concerned with economic integration.

The impact of the article reaches further than would seem at first sight. It implies that sporting issues would not escape from the application of European Union law and so differ from what has been held up in the case of Walrave and Koch.

The Lisbon Treaty of 13 December 2007, amending the EC Treaty, provides a new article on sport. Article 165 now reads:

1. (. . .) The Union shall contribute to the promotion of European sporting issues, while taking account of the specific nature of sport, its structures based on voluntary activity and its social and educational function.
2. Community action shall be aimed at: (. . .) developing the European dimension in sport, by promoting fairness and openness in sporting competitions and cooperation between bodies responsible for sports, and by protecting the physical and moral integrity of sportsmen and sportswomen, especially the youngest sportsmen and sportswomen.
3. (. . .)
4. In order to contribute to the achievement of the objectives referred to in this Article:

   - the European Parliament and the Council, acting in accordance with the procedure referred to in Article 251, after consulting the Economic and Social Committee and the Committee of the Regions, shall adopt incentive measures, excluding any harmonisation of the laws and regulations of the Member States;
   - the Council, on a proposal from the Commission, acting by a qualified majority on a proposal from the Commission, shall adopt recommendations.

In order to assess the relative impact of the sport article, it is necessary to recall the nature, the purposes and subject fields, as well as the methods of interaction between the EU-level and the Member States and the required majority for European decisions.

The nature of the interaction in the area of sport is determined as a 'competence to carry out actions to support, coordinate or supplement the actions of the Member States.'

This seems to give the European Union a rather wide spectrum for intervention in the field of sport.

The sport article nevertheless provides that the methods to be used should not be confined to 'any harmonisation' of laws and regulations of the Member States. The wording 'any harmonisation' would imply that purposes of partial harmonisation are also excluded.

The aims and scope of EU activity in the area of sports are laid down in the sport article itself. It provides a basis for the various areas of sport that the EU wishes to approach in its policy.

The sport article provides that the Union shall contribute to the promotion of European sporting issues, while taking account of the specific nature of sport, its structures based on voluntary activity and its social and educational function. It also provides that community action shall be aimed at developing the European dimension in sport, by promoting fairness and openness in sporting competitions and cooperation between bodies responsible for sports and by protecting the physical and moral integrity of sportsmen and sportswomen, especially the youngest sportsmen and sportswomen.

It is clear that the wording used to indicate the areas of activity, in the field of sport, will be subject to interpretation. Due to the fact that some rather abstract terms are used, like 'European sporting issues' or 'the European dimension in sport', it has the potential of covering a wide range of issues.

The question is, therefore, not whether the Treaty does allow the European Union to take initiatives in the area of 'sports ethics' because it clearly falls within the broad range of sporting issues. The question is rather how this is to be done.

This is something that is addressed in the sport article. In order to contribute to the realisation of the objectives referred to in the sport article, two sets of measures are envisaged, incentive measures and recommendations.

It is not exactly clear what is meant by 'incentive measures', as this concept refers to the purpose of measures to be adopted rather than the legal instrument to be chosen. Though it is indicated that incentive measures cannot be confined to the harmonisation of laws of the Member States, in principle, these measures do not exclude certain forms of regulation and could, therefore, be combined with acts that are legally binding.

With regard to the required majority in European decision-making in the area of sport, the sport article allows for qualified majority voting. For the incentive measures, reference is made to article 251 of the EC Treaty, whereas for recommendations, qualified majority voting is also used.

When looking at EU competences in the field of sports it is clear that more than one legal strategy is going to be followed in the area of sports ethics.

In the 'youth sport ethics' area one can infer from the European Commission's White Paper on Sport,[5] that a double strategy (hard versus soft) is being pursued.

On the one hand (cf. §42) the Commission will continue to monitor the implementation of EU legislation, for example the Directive on the Protection of Young People at Work. The Commission has recently launched a study on child labour as a complement to its monitoring of the implementation of the Directive. The issue of young football players falling within the scope of the Directive will be taken into account in the study.

On the other hand (cf. §43) the Commission will propose to Member States and sport organisations that they cooperate on the protection of the moral and physical integrity of young people through the dissemination of information on existing legislation, the establishment of minimum standards and the exchange of best practices.

This fits rather well into the above theoretical analysis, which refers to a need for an optimised or gradual mix of soft and hard approaches.

CONCLUSIONS

The tension between public governmental intervention in sports issues and the autonomy of sports organisation can be found in the very nature of sports law. It is both public and private. Sports law emanates primarily from the sports movement, in essence a private initiative. The specific characteristics of sports law have given rise to a doctrine of the specificity of sport, developed in an EU legal context, which shields sports bodies from public regulatory initiatives.

In both the design and the practice of public policy it is a requirement to determine the right (legal) method of operation in ethical issues in sports. In order to define policy intervention, it can be said that two main considerations play an important role: how can we keep the respect for individual and organisational freedom? Do we want to promote or prohibit specific (ethical) behaviour?

Within this consideration, the following principles have to be taken into account. In the area of sports ethics, the topics often referred to are general ethical obligations that express desires or programmes rather than strict legal obligations. This could imply that hard legal or governmental interference and top-down approaches, should be recommended in only those areas of sports ethics that concern the most severe forms of malpractice or improper behavior. This would concern policies prohibiting certain types of behaviour.

For less extreme and therefore, broader ethical themes, a less interventionist approach could be more feasible. Given the vague and broad scope of real ethical issues and the problematic nature of consensus, a bottom-up approach may be more desirable. This would fit policies promoting certain types of behaviour.

Given the value of alternative modes of regulation in ethical issues in sports, the value of interventions through soft law, self-regulation or disciplinary law needs to be looked at. At a theoretical level, these alternative forms of policy intervention are supported by the theory of responsive regulation.

It would appear that the open method of coordination (OMC) offers added value in a perspective that demands a plurality of initiatives in the regulation of sports ethics. It may serve as a bridge between public policy concern and private autonomy.

When looking at the EU competence in the field of sports, it is clear that more than one legal strategy is going to be followed in the area of sports ethics.

NOTES

1. Case 36/74 Walrave v Union Cycliste Internationale [1974] ECR 1405, paragraph 4.
2. Case C-13/76 ECR (1976).
3. Case C-415/93, ECR I-4921.
4. Case C-519/04.
5. COM(2007) 391 final Brussels, 11.7.2007.

REFERENCES

Ayres, I. & Braithwaite, J. (1995), *Responsive Regulation. Transcending the Deregulation Debate*, Oxford: Oxford University Press.

Bladwin, R. & Black, J. (2008), 'Really Responsive Regulation', *Modern Law Review*, 71: 59–94.

Borchardt, G., et al. (1989), 'Soft Law in European Community Law', *European Law Review*, n°5, 285.

Braithwaite, J. (2006), 'Responsive Regulation and Developing Economies', *World Development*, 34(5): 884–898.

Canadian Centre for Ethics in Sport (1997), *A Guide to Moral Decision Making in Sport*, accessed 12 March 2012 at: http://www.cces.ca/en/files-33?page=2.

de la Porte, C. & Pochet, P. (2004), 'The European Employment Strategy: Existing Research and Remaining Questions', *Journal of European Social Policy*, 14(1): 75.

Eijlander, P. (1993), *De wet stellen. Beschouwingen over onderwerpen van wetgeving*, Zwolle: W. E. J. Tjeenk Willink, p. 230.

European Convention of Human Rights (1959).

Guzman, A. T. (2005), 'The Design of International Agreements', *European Journal of International Law*, 16(3): 577–612, at 592.

Hepple, B. (1995), 'The Development of Fundamental Social Rights in European Labour Law', in A. C. Neal & S. Foyn, *Developing the Social Dimension in an Enlarged European Union*, Oslo: Universitetsforlaget, pp. 23–34.

Howe, J. & Landau, I. (2007), '"Light Touch" Labour Regulation by State Governments in Australia', *Melbourne University Law Review*, 393: 367–399.

Kenner, J. (1999), 'The EC Employment Title and the Third Way: Making Soft Law Work?', *International Journal of Comparative Labour Law and Industrial Relations*, 15(1): 33–60.

Mitten, M. J. (1997), 'Sports Law as a Reflexion of Society's Laws and Values', *South Texas Law Review*, 38: 999–1006.

Morand, A. (1970), 'Les recommendations, les resolutions et les avis du droit communautaire', *Cahiers de Droit Européen*, n°2, 626–627.

Nafziger, J. (2006), 'Lex Sportiva and CAS', in *The Court of Arbitration for Sport*, The Hague: Asser Press, pp. 409–419.

Parrish, R. (2003), 'The Politics of Sports Regulation in the European Union', *Journal of European Public Policy*, 10(2): 246–262.

Scharpf, F. W. (2001), 'European Governance: Common Concerns vs. the Challenge of Diversity', in C. Y. Joerges, Y. Meny & J. H. H. Weiler (eds), *Symposium: Responses to the European Commission's White Paper on Governance*, Cambridge: EUI/RSC/Harvard Law School.

Senden, L. A. J. (2005), 'Soft Law and Its Implications for Institutional Balance in the EC', *Utrecht Law Review*, 1(2), accessed at: http://www.utrechtlawreview.org/.

Siekmann, R. (2008), 'Is Sport Special in EU Law and Policy?', in R. Blanpain, M. Colucci & F. Hendrickx (eds), *The Future of Sports Law in the European*

Union. Beyond the EU Reform Treaty and the White Paper (*Bulletin of Comparative Labour Relations*, 66: 37–49).

Snyder, F. (1994), 'Soft Law and Institutional Practice in the European Community', in S. Martin (ed.), *The Construction of Europe: Essays in Honour of Emile Noël*, Dordrecht: Kluwer Academic Publishers, p. 198.

Szasz, C. (1992), 'International Norm making', in E. Brown Weiss (ed), *Environmental Change and International Law, New Challenges and Dimensions*, Tokyo: United Nations University, pp. 41–70.

Thürer, D. (1990), 'The Role of Soft Law in the Actual Process of European Integration', in O. Jacot-Guillarmod et al., *L'avenir du libre-échange en Europe, vers un Espace economique européen?*, Zürich: Schulthess Polygraphischer Verlag, p. 132.

WRR (The Netherlands Scientific Council for Government Policy) (2003), Effective Policy Making in the Pan-European Union (nr. 65), Den Haag: SDU.

Contributors

Hans Bruyninckx is professor of International Relations and Global Governance, Institute for International and European Policy, KU Leuven and Director of HIVA Research Institute for Work and Society, KU Leuven, Belgium.

Cora Burnett is professor in the Department of Sport and Movement Studies at the University of Johannesburg in South Africa. She has extensively published in the field of the sociology of sport, addressing issues of inequality, inclusion, and socio-political dynamics and preparing impact assessments of sport-for-development projects.

Fred Coalter is professor of Sports Policy at the University of Stirling. His research relates to the contributions sport is claimed to make to various aspects of social policy. He is responsible for compiling Sport England/ UK Sport's on-line research-based 'Value of Sport Monitor' and his latest publication is *Sport and International Development* (Routledge, 2012).

Richard Giulianotti is professor of Sociology in the School of Applied Social Sciences at Durham University. His research focuses on sport, globalization, crime and deviance and urban studies. His most recent publications are (with Roland Robertson) *Globalization and Sport* (Blackwell, 2007) and *Globalization and Football* (Sage, 2009).

Reinhard Haudenhuyse is a doctoral student in the Department of Sport Policy and Management at the Vrije Universiteit Brussels, Belgium with an MA in Physical Education and an MA in Conflict and Development. In his PhD (2008–2011) he tries to understand the conditions in which broader outcomes can be generated for socially vulnerable youth through sports practices.

Frank Hendrickx is professor of Law at the University of Leuven (KU Leuven), Belgium, where he teaches labour law and sports law and Jean Monnet Professor at Tilburg University (ReflecT institute). He is the editor of the *International Encyclopaedia of Sports Law* and author of the Belgian 'Sportcodex'.

Marion Keim is associate professor at the University of the Western Cape. She has been lecturing, conducting and supervising research in the areas of sport and social transformation, community and youth development, multiculturalism, conflict transformation and peace building in Africa, Europe and the United States since 1989.

Stefan Késenne is professor of Sports Economics at the University of Antwerp (UA) and at the University of Leuven (KU Leuven), Belgium. He is vice-president of the International Association of Sports Economists and a founding member of the European Sports Economics Association.

Lian Malai Madsen is a postdoctoral researcher at the University of Copenhagen, Department of Scandinavian Studies and Linguistics. She has carried out a research project in a Taekwondo club and holds a PhD from 2008 in interactional sociolinguistics. Her research focuses on identities, social relationships and linguistic practice.

Bert Meulders is a former doctoral researcher at the Department of Human Kinesiology of the University of Leuven (KU Leuven), Belgium. His doctoral project examines the development agenda of the 2010 FIFA World Cup in South Africa from a governance perspective. He is co-editor of *Sport and Development* (2006) providing an overview of this new field of research and of *Wedijver in een internationale arena—Sport, bestuur & macht* (2009), a book that deals with governance issues in sport.

Joel Rookwood studied Football Science at undergraduate level, earned masters degrees in Notation Analysis and Sport Sociology and a PhD in Football Fandom. He is a lecturer at Liverpool Hope University, where he is leader of the Sports Development and Football Studies pathways.

Bettina Rulofs is assistant professor at the German Sports University Cologne, Institute of Sociology of Sport, Gender Studies. She is a member of the extended board of the International Sociology of Sport Association. Her fields of specialisation are social inclusion in sport, social construction of gender in sport, gender representation in sports media, sport and violence, and sport and social work.

Jeroen Schokkaert is a doctoral student at LICOS Centre for Institutions and Economic Performance at the University of Leuven (KU Leuven), Belgium. He holds a masters degree in Advanced Studies in Economics and his main research interests are sports, migration and economic development.

Barbara Segaert holds an MA in Oriental Studies, Islamic Studies and Arab Philology (KU Leuven, Belgium) and an MA in the Social Sciences (Open University, UK). Since 2002 she is scientific coordinator at the University Centre Saint-Ignatius Antwerp where she develops academic programmes on various topics of contemporary relevance to society.

Jens Sejer Andersen is former journalist on sports culture and director of 'Play the Game', an independent institution funded by the Danish Ministry of Culture, the Danish Gymnastics and Sports Associations and the Danish Federation of Company Sports, aiming to strengthen the basic ethical values of sport and encourage democracy, transparency and freedom of expression in world sport through, for example, international conferences with stakeholders from the world of sport.

Johan Swinnen is professor of Economics and Director of the LICOS Centre for Institutions and Economic Performance at the University of Leuven (KU Leuven), Belgium. His research focuses on institutions and development, transition, political economy, globalization and trade. He is a senior research fellow at the Centre for European Policy Studies (CEPS), Brussels.

Marc Theeboom is professor and vice-dean at the Faculty of Physical Education and Physiotherapy and the Faculty of Psychology and Educational Sciences of the Vrije Universiteit Brussel, Belgium and chairs the Sports Policy and Management Department. His research primarily focuses on pedagogical and policy-related aspects of youth sport in general and specific target groups in particular (e.g., socially deprived youth, ethnic minorities, elderly).

Christiane Timmerman holds an MA in Psychology and a PhD in Social and Cultural Anthropology. As head of the Centre for Migration and Intercultural Studies, she co-ordinates research on Ethnic Minorities and Migration at the University of Antwerp, Belgium. She is in charge of several large-scale (international) research projects (e.g., FP7) and PhD projects. Until September 2011 she was also Director of Academic Affairs of the University Centre Saint-Ignatius Antwerp.

André Travill is professor in the Department of Sport, Recreation and Exercise Science and Deputy Dean of the Faculty of Community and Health Sciences at the University of the Western Cape Bellville, South Africa.

Thijs Vandemoortele is a postdoctoral researcher at LICOS Centre for Institutions and Economic Performance at the University of Leuven (KU Leuven), Belgium. He has published several articles in international journals on political and economic theory of standards.

Bart Vanreusel is professor in Sport Sociology and head of the Department of Human Kinesiology at the University of Leuven (KU Leuven), Belgium. He published on issues of human movement culture such as play, physical activity, sport for all and elite sport.

Name Index

Subject Index